Lines of Resistance

LINES OF RESISTANCE

Essays on British Poetry from Thomas Hardy to Linton Kwesi Johnson

Edited by Adrian Grafe *and* Jessica Stephens

McFarland & Company, Inc., Publishers
Jefferson, North Carolina, and London

LIBRARY OF CONGRESS CATALOGUING-IN-PUBLICATION DATA

Lines of resistance : essays on British poetry from Thomas Hardy to Linton Kwesi Johnson / edited by Adrian Grafe and Jessica Stephens.
　　　p.　　cm.

Includes bibliographical references and index.

ISBN 978-0-7864-6283-4
softcover : acid free paper ∞

1. English poetry — History and criticism — Theory, etc. 2. Literature and society — Great Britian. I. Grafe, Adrian. II. Stephens, Jessica.
PR503.L56 2012
821.009 — dc23   2012008869

BRITISH LIBRARY CATALOGUING DATA ARE AVAILABLE

© 2012 Adrian Grafe and Jessica Stephens. All rights reserved

No part of this book may be reproduced or transmitted in any form or by any means, electronic or mechanical, including photocopying or recording, or by any information storage and retrieval system, without permission in writing from the publisher.

Front cover image © 2012 Shutterstock. Background: 1901 poem entitled "The Self-Unseeing," part of Hardy's volume entitled *Poems of the Past and the Present.*

Manufactured in the United States of America

McFarland & Company, Inc., Publishers
　Box 611, Jefferson, North Carolina 28640
　　www.mcfarlandpub.com

Table of Contents

Acknowledgments — vii

Introduction (ADRIAN GRAFE and JESSICA STEPHENS) — 1

Part I: From Constraint to Release

1. The Self-Resisting: Hardy's Ambivalent Evocation of Romantic Childhood (GALIA BENZIMAN) — 15
2. Hardy's Cunning in Form and Diction (EMILIE LORIAUX) — 29
3. "Minds" and "Manacles" in Late Lawrence (ELISE BRAULT-DREUX) — 41
4. Lawrence Between Resistance and Dissolution (SARAH BOUTTIER) — 55

Part II: Against the Odds

5. The Poem or the "Fierce Desire" to Live: Isaac Rosenberg and Robert Graves (ANNE MOUNIC) — 70
6. Resisting Theological Error as a Means of Political Salvation: Charles Williams' and Dorothy L. Sayers' Second World War Poetry (SUZANNE BRAY) — 88
7. Resilience and Regeneration: *Four Quartets* in French Translation (JESSICA STEPHENS) — 104

Part III: Northern Resistance

8. Basil Bunting: Resistance, History and Myth (CHARLOTTE ESTRADE) — 120
9. Ted Hughes and "That Built-In Resistance": Versions of the Calder Valley (CLAIRE HÉLIE) — 135

Part IV: The Celtic Strain

10. "The Embattled Stance": Late Yeats (ELIZABETH MULLER) — 149

11. W.B. Yeats and Resistance (CATHERINE PHILLIPS)		166
12. Responding, Rewording and/or Resisting: Edwin Morgan (SHONA M. ALLAN)		179

Part V: Irony, Play and Pleasure

13. Auden's Irreducible Art (BOUTHEINA BOUGHNIM LAARIF)		194
14. Hugo Williams: Standing the Test of Time? (ADRIAN GRAFE)		206
15. "Wi Naw Tek Noh More A Dem Oppreshan": Linton Kwesi Johnson's Resistant Vision (EMILY TAYLOR MERRIMAN)		218
About the Contributors		235
Index		237

Acknowledgments

Grateful acknowledgment is made for permission to reproduce copyrighted material as follows:

Bloodaxe Books for quotations from Basil Bunting, *Complete Poems* (2000). Carcanet Press Limited for quotations from the poems of Robert Graves taken from Complete Poems in One Volume; David Higham for quotations from Dorothy L. Sayers and Charles Williams; Linton Kwesi Johnson for permission to quote from his *Selected Poems* (Penguin); Claude Vigée, Menard Press, Anthony Rudolf, King's College, for all quotations taken from T. S. Eliot, *Quatre Quatuors*, the translation of *Four Quartets* by Claude Vigée (London, 1992); "Fish," "Humming-Bird," "Trees in the Garden," "Butterfly," "Corot," "Michael-Angelo," "Almond Blossom," "Hibiscus and Salvia Flowers," "Turkey-Cock," "Only the Best Matters," "Bat," "Lucifer — 8 lines," from THE COMPLETE POEMS OF D.H. LAWRENCE by D. H. Lawrence, edited by V. de Sola Pinto & F. W. Roberts, copyright © 1964, 1971 by Angelo Ravagli and C. M. Weekley, Executors of the Estate of Frieda Lawrence Ravagli. Used by permission of Viking Penguin, a division of Penguin Group (USA) Inc. Reproduced by permission of Pollinger Limited and the Estate of Frieda Lawrence Ravagli. Linton Kwesi Johnson and LKJ Music Publishers Ltd. for permission to quote from the poetry of Linton Kwesi Johnson.

The editors acknowledge the backing of: the University of Artois, especially Francis Marcoin, head of the research center *Textes et Cultures*, as well as Claudine Nédelec and Jean-Pierre Martin; Laurent Lepaludier and the C.R.I.L.A. research laboratory at the University of Angers, Marie-Annick Montout and the English department. They also wish to thank René Gallet, Stephen Rowley and Paul Volsik. Katy Loffman (Pollinger Ltd.) has been unstinting in her assistance. Special thanks are due to Emily and Stephen Merriman. Hugo Williams has been more than generous. The editors are particularly grateful to Catherine Phillips.

Natacha, Julia, Dylan, John, Mary-Carolyn and James Grafe have been patient and supportive (and curious) throughout the preparation of this book.

Introduction
Adrian Grafe *and* Jessica Stephens

What is it that resists in a poem? What is the poem resisting, and how does it resist? And what is the reader resisting in the poem? Poets are caught up within time and history, but also, through their work, try to resist being conquered by time and go against its sometimes destructive course. Poetry at its most perfect pitch is by definition an art by which the individual — the poet — resists current cultural standards and the lowest common denominator. The poet calls into question the established order. In a relativistic world, poetry is a quest for the Absolute, be it linguistic, philosophical or religious, or all three. Geoffrey Hill argues that through the beautiful and moving character of the poem, the poet works against what Hill calls "the debasement of words."[1] Poetry resists the dominant trends, a lukewarm or indifferent social consensus, the standardization of society, so that, as Hill writes, the poem becomes "one of the instruments of resistance to the drift of the age."[2]

This volume aims to show how British poetry and resistance fruitfully interact and combine in a multiplicity of ways. Resistance, in the sense of fortitude and resilience, is a valued quality when it applies to an individual's ability to endure the wear and tear of life: an ability that is acquired through experience and is the result of an ongoing learning process. On the political and social fronts, those which come to mind most readily, does resistance as civil disobedience still have a part to play in changing attitudes, if not government policy? In the twenty-first century, such movements as Ghandi's non-violent resistance, the French Resistance, and Martin Luther King's civil rights movement may seem remote. Yet they still keep their historical and ethical resonance. Resistance, according to Edgar Morin, member of the French Resistance and sociologist, is first and foremost creative and liberating.[3]

The etymology of the word "resistance" itself is peculiar because it is composed of a prefix and a root form that are inseparable; in other words, it differs from "reread" or "undo" to the extent that if the prefix is removed one is not left with a word in its own right. The OED gives Latin *sistere*, "to stand," combined with the prefix "re" as a reduplication, meaning a doubling, a reinforcing, so that the whole word in Latin means "to stop." If one looks up "assistance," morphologically similar to "resistance," with a prefix followed by a root form derived from *sistere,* the OED gives the meaning of *sistere* not as "to stand" but as "to take one's stand." This seems to be more appropriate for defining "resistance": taking a stand with insistence; "the act of resisting, opposing, or withstanding."

In the Judeo-Christian tradition, one of the first and most powerful instances of resistance is Jacob wrestling with the angel in Genesis (32, 24–32). This famous episode symbolizes the spiritual combat of man with God, and it has inspired many poets, artists and philosophers. In the New Testament resistance is presented in a different, more subversive and provocative light. Christ's Sermon on the Mount says: "You have heard it said: an eye for an eye, and a tooth for a tooth. But I say to you, Do not resist evil: whoever strikes you on your right cheek, turn your left one to him, too" (Matt. 5, 38–39). St Paul's epistle to the Ephesians (6, 11ff) is a variation on that very theme, and makes full use of both the verbs "to resist" and "to stand": "You must wear all the weapons in God's armory, if you would find strength to resist the cunning of the devil.... Take up all God's armor, then, so you will be able to stand your ground when the evil time comes, and be found still on your feet when all the task is over. Stand fast...." In the nineteen-sixties, Martin Luther King addressed a black crowd about to attack white racists who had thrown a bomb onto the porch of King's house along the same lines: "Our weapon is to have none."[4] Whether it be in the Sermon on the Mount, the epistle to the Ephesians, or King's statement, striking back is not the best solution. In *The Silent Cry: Mysticism and Resistance,* Dorothee Soelle argues that mysticism can free people from what she calls "the compulsion to win."[5]

In psychoanalytical terms the word refers to "the opposition, frequently unconscious, to allowing memories or desires which have been repressed as unacceptable or disruptive to emerge into the conscious mind." The grit of much poetry lies in its unacceptable, disruptive, irritant or opaque dimension. On the other hand, the OED cites Freud's assertion concerning "the resistance with which the patient clings to his disease and thus even fights against his own recovery" (*On Psychotherapy*). Resistance in the psychotherapeutic and medical fields has a self-sabotaging character: one thinks of patients who refuse to take their treatments, or indeed of doctors who may be reluctant to see their patients cured. This phenomenon might seem perverse, and only recently have French philosophers like Claire Marin begun to take account of it. Marin has examined the view that the patient is often considered as someone who either resists and fights, or gives up. She says that illness is a manifestation of life.[6] Before Marin, Françoise Proust in *De la résistance*, argued that life itself with its irreducible energy and blind thrust resists whatever diminishes it and even more, threatens to destroy it—death, in other words. From the first second, with the innate immune system, life resists the forces of death and destruction with all its might. Even more crucially, she goes on to ask whether this struggle "isn't precisely what makes life lively"— lively, rather than merely livable.[7] If death is resistance to life, life is ingenious in coming up with ways of resisting death's resistance; the relationship of the forces of life and death becomes a narrative of resistance—what Anne Mounic, in her essay below, calls, after Isaac Rosenberg, the "fierce desire to live"— and counter-resistance. Resistance is according to Proust "the joy of invention" and "the affirmation of something different," meaning a better alternative to a given situation; one can see that such phrases as Proust uses are quite close to a description of artistic creation.[8] Such phrases are also surprisingly reminiscent of the work of the theologian Dorothee Soelle, who expresses her belief in the oppositional power not only of mysticism but of "joy, laughter, and delight."[9]

Is there a common denominator in the forms that the process of resistance takes? In other words does not resistance come down to a kind of questioning? The kind of questioning that breaks an individual and turns him into a new man as in Socrates' maieutics? If *resistere* means, among other things, "to cause to stand back," resistance is a form of critical awareness—learning to think for ourselves and opening up to other voices and alternatives. Instead of seeing resistance as a negative but sometimes wholesome drawing back from a situation, or the repression of emotions in the unconscious mind, resistance can thus be seen as an active process geared towards the future, geared towards the hope of a better future.

In an apparent paradox, resistance is intimately connected to flux. Resistance is a state of mind, an acceptation of a situation that allows us to position ourselves in such a way as to be able to bring about change. In Shelley's *Prometheus Unbound*, Prometheus is freed and Jupiter crushed when he—Prometheus— lets go of his hate, stops fighting, opposing, resisting Jupiter and the punishment inflicted on him daily. Then and only then does the world begin to change and the fixity of hatred give way to flux and the coming of spring.

How does resistance differ from opposition, to which it is closely connected? In contrast to opposition, it would seem that resistance applies to a much more structured, deliberate process targeted at some form of oppression—be it political, social or intellectual—that is perceived as deeply unjust. An equilibrium or balance is upset; a situation that is wrong needs to be addressed and redressed. The concept of resistance implicitly also suggests a higher ideal and motive under which acts of resistance are subsumed. Something vital, something to do with the very essence of human nature is at stake.

Resistance is often associated with disruption, not only in the realm of psychoanalysis but as applied to society—in the case of civil disobedience, for example; the concept proves ambivalent, for if resistance engenders disruption it is also cohesive, bringing together categories of people or individuals who are committed to change. In this respect, resistance testifies to our desire to stand against and to stand straight, to act according to a set of deep and valid beliefs—to fight barbarism which is a form of human entropy, refusing to let go of our humanity at one end of the spectrum or, at the other, simply to improve our lot. At different historical periods, resistance has been a way of staying alive: "Writing meant living and surviving," wrote the German poetess Rose Aüslander about her experience in a ghetto during World War II.[10] Resistance is a way for man to assert his integrity, to come alive by coming into his own. In this perspective, acts of resistance can be seen as connected with the evolution of society, our striving towards the good life. What George Steiner has to say about man's refusal "to accept the world as it is" also applies to resistance. "Without that refusal, without the unceasing generation by the mind of 'counterworlds'—a generation which cannot be divorced from the grammar of counter-factual and optative forms—we would turn forever on the treadmill of the present."[11]

Indeed, as there are acts of resistance, there are also modes of resistance. Man has at his disposal such tools of resistance as art and language. Artists and poets, because they are able to stand still, question our beliefs and create a meaningful, resistant hiatus. Some works of art can be considered as resistant to social or cultural trends or norms, but more often than not they are only—or only intended to be—subversive. However, a painting like *Guernica* can be considered as a form of resistance to war or a testimony against war.

Faith, humor, simple images of desire or past happiness are integral to the process of resistance. They enrich our perception of reality by giving the self a space where it can provide an alternative to the given, and be strengthened; in that fleeting moment the self escapes and is set free: "in resistance to cruelty in the world and human barbarism, there is always a 'yes' animating the 'no', a 'yes' to freedom, a 'yes' to the poetry of living."[12]

Contrary to paintings and installations, poems, songs and novels, because they can be printed, circulated and translated into other languages, have proved over the years more powerful and effective tools. This has to do with the nature of and possibilities afforded by language. Poems can also be easily committed to memory, brought to mind and recited in times of trouble; in Ray Bradbury's *Fahrenheit 451*, political or social opponents who choose to live in

the forest, on the fringe, are required to learn off by heart a great classic, thereby keeping books, experience and the power of language alive.

If writing — and more specifically poetry — contributes to our ability to withstand the difficulties inherent in life, it is because poets, in spite or because of the constraints of poetry writing, come up with the right words, words that match a situation to which we can relate exactly. Someone else has expressed what we feel and what we can therefore express and construe more meaningfully. Someone else has both expressed and transcended an experience by structuring it through art. Our resistance to pain and extreme suffering is increased because, in a way, through writing and art, we step into the solace of the brotherhood of man; we are reminded that we are links in a chain. Someone has felt thus, someone who stands as an examplar.

At one level or another — at exactly which level or levels is something this book attempts to find out — the place of art in civilization must be contrary; otherwise it won't stand out, it won't stand up and be counted, and will sink back into the general diffuseness of the commodity culture. In *Aesthetic Theory*, Theodor Adorno writes: "Art's opposition to the real world is in the realm of form."[13] In formal terms, poets bring their chosen medium, language, to its highest pitch. Language, however, including poetic language — especially poetic language — is a notoriously shifting, unstable, unreliable means of expression and communication: in *The Resistance to Poetry*, James Longenbach claims that the poem resists because its "words leap just beyond our capacity to know them certainly."[14] The resistance of a poem to interpretation and translation is a sign of its fecundity, as is the multiplicity of interpretations and translations it generates.

The poem exists because, in one way or another, it resists. Knowledge of a person's or a thing's "independent reality," according to J.H. Prynne, comes from their resistance: "the stone's hard, palpable weight is the closest I can come to the fact of its existence, and the resistance or disagreement of my neighbor is my primary evidence for his being really there."[15] Nevertheless, the surrealistic modernism practiced by Prynne, which is a form of poetic resistance, clearly stands apart from the two strands of English poetry that one might most readily associate with resistance. One is the dissenting tradition, being a branch of Protestant prophesying to which Milton, Blake, Lawrence and Hughes belong, while Geoffrey Hill also has links to this category. Hughes is also a towering figure in this context, to the extent that he participated in the seventies and eighties, along with Heaney and others, in translating Eastern bloc poets into English: here was a cipher for political and cultural resistance that could speak to British culture, and was clearly intended to do so. As for Hill, he paid tribute to the German resistance to Hitler and the Kreisau Circle in *Canaan* and *The Triumph of Love*, just as Thom Gunn, before him, wrote a poem celebrating "Claus von Stauffenberg of the bomb-plot on Hitler, 1944." The other trend is Pastoral which, post–Renaissance, might include Traherne and Marvell; the first-generation Romantics including Clare; Hopkins, and Hughes.

Two components of this trend are Romantic idealization and nostalgia. It is precisely such defining qualities of the pastoral genre which can be found in Hardy. With a deft use of irony and paradox, Hardy delicately subverts these Romantic pastoral features, as Galia Benziman shows in the opening chapter of the first section of the volume, the section entitled "From Constraint to Release," which features two essays each on the two earliest-born poets to be considered. In two childhood poems, "The Self Unseeing" (1901) and "Childhood among the Ferns" (1928), Hardy questions the value of growing up. The wish that the child should not "look away" toward the future in the earlier poem, and the child speaker's fantasy of remaining forever "among the ferns" of eternal childhood in the later poem, manifest a Romantic resistance to the necessity of growing up, and an ethical revolt against a noisy, callous, aggressive adult world. The form of the poems also echoes this resistance, as the ending seems to invert — that is, to resist — the previous direction of the poem. Hardy's own irony regarding the Romantic desire to remain a child reveals this resistance as paradoxical. While resisting the adult world, Hardy also resists the very fantasy of remaining forever under the dominion of the childlike — as a regressive delusion, in fact. The child-speaker of "Childhood among the Ferns," for instance, desires to "live on here thus till death"; he longs for a sense of shelter and permanence that will outweigh the powers of time and the social. Yet in the same breath he talks of his own growing up, entrance into the world, and eventual death, implying that although a child, he knows that he is already exposed to the forces he aims to resist. This chapter shows how this paradoxical staging of the reluctance to grow up is part of Hardy's ambivalence toward Romantic ideology. Conversely, and in complementary fashion, Emilie Loriaux's "Hardy's Cunning in Form and Diction," examines Hardy's poetic language, above all in three poems dating from around the turn of the century, not long after Hardy had taken his decision to give up fiction for poetry — a major act of resistance, or protest, in relation to the literary critics of his day who had so savagely treated his later novels. This being Hardy, however, Loriaux also shows how the poet works prosaic elements into his prose, thus calling into question conventional and indeed Romantic ideas about what, in a poem, was poetic and what was not. Hardy's linguistic ingenuity enables him to circumvent standard stylistic constraints and norms, counter and subvert the given, and provide poetic alternatives.

Nevertheless, poetic form and the framework provided by stanza, rhyme and meter are paramount for Hardy: tradition and invention overlap. As for Lawrence, he came to resist formal poetry, as Elise Brault-Dreux reminds us in "'Minds' and 'Manacles' in Late Lawrence." Lawrence opposed "restricted, limited unfree verse" with his flowing poetry. Poetry should, according to him, be all utterance, "the insurgent naked throb of the instant moment. "He used poetry as a means to resist modernity and what were for him contemporary ideals — "money, hypocrisy, greed, machines." Deeply aware of the circumstances of his immediate surroundings (though often considered a late nineteenth-century man), Lawrence formulated strong calls for resistance to modern mechanization and exacerbation of the powers of the mind and of the "single ego" which, he argued, were all annihilating the life and instincts of the body. In his poems, he meant to fight against modern "*mind*-forged manacles": the body must resist the mind, and both must reach, in Lawrence's word, an "equilibrium." In fact, at least two kinds of resistance appear in Lawrence's poetry: one, subversive, the other apparently passive — subversive in Lawrence's choice of words, poetic rhetoric and arguments (and in his conviction that, in the end, man's natural and physical instincts would triumph), and passive in his use of unresisting poetic form. However, Brault-Dreux asks, is this (apparent) passivity not a means of resistance in itself, a poetic model for resistance to the "manacles" forged by modern cerebral machines? Resistance is not so much a matter of confrontation as of connection with one's instinctual life. As this connection occurs, poetry is released from constraints: *Pansies* and *More Pansies* demonstrate this.

On the other hand, Sarah Bouttier shows "Lawrence Between Resistance and Dissolution." She highlights ways in which Lawrence uses images of resistance to assert the presence of his creatures, echoing the theories of many thinkers of the turn of the century such as Bergson, Haeckel or Spencer, who considered resistance as the shaping force of any living thing. However, gradually, the poems acknowledge that the forces the creatures resist also sustain them. Lawrence's late poems seem, in fact, to celebrate the creatures' final dissolution into the great flow of life, and thereby the end of resistance. As physical resistance in the creatures becomes ephemeral, their presence becomes more resistant to poetic expression, and Lawrence's response consists in building "yielding lines" with fleeting, evanescent images. Lawrence monitored the world around him and the changes that affected his cultural and social environment; resistance was something he worked through experientially. It also proved to be a protean concept as applied to his poetry since he evolved from an oppositional standpoint to the opening up to flux.

It was surely inevitable that, in a volume on the topic of British poetry and resistance, the problematics of war should feature in relation to the twentieth century, even though much British war poetry is not necessarily considered as protest poetry, or expressing resistance. The second section entitled "Against the Odds" tackles poetry's response to war. It is war and the response to war, as much as literary Modernism, which changed the shape of British poetry from 1914 onwards. Of the poets considered here, the lives of several straddle both World Wars: Robert Graves (1895–1985), Eliot (1888–1965), Dorothy Sayers (1893–1945), Charles Williams (1886–1945; Williams died on May 15, just long enough to see in V-E Day, 8 May), and Auden (1907–1973). Incidentally, co-editor Adrian Grafe suggests further on in the volume that the contemporary poet Hugo Williams, born in mid-war (1942), can be deemed a war poet, and a resistant one at that.

Anne Mounic shows how Isaac Rosenberg and Robert Graves, who were both involved in the Great War, resisted through writing their "fierce desire" to live into their poems, and resorting to myth. What the soldiers had to face in the trenches was not only the enemy, death, and warfare, but also boredom since they were deprived of any individual privileges. As for Graves, poetry and myth helped him to apprehend the specter of death and resist it. When he wrote *The White Goddess* during the Second World War, he elaborated the trauma and the figure of the poet, half resistant, half submitting to fate. With both poets, the Bible is a key reference. The figure of Jacob contending with the angel is crucial for Robert Graves. What ultimately transpires is the human being as he grapples with higher forces. In a way, Robert Graves also resisted the "mind-forged manacles" of the time, the dictates of society and religion concerning the perception of the sacrifice expected. Lawrence's work testifies to a binary opposition to society—a rebellion even, whereas Graves pursued a private, poetic and intellectual itinerary by tapping into and giving shape to forces stemming from the collective cultural and spiritual reserves. His resistance, then, involved coming into his own by developing and drawing on his personal poetic mythology.

In Dorothy L. Sayers' and Charles Williams' poetry, it is not the fate of the individual but rather, as Suzanne Bray argues in "Resisting Theological Error as a Means of Political Salvation," the spiritual fragmentation of the entire European continent, that poetry resists. Bray considers two, now little-read war poems from 1944—Sayers' "Target Area" and Williams' "The Prayers of the Pope." The two poets were not afraid to court controversy. For Bray, these poems are affirmations of solidarity in guilt and co-inherent responsibility, and they resist the tendency of the time to demonize, hate or refuse forgiveness of or solidarity with the enemy. Although the two poems are stylistically very different, from a Christian point of view, they both maintain an unpopular vision of the brotherhood of man and the unity of the Church, which they see as necessary for any realistic project of reconstruction. This is, incidentally, an instance of what Eliot, in his Nobel Prize acceptance speech, called, "the supra-national value of poetry."[16]

Concomitantly, in "Resilience and Regeneration: *Four Quartets* in French Translation," co-editor Jessica Stephens examines the spiritual regeneration that can arise from resistance. In *Four Quartets*, resilience is closely connected to the poet's ability to structure events and experience through language, but regeneration occurs through letting go and the alignment with the Divine. The two French translations of *Four Quartets*, by Pierre Leyris and poet Claude Vigée, also bear upon what is at stake in Eliot's poem : survival, resilience as perhaps leading to the good life. Claude Vigée's poetic translation rubs up creatively against the source text, whereas Pierre Leyris's work, because it aligns itself with the wording, opens up to the experience in the poem so that his French version is not only a translation but an offshoot of the source text.

The next section of the volume, "Northern Resistance," considers the opposite extreme of Eliot's point about the supra-national dimension of poetry, by considering it as, in the first instance, a peculiarly local art. Hence, first, Charlotte Estrade demonstrates how Basil Bunting grounds his resistance to mainstream British English poetry in his native Northumbrian culture and language. Bunting was a conscientious objector with social concerns; he also stands for poetic resistance to facile, diluted poetry. His poetics of condensation — sometimes leading to obscurity — make him a lonely figure producing poems which resist comprehension: Bunting is a poet of the "British dissonance."[17] His poetry of the margins involves mythological and semi-historical figures. Although these may seem familiar, the poetic use of such presences serves to mystify the reader and adds to the recondite intricacies of the texts. Ted Hughes explores several kinds of resistance, drawing on his own native region, West Yorkshire, and more especially to the Calder Valley, situated to the west of that region, and some distance south of Bunting's Northumbria. In her chapter "Ted Hughes and 'That Built-In Resistance': Versions of the Calder Valley," Claire Hélie shows that the resistance of the Celts of the ancient kingdom of Elmet to dominion by the British provided a template for Hughes for his identity as a dissenting poet. Resistance appears in various guises in his work on the region and writing itself becomes a site of resistance: against the autobiographical interpretation of poetry, the confessional mode, conformism. "The Rock" (1963) traces the *gravitas* which imbues the mineral Yorkshire landscape and figures Sylvia Plath's "absentia." *Remains of Elmet* (1979) focuses on regeneration, and *Elmet* (1994) on survival. This form of resistance — a grappling with grief at a creative and psychic level — in turn resists completion in writing, as the same sequence is written over and over again. In these poems by Hughes, resistance produces energy.

In the next section, "The Celtic Strain," resistance to change, modernity and (the) English is the driving force behind the life and work of W. B. Yeats. Indeed, Yeats's early poetry was devised as a form of intellectual mutiny against England; later he denounced the philistinism of the Dublin middle classes. Finally, he fought against the Catholic clergy of Ireland, defended Irish Protestants — without ever really embracing the tenets of Christianity — and his lifelong commitment to esotericism amounts to another refusal to please the world. In her essay, Elizabeth Muller demonstrates the way in which Yeats's "embattled stance" in relation to the world of progress, science and democracy evolved. The apotheosis of such rebellion is the famous poem Yeats wrote on his deathbed, "The Black Tower," where mysterious "oath-bound men" resist the banners of modernity whilst waiting for a hypothetical king. Yeats's syntax and diction became radically stripped down to the bare essentials — a few nouns and particularly telling verbs — as if the poem had been hammered out of a block of marble. Thus, Yeats's whole artistic endeavor sometimes results in poems of ruthless efficacy and brutal assertion which, in turn, have often been resisted by critics. In the end, Yeats's struggle against the "drift of the age" has been amply reciprocated and Muller also addresses the issue of critics' and readers' resistance *to* Yeats. Catherine Phillips for her part considers that "Yeats's resists both Irish conformism and modernity — because of the way in which the latter 'dilutes individuality'" while, in "Among Schoolchildren," Yeats takes to task the Church for the standardizing effect of the education it provided. Yeats's poetic voice becomes the voice of protest, as in his poems about Roger Casement. Phillips shows how in his later poetry Yeats turns against the self of the poems of his youth, and this kind of self-resistance is part of Yeats's ongoing "quarrel" with himself. Yeats's work is seen in this essay as a quarrel and an attempt to strike a balance between opposites — between beauty on the one hand, for example, and strength of personality on the other.

Poetry can come out of a quarrel with the self, but it also stems from the desire to look for aesthetic models elsewhere and observe other social environments. Until his death on August 17, 2010, Edwin Morgan was undoubtedly Scotland's pre-eminent poet of the late 20th and early 21st century. As a young man searching for his own poetic voice, translation of poetry from Anglo-Saxon into modern English also proved inspirational. However, because he was utterly antagonistic to the right-wing politics linked with the still-influential Pound and Eliot, Morgan soon turned to the Russian avant-garde poets, particularly Mayakovsky. Translation from Russian and Hungarian but also French, Italian and Spanish formed a significant part of Morgan's output as is more than evident from his hefty tome *Collected Translations* (1996). As Shona M. Allan argues in her essay, "responding and rewording" are modes of intellectual and linguistic resistance for the translator Morgan was — he looked far from home, perhaps because he could not draw on the contemporary poetry of his southern neighbor, perhaps in a conscious or unconscious desire to resist English dominion; perhaps also because he felt a certain kinship with these Eastern European countries and poets. Seeing his environment through a fresh new lens may have contributed to an enhanced awareness of his immediate surroundings but, mostly, translating Eastern European poetry led to vigorous linguistic experimentation — a fresh way of saying.

The three poets examined in the concluding section of the volume "Irony, Play and Pleasure," have all put their stamp on poetic language in English, reveling in both the possibilities and playing with language.

The young Tunisian scholar Boutheina Boughnim Laarif argues that this is an age turned towards "reducibility" and digitalization. However great poetry exceeds the bounds of understanding, it constantly eludes our grasp. Indeed, due to the dynamics inherent in poetic language, the poem constantly generates new meanings, just as criticism over the period covered by the volume has constantly evolved. Poetry confers something beyond the semantic confines of language. The irreducible bodily experience of poetic rhythm is salutary for the reader in that it allows him/her to recognize the limitations of language and if only momentarily break free from them. Laarif makes a case for the "heart," which refers both to emotional inwardness and to the universal dimension of prosodic rhythm; the "poematic" experience, a concept developed by Derrida, brings together this inwardness and the experience of learning the poem by heart. Laarif reads Auden's "September 1, 1939" and "Spain 1937" as examples of the fusing of intimacy and mnemotechniques and this, in turn, enables the poems to be offered and confided to the reader or listener.

Hugo Williams might at first sight seem an unlikely inclusion in a volume devoted to the poetics of resistance. Yet Adrian Grafe's essay "Hugo Williams: Standing the Test of Time?" justifies his poetry's inclusion in the volume, for tone alone can be a kind of resistance, and Williams's wry poetic tone, sometimes absurdist, always undeceived, is in itself a form of resistance to the world. The essay argues that Williams, born half-way through the Second World War in 1942, is a war poet: his many poems on the subject, or which take military matters as their central metaphor, bear this out. Williams and his father are the major enemies in his war poems, the main assailant being the father; the essay examines how the son makes poetry out of resisting, or failing to resist, his father. The essay broadens the argument to focus on Williams's poetic approach as resistance to poetry of the Modernist kind that entered British poetry with *The Waste Land* (1922). Finally, as its title suggests, Grafe's essay seeks to probe whether Williams's poetry has the fragility of ice on the surface of a lake, or whether it will, like gold, survive. The conclusion is that it will — thanks, in a way, to its very fragility.

Another kind of language altogether, that of Caribbean British dub poetry, informs the work of Linton Kwesi Johnson who, in the 1970s and 1980s, used his art to fight British racism, including police brutality, and protest against Thatcherite policies. In 2008 he headlined the "Cultures of Resistance" concert at the Marxism Festival in London. Emily Taylor Merriman asserts that Johnson's role as spokesperson for the oppressed and rebuker of the oppressor renders him resistant to easy accommodation or appropriation. An underlying motivation for Johnson's righteous rage is a vision of the human capacity for joy. In Johnson's work, young people's irrepressible desire to "Goh Rave" should be met, not negated, while adults also have the right to "More Time" for leisure, pleasure, education, and relation. Together with the mourning and anger, Merriman shows how the beat and the linguistic playfulness of Johnson's poetry witness and resist the joylessness that plagues people of all races and classes in an unjust society.

The British poetry of the past hundred and fifty years finally typifies the ways in which the human spirit itself is able to thrive in the most unpropitious of circumstances, be they linguistic, political or cultural, or indeed personal. The diversity of the lines of resistance taken by the poets discussed in this volume and the variety of views expressed by the contributors show that the notion of resistance is not static or fixed as applied to poetry at least. It exceeds mere opposition; resistance is associated with flux, letting go and sidestepping. Resistance proves its effectiveness when allied to adaptability and the capacity to provide alternatives to the given, which is not the least dimension of poetry itself.

Notes

1. Interview with Hill in John Haffenden, *Viewpoints: Poets in Conversation* (London: Faber & Faber, 1981, 76–99), 88.
2. Hill, 88.
3. Edgar Morin, interview in *Le Monde*, 11 June, 2010, 19.
4. Dorothee Soelle, *The Silent Cry: Mysticism and Resistance*, trans. Barbara and Martin Rumscheidt (Minneapolis: Fortress Press, 2001), 272.
5. Soelle, 197.
6. Claire Marin, "Différentes formes de résistance consciente et inconsciente dans la

relation patient/médecin" (Different kinds of conscious and unconscious resistance in the patient/doctor relationship), unpublished lecture given at the Human Sciences Center in Paris on April 2, 2009.

7. Françoise Proust, *De la résistance* (Paris: Cerf, 1997), 117.

8. F. Proust, 12.

9. Soelle, 180.

10. This phrase is taken from a collection of prose texts by Rose Aüslander, *Die Nacht hat zahllose Augen* [The Night Has Countless Eyes] (Francfort-sur-le Main: Fischer Verlag 1995).

11. George Steiner, *After Babel* (London, New York: Oxford University Press 1975), 228.

12. Morin, *Le Monde* interview.

13. Cited in Sidney Burris, *The Poetry of Resistance: Seamus Heaney and the Pastoral Tradition* (Athens: Ohio University Press, 1999), xii.

14. James Longenbach, *The Resistance to Poetry* (Chicago: Chicago University Press, 2000), 108.

15. J. H. Prynne, "Resistance and Difficulty," *Prospect* 5 (Winter 1961, 26–30), 28.

16. http://nobelprize.org/nobel_prizes/literature/laureates/1948/eliot-speech.html.

17. A. K. Weatherhead's *The British Dissonance: Essays on Ten Contemporary Poets* (Columbia, London: University of Missouri Press, 1983), 144.

PART I: FROM CONSTRAINT TO RELEASE

1. The Self-Resisting
Hardy's Ambivalent Evocation of Romantic Childhood
Galia Benziman

As a Post-Romantic poet, Thomas Hardy (1840–1928) is often taken to be a somewhat untypical modernist who, unlike his contemporaries, is still caught by an old-fashioned longing for the pure innocence and harmonious beauty idealized by poets such as Wordsworth, Shelley and Keats. His irony about the applicability of their ideals and aesthetics to his own times notwithstanding, Hardy is indeed unique among the poetic voices of the early twentieth century in his strong attachment to the poetry of the century-old poets he resists. In poems such as "Shelley's Skylark"[1] or "The Darkling Thrush,"[2] he fondly mocks Romantic hyperbolic rhetoric and ideology figured in the trope of the visionary bird, an image that embodies the world's beauty and poetry's grand, sanctified position as its representative. Yet, intent as he is upon "exorcizing that famous bird of its deluding spirit," he still wishes to be "able to experience what Shelley himself had experienced upon hearing the bird sing."[3]

The great influence on Hardy of Romantic poetry, especially Wordsworth's, has been recognized.[4] Clearly, this influence is far from simple. Critics note Hardy's ironic or critical treatment of Romantic images and his use of Wordsworthian vocabulary in a manner that achieves a mock-Romantic style, exposing "some unromantic aspects of life by the very use of Romantic diction."[5] I suggest that more can be said about the ways in which Hardy, while ironizing or inverting them, employs the ideological substance of familiar Romantic tropes. Critical evaluations of Hardy's Post-Romantic position often discuss linguistic and structural patterns; the examination of thematic concerns tends to center around his treatment of Nature. Yet childhood is a no less significant trope, whose important presence in Hardy's work sheds new light on his complex relation to Romantic poetics.

There is a double resistance at work in Hardy's evocation of childhood. His adult speakers often not merely mourn the loss of their earlier innocence but question its very existence in the first place, thus suggesting some self-doubt about the validity of the speaker's own nostalgia. Hardy deeply laments something that has been lost, while craftily exposing it as inherently unreal in the first place, unattainable even by what he constructs as the child that he was. Furthermore, the Romantic idealization of childhood, translated in some of Hardy's works into a refusal to grow up, is shown to nurture, potentially, some self-destructive, irresponsible, or nihilistic impulses. Resisting Romantic idealization, Hardy's poetry also resists its own participation in reproducing it.

In various poems Hardy invokes the topos of the child's ideal innocence that is no longer accessible to the adult, often in a way that seems to manifest relative conformity with the Wordsworthian paradigm of development. In "To Outer Nature,"[6] for example, the speaker's ability to regard nature as spiritually, aesthetically and morally uplifting as it once was, is represented as lost. It had been the child's intuitive gift, sadly taken away from him as he turned into an adult. For Wordsworth and other Romantic poets, the loss of this ability is to be rectified by producing poetry — it is the mission and substance of the poetic project to reawaken the sensibility of the child's response and enable the adult to become a poet, i.e. someone capable of grasping once again, and expressing afresh, the deep meaning and beauty of the world. Like the speakers of "Tintern Abbey" or the *Prelude*, Hardy cherishes this former ability as, in a mixture of gentle irony and affection, he grieves for its loss. Unlike the Wordsworthian speaker, however, he knows that he can no longer retrieve it, as Nature's "first sweetness, / Radiance, meetness, / None shall reawaken."[7] Yet this is not the only difference. For Hardy's speaker, Nature's earlier harmonious, glad, and inspiring beauty has never been clearly, firmly and unquestionably "there." It only offered itself "as I thought thee"[8] i.e., merely as reproduced by the child's fancy.

Similarly, in "The Oxen,"[9] Hardy's speaker expresses his longing for the earlier simplicity and spiritual innocence that allowed him to believe, as a child, in the Christian fable that the farm animals knelt on Christmas Eve, at midnight, to honor the birth of Christ. Though as an unbelieving adult he can no longer cling to the former creed, he wishes he could, feeling even now that "If someone said on Christmas Eve, / 'Come; see the oxen kneel, / In the lonely barton by yonder coomb / Our childhood used to know,' / I should go with him in the gloom, / Hoping it might be so."[10] The fancy that someone should offer to show him the oxen kneel, however, is clearly presented in the poem as far-fetched. Beneath the World-War-One disillusionment that hovers over this 1915 poem, it is mainly "the gloom" that remains.

As critics have suggested, Hardy's deviation from, and resistance to, the Romantic tradition are conflicted. Longing for the Romantic unity of subject and object, yearning for the inspiring harmony between mind and nature, he reproduces some of the thematic patterns and poetic techniques of his literary predecessors while avowing to refute them. Satoshi Nishimura argues that in "To Outer Nature" for example, Hardy does not break with Romantic forms altogether as we might suppose, because he uses the pathetic fallacy and personifies Nature repeatedly in the poem; it is the trope of personification that makes his writing possible.[11] Constructing a speaker who, like Wordsworth, looks towards Nature in order to find meaning, Hardy scorns his own prior childlike innocence although he is not completely free of it.

However, I want to make a stronger claim for Hardy's conflicted resistance to Romantic poetry by locating the ambivalence at an even earlier stage. Not only does the adult in Hardy fail to abandon a Romantic worldview about which he is so skeptical, but the very core of the early childlike innocence and sense of beauty whose loss he mourns is in itself already given as ambiguous. Hardy does not question the child's moral innocence; clearly, his concept of childhood implies that it is free of blame. It is rather the notion of cognitive innocence — the child's guileless unknowingness — that he interrogates. Skeptical about his own childlike cognitive innocence, Hardy's adult speaker often subverts the Wordsworthian paradigm from its foundation.

Focusing on two poems about childhood, "The Self-Unseeing"[12] and "Childhood Among the Ferns,"[13] we should observe that it is not merely the pain over the loss of childlike sensibilities that renders Hardy's critique of Romantic poetics ambiguous, but also the initial sensibility itself that turns out to be already self-contradictory. Hardy resists his own Romantic longing by deconstructing and collapsing the very object of his nostalgic desire.

In both "The Self-Unseeing" and "Childhood Among the Ferns," Hardy's speaker goes back to a scene he remembers from childhood and expresses regret for something that since then was lost. Yet what might seem like a nostalgic mood that underlies these two poems is very mildly, very subtly, inverted or complicated by the accompanying suggestion that this feeling of loss was already embedded in the moment now recalled as the one that evokes longing. What is now longed for as that which can no longer be retrieved, was never fully there to begin with. Hardy's double resistance is, first, the resistance to the necessity to abide by the passage of time, to the coercion to accept change, expressed in the longing for a lost feeling of permanence. Second, in addition to this resistance to the need to grow up and undergo change, there is also Hardy's paradoxical resistance to this very longing. This double resistance creates an internal conflict in each of the two poems. Besides its personal, introspective nature, this conflict is also cultural, poetical and ideological, as it expresses Hardy's undermining of a major Romantic convention: the idealization of the bliss of early life and the elevation of the experience of childlike innocence.

The later poem, "Childhood Among the Ferns," was published posthumously in March 1928, a few weeks after Hardy's death at the age of 88. The explicit theme of this 15-line poem is the child's reluctance to grow up and become a man, envisioning adulthood as a fall from an Edenic beginning — a familiar Romantic trope.

> I sat one sprinkling day upon the lea,
> Where tall-stemmed ferns spread out luxuriantly,
> And nothing but those tall ferns sheltered me.
>
> The rain gained strength, and damped each lopping frond,
> Ran down their stalks beside me and beyond,
> And shaped slow-creeping rivulets as I conned,
>
> With pride, my spray-proofed house. And though anon
> Some drops pierced its green rafters, I sat on,
> Making pretense I was not rained upon.
>
> The sun then burst, and brought forth a sweet breath
> From the limp ferns as they dried underneath:
> I said: "I could live on here thus till death";
>
> And queried in the green rays as I sate:
> "Why should I have to grow to man's estate,
> And this afar-noised World perambulate?"[14]

It is remarkable that in his late eighties, facing death, Hardy was still attached to a childhood memory shaped by the reluctance to grow up. Constructing a child speaker who expresses a wish to remain forever among the ferns, in an eternal childhood, he seems to echo here a familiar Wordsworthian longing. The main sentiment of the poem follows the Pastoral and Romantic preference for a pure, sustaining unity with nature over the unwelcome involvement in social life; the child-speaker laments the need to depart from the far-from-the-madding-crowd setting of his childhood in order to enter the undesirable "afar-noised world" of adult society. Also Romantic is the way in which the poem gives priority to the imagination and to the child's interiority over external fact. The imagination serves to shape reality, as the child's fancied "spray-proofed house" is constructed, subjectively, in order to fend off the rain.

However, as much as the state of childhood may be perceived as protected, Hardy knows that this protection is delusory. But not just Hardy and his adult speaker possess this knowledge in retrospect. The child-speaker himself feels the drops pierce the green leaves, which he calls rafters, and has to pretend that he is not rained upon. This is not the only painful knowledge with which he has to contend. He also knows about his own mortality, introducing into the text the word "death" at the supposedly most life-affirming moment of the poem: his desire to "live on here thus till death" is formulated in a way that highlights its paradoxical nature. This child, like its Romantic precursors, longs for a sense of shelter and permanence that will outweigh the destructive and impersonal powers of time. The emblem of this sense of shelter and permanence, besides the ferns, is childhood itself, the two being merged into an almost vegetative oneness shared by the rained-upon child and the soaked ferns accumulating the drops.

Yet this idealizing concept of childhood, which follows familiar conventions from the Romantic repertoire, is deconstructed in the poem. It is deconstructed by the words Hardy puts into the child's mouth — what appears in the poem as a direct quote in inverted commas, allegedly the child's own voice, unmediated by the adult speaker. These words show us that the child is no longer, perhaps never was, imbued with timeless innocence and a sense of sheltered permanence; he merely yearns to be thus sheltered. The last four lines of the poem invert our expectations, as the child's direct quote, with its surprisingly adult discourse and sentiment, indicates awareness of the negative aspects of growing up and of what it would mean to become a part of the social world. Hardy implies that the child knows about these changes and about his own mortality. Both this awareness and the child's use of a not-particularly-childish diction ("afar-noised," "man's estate," "perambulate") draw our attention to the incongruity of this childlike voice and make us wonder about the child speaker's strangely early fit of nostalgia for childhood, which he experiences somewhat prematurely. More than that, it alerts us to the extent to which adult consciousness overshadows what otherwise would have been a conventionally naïve childlike perspective — a convention that Hardy eschews. Adult projection is, of course, a central factor in the creation of this child's voice. Whether based on actual memories of himself as a precocious child or because of his resistance to Romantic idealization, Hardy abstains from imagining a childlike consciousness that is purely innocent and timeless. If judged by Romantic parameters, Hardy constructs a child who is far more adult than he pretends, or prefers, or would like, to be. This is not a case of double consciousness, in which a speaker is split between the innocent child that he was and the present-day reminiscing adult that he is. The use of direct speech in these four lines, just like the earlier emphasis on the child's pretending, is Hardy's way of presenting us with a child who is already vulnerable to temporality and death, and more than that, a child who already knows the extent of his own vulnerability.

The sheltered innocence of Hardy's child speaker in "Childhood Among the Ferns" is fabricated, implying that although still a child, he is already split. One of the chief categorical distinctions between child and adult according to Romantic thinkers and writers such as Jean-Jacques Rousseau, William Blake or William Wordsworth, is that the child represents the authentic, unified self, which precedes the adult social self. The adult self is irrevocably split between the core of the earlier, authentic self and the acquired, artificial, social self. Yet for Hardy, these binary categories of childhood and adulthood, innocence and experience, which have underlain poetic constructs since Romanticism, are no longer valid. The child knows that this is only a make-believe shelter, and that time will conquer supposed permanence as much as reality will defeat imagination, and raindrops will outweigh green ferns.

The boy's imagination in Hardy's poem is only tentatively and partially granted the power to integrate subject and object in the way that Wordsworth envisions in *The Prelude* or in *The Excursion*, when he tells us how "exquisitely the individual mind [...] / to the external World / Is fitted: — and how exquisitely, too [...] / The external World is fitted to the Mind."[15]

The apparent paradox expressed in "Childhood Among the Ferns" — describing a supposed phase of a child's early blissful sense of timelessness and permanence and at the same time his early recognition of transience and mortality — is a recurrent motif in Hardy's work that is time and again linked to childhood or the childlike. Notably, we encounter this motif in Hardy's last novel, *Jude the Obscure*, where the boy-protagonist feels that he should never consent to the coercion to grow up, but reveals, via this very resistance, the illusory nature of his own state of childlike innocence.

The similarity of the scene in *Jude the Obscure* to the one evoked in "Childhood Among the Ferns" is striking. Based on an actual childhood memory recounted in Hardy's *Life* (an autobiography written in the third person and dictated by the author to his second wife, Florence Emily Hardy), the recurrence of this scene, with variations, indicates that the issue of the child's refusal to grow up had occupied Hardy intensively long before the 1920s poem. In the *Life* he recalls lying on his back, pulling his straw hat over his face, looking at the light between the chinks, and reflecting that he did not want to grow up.[16]

The scene in *Jude the Obscure*, published in 1895, at least thirty years before the posthumously published poem, is almost identical. Lying on his back, the boy Jude "pull[s] his straw hat over his face, and peer[s] through the interstices of the plaiting at the white brightness, vaguely reflecting." He then thinks how

> Nature's logic was too horrid for him to care for [... and] sickened his sense of harmony. As you got older, and felt yourself to be at the centre of your time, and not at a point in its circumference, as you had felt when you were little, you were seized with a sort of shuddering, he perceived. All around you there seemed to be something glaring, garish, rattling, and the noises and glares hit upon the little cell called your life, and shook it, and warped it. If he could only prevent himself growing up! He did not want to be a man.[17]

The focus on internal dynamics is illustrated by the fact that the chief anxiety sensed here is that of being invaded. The cause of suffering is abstract and all-engulfing — it is a "something," that glares and rattles at you, a cluster of "noises." The external world as a whole is perceived as a violent, vulgar intrusion into the child's interiority, the fragile "little cell called your life." Rather than feeling bitter about his concrete experiences with particular people, Jude is oppressed by the broader conditions of existence, Nature's logic being too "horrid" for him to bear.

Ironically, even if Jude had been able to remain a child, he would not have been sheltered from this awareness, because no blessed initial innocence is available to him. There is indeed some difference between childhood and adulthood even in Hardy, a difference that indicates that the child is still somehow protected — Jude, in the passage quoted above, thinks of the shudder that seizes you as you grow up. However, unlike the Romantic paradigm, the difference is not categorical but merely one of degree. The previous state Jude contemplates — his early childhood — differs from his present one (the age of eleven) merely in being located at the "circumference" of his life or at its center. There is an ongoing movement toward this center, and though Jude has not arrived there yet, he can already see what it looks like. There is no possibility of fully enjoying innocence, and even if there had been, it would have only been illusory, the result of observing life from a point that blocks it from sight rather than seeing it for what it really is. The child's dismal thoughts about the world present him as already intruded on by these negative forces. The child is so fully aware of the meaning of growing up, that in a sense he is already "grown-up." He already knows the anguish and pain of adult life. The yearning for a phase of innocence is there, but it is filtered through the poet's realization that its existence is no more than a Romantic construct.

Although shown by Hardy as highly appealing, the boy's Romantic idealization of childhood and resistance to adulthood are simultaneously represented as far-fetched, even false. In the novel, this idealization is also represented as ethically problematic, as the narrative of the boy Jude's growth into a man complicates the pure idealism of the wish to remain a child, and exposes its destructive and irresponsible aspects. This is fully revealed in the narrative sequence that the lyrical poem cannot encompass.[18] For the non-narrativized child of the lyrical poem, the refusal to grow up contains no temporal process of growth, only a frozen moment of resistance to the necessity to enter the adult world with all its complexity and self-contradictions.

The hat on the boy's face in both the *Life* and the novel, as well as the green shelter of the boy in "Childhood Among the Ferns," signifies the distance between these scenes in Hardy and the familiar Romantic evocations of childhood. Rather than looking at nature as a Wordsworthian child would do, in Hardy's writings, the child who wishes to remain a child retreats back into his interiority, away from the outside world, hiding his face, but mainly keeping the world out of his gaze. The child in "Ferns," too, although placed in a natural setting, relies on nature as a device for constructing a closed, secure space, a "home" built by ferns and the imagination to shield him from the menace of the outside. Despite the charm that this verdant home yields, it is also a regressive site, a womblike space associated with maternal protection, where the child hopes to hide himself from his own growth and retreat into his interiority. This retreat is potentially self-destructive — a going back to a prenatal state of non-individuation, before separation, which Freud, in *Beyond the Pleasure Principle*, identifies as a death wish. Hardy, too, recognizes the dark side of this desire to imagine such enveloping natural protection. Sitting in the rain, the child in the poem clings on to the uncertain shelter of mere leaves and stalks, with the risk of being submerged.

Some of the complexity of Hardy's skepticism about the Romantic image of childhood is also revealed in the 1901 poem "The Self-Unseeing," part of Hardy's volume entitled *Poems of the Past and the Present*. It is indeed a poem precisely about, and of, the past and the present, and about the tricky connection between the two. Here, as above, we may observe a dialectical relationship between, on the one hand, a strongly nostalgic mood that idealizes and Romanticizes early childlike bliss, and on the other, an ironic undertone that resists and undermines this nostalgic option by exposing it as deceptive.

> Here is the ancient floor,
> Footworn and hollowed and thin,
> Here was the former door
> Where the dead feet walked in.
>
> She sat here in her chair,
> Smiling into the fire;
> He who played stood there,
> Bowing it higher and higher.

> Childlike, I danced in a dream;
> Blessings emblazoned that day;
> Everything glowed with a gleam;
> Yet we were looking away![19]

Though not explicitly "about" growing up, the three stanzas of this poem, read together with "Childhood Among the Ferns," articulate, in a similar way, a longing for an early, childlike experience of permanence and security that was snatched away by time, growth and death. This poem may seem to lend itself easily and readily to a nostalgic reading: reentering his childhood home, now a dilapidated ghost of a house, the speaker juxtaposes the present-day ruin with the memory of a warm, glorious scene out of early childhood when this was still a home with a family, a father playing the violin, a mother smiling, a fire burning, a child dancing.[20] Critics have indeed read it this way. David Bromwich states that in its lament over the loss caused by temporality, "the poem feels like a small romantic piece."[21] Peter Simpson sees Hardy's glorification of childhood in this poem as closely akin to that of Wordsworth in the *Immortality Ode*.[22] U. C. Knoepflmacher reads the poem as expressing Hardy's "profound yearning for the lost maternal shelter he wants to preserve" and as articulating the adult poet's longing for the oneness he once experienced as a boy, when he was still "presided over by the approving mother."[23]

Yet, as we get to the end of this short poem, we have to realize that in its exploration of the relation between past and present, "The Self-Unseeing," if anything, is about the deceptive side of nostalgia. The last line of the poem inverts what up to this point has indeed seemed to be the speaker's strongly nostalgic gaze. Whatever it is that is missed upon revisiting the house after so many years—whether the visit takes place in reality, in the imagination, or in a dream—that which is now missed has not been lost over time. It is a loss already embedded in the early scene itself. Emblazoned, beautiful, musical and elevating as the early scene may have been, at its core was this failure of the three characters present to see value, beauty or meaning in it.[24]

As in the last lines of "Childhood Among the Ferns," the ending of "The Self-Unseeing" resists the poem's own movement. In "Ferns," it is the mentioning of death by the child speaker that inverts more clearly than anything that precedes it the Romantic supposition that the child is indeed innocently unconscious of time and change. Here, in "The Self-Unseeing," the reversal of the nostalgic suggestion occurs in the last line, with the disturbing insertion of the plural pronoun that creates a jarring effect. If everybody was looking away, what does the speaker have to long for? The use of the "we" instead of the "I," which would have been the more conventionally expected pronoun here, belies the simplistic assumption that the child was so completely surrounded by bliss that he was just too ignorant and innocent to appreciate his own happiness. The fact that the mother and father, too, were looking "away" rather than at each other, or even at themselves, suggests that the sense of family unity and warm, loving proximity was, at least to some extent, an illusion — an illusion for the readers until they reach the last line, and to some extent also for the three actors in this ancient drama, the mother, the father, and the little boy, despite the blessings that emblazon around them. To "look away" means not merely "not to notice"; it signifies active avoidance. What was this family avoiding? Was it resisting its own togetherness? Going back to the ancient-home synecdoches that produce the uncanny atmosphere of the first stanza — the dead feet, and the hollow floor, and the absent door — we should ask ourselves whether the eerie, desolate impression these images create is merely the result of the damage caused by time, change and death. It is possible to see these images as projected back onto the past, as the strange use of tenses suggests.[25] The dead feet are dead in the present, but the use of past tense ("the dead feet walked in") sheds ambiguous light on a far-from-ideal, less-than-blessed, potentially hollow beginning that was this speaker's childhood.

 The knowledge that not merely himself but the parents, too, were looking away is no belated realization arrived at by the now-adult speaker. The less than satisfactory familial set-up, the less than idyllic condition of the speaker's childhood, is not a retrospective epiphany but one of the defining features of the scene from the outset. Looking away and not at each other, the three are indeed hopelessly "unseeing," as the title of the poem suggests. Bearing in mind that sight is the sense that prevails in Romantic poetry, Hardy's emphasis on "unseeing" is significant, exposing the way in which looking away with the mind's eye obscures those things that are near. Like the child with the hat on his face, who Romantically refuses to grow up and face the external world of social interaction, the gaze of the family members in the poem — directed away from the present scene and from their own kin — is suggestive of solipsistic evasion, represented by Hardy as psychologically appealing yet ethically problematic.

 Looking back at the first line of the last stanza, still part of the heart of the poem — the remembered scene itself — we may also notice the strange use of the adjective "childlike" attached to the speaker-as-child. A more simple meaning, as Marjorie Levinson suggests, would require a different phrasing; it would have been more natural to say "a child, I danced" instead. According to Levinson, "Child*like* measures the inauthenticity of the innocence, or its status as impersonation rather than a state of immediate and unself-conscious being."[26] Impersonating a child's innocence, this younger self of the speaker will be replicated in the child speaker of the later "Childhood Among the Ferns"—a speaker who must actively pretend he is not rained upon, acting as if his childhood grants him absolute and permanent innocence, massively denying all along the deeper understanding that this is not the case. Asserting his childlike position, the speaker of "The Self-Unseeing" similarly uses emphatically non-childlike diction as he recounts his childhood experience.[27]

Significantly, the plural pronoun "we" of the last line of "The Self-Unseeing" also undermines the categorical, conceptual separation of child and adult. The failure is shared by all three participants in the early drama, and this unity serves to deconstruct even further the Romantic dichotomy according to which childhood is not merely an ideal phase, but one that is categorically and diametrically different from the state of adulthood. For Hardy, as this line and the mixed linguistic register of the final stanza indicate, there is no such separation.

The wish that the child should not "look away" in the 1901 poem, and the child speaker's fantasy of remaining forever among the ferns of eternal childhood in the 1920s poem, both manifest, to some extent, a familiar Romantic resistance to the necessity to grow up and a Romantic stance of revolt against the need to join the noisy, potentially callous adult world of impersonal social interaction, artificial social selves, the world of mortality and loss. Hardy shares this stance to some extent. Yet the form of the poems highlights his ambiguity about this resistance, as the poems' very endings conflict with their own nostalgic and regressive drift and imply that "adulthood" is already imprinted on the child.

Notes

1. Thomas Hardy, *Complete Poems*, Ed. James Gibson (London: Macmillan, 1976), 101. Written in 1887, the poem was included in Hardy's *Poems of the Past and the Present* (1901).
2. *Complete Poems*, 150. Written on 31 December 1900, the poem was published in *The Times* on New Year's day, 1 January 1901, under the title "By the Century's Deathbed." It was later included, under the current title, in *Poems of the Past and the Present*.
3. Iris Tillman-Hill, "Hardy's Skylark and Shelley's" in *Victorian Poetry* 10/1 (Spring 1972, 79–83), 79, 81.
4. Peter Casagrande provides ample evidence for Wordsworth's early major influence on Hardy, and argues that even at the final stages of his career, as late as 1922, Hardy "continued to wish to be seen as a descendant of Wordsworth." See Casagrande, "Hardy's Wordsworth: A Record and a Commentary" in *English Literature in Transition* 20/4 (1977, 210–37), 222, 226. Walter Wright states that "the influence of Wordsworth permeated Hardy's work [as both] were again and again trying to express similar feelings." See Walter Wright, *The Shaping of* The Dynasts (Lincoln: University of Nebraska Press,

1967), 79–80. Bernard Jones brings evidence from Hardy's "*Studies, Specimens &c.*" *Notebook* indicating that from about 1865 he had been a close reader of Wordsworth's poetry. See "1798–1898: Wordsworth, Hardy, and 'The Real Language of Men': A Centenary Note" in *English Studies* 80/6 (December 1999, 509–17), 509. Dennis Taylor maintains that Wordsworth is "so pervasive an influence that he cannot be confined to specific parallels and contrasts." Dennis Taylor, "Hardy and Wordsworth" in *Victorian Poetry* 24/4 (Winter 1986, 441–54), 441–42.

5. Kenkichi Kamijima, "The Terrestrial Imagination: The Poet Hardy in the Romantic Tradition" in *The Wordsworth Circle* 29/1 (Winter 1998, 79–84), 80. According to Kamijima, Hardy's relation to Wordsworth was ambivalent, a "paradoxical alienation from what he had been longing for in heart" (81). Dennis Taylor, too, claims that several of Hardy's poems seem to "parody and reverse Wordsworth's poems" ("Hardy and Wordsworth," 443). Peter Casagrande defines Hardy's use of Wordsworth as an effort toward "intellectual revisionism" ("Hardy's Wordsworth" 211), i.e., a swerve from Wordsworth's views, in Hardy's mind closely associated with Christian orthodoxy, on God, Man, and Nature. Casagrande observes that Hardy did not regard influence as anxiety (211). It is indeed interesting that in *The Anxiety of Influence*, Harold Bloom famously maintains that Hardy is one of the very few poets who "attain the poetry of discontinuity" (London: Oxford University Press, 1973), 80.

6. *Complete Poems*, 61. Published in Hardy's 1898 *Wessex Poems and Other Verses*, the title in the manuscript had been "To External Nature."

7. "To Outer Nature," ll. 23–25.

8. "To Outer Nature," l. 1.

9. *Complete Poems*, 468. First published in *The Times* on Christmas Eve, 24 December 1915.

10. "The Oxen," ll. 11–16.

11. Satoshi Nishimura, "Thomas Hardy and the Language of the Inanimate" in *SEL* 43/4 (Autumn 2003, 897–912), 901.

12. *Complete Poems* 166. First published in *Poems of the Past and the Present*, 1901.

13. *Complete Poems* 864. Published posthumously in March 1928. The date of composition is unknown, but it is assumed that the poem was written between 1924 and 1928. See Dennis Taylor, "The Chronology of Hardy's Poetry" in *Victorian Poetry* 37/1 (Spring 1999, 1–58), 57.

14. *Complete Poems*, 864.

15. *The Excursion* V, ll. 63–70 (1814). Kenkichi Kamijima uses this passage to offset the different subject-object relations in Hardy's poems with the Romantic paradigm, according to which the inner mind, or imagination, transforms the physical universe ("The Terrestrial Imagination," 82–83).

16. See F. E. Hardy, *The Life of Thomas Hardy, 1840–1928* (London: Macmillan, 1962), 15–16.

17. Thomas Hardy, *Jude the Obscure* (New York: W. W. Norton, 1999), 17.

18. A major difference between narrative and lyric is that the former is usually understood to be a mode that foregrounds a sequence of events, whereas lyric is seen as a mode that foregrounds "a simultaneity, a cluster of feelings or ideas that projects a gestalt in stasis." See Susan Stanford Friedman, "Lyric subversions of Narrative in Women's Writing: Virginia Woolf and the Tyranny of Plot" in *Reading Narrative: Form, Ethics, Ideology*, Ed. James Phelan (Columbus: Ohio State University Press, 1989), 164.

19. *Complete Poems*, 166.

20. It is assumed that the poem is based on an actual early-childhood memory

recounted in Hardy's *Life*. See Peter Simpson, "Hardy's 'The Self-Unseeing' and the Romantic Problem of Consciousness" in *Victorian Poetry* 17/1–2 (Spring-Summer 1979, 45–50), 45.
  21. David Bromwich, "Poetic Invention and the Self-Unseeing" in *Grand Street* 7/1 (Autumn 1987, 115–29), 115.
  22. Peter Simpson, "Hardy's 'The Self-Unseeing' and the Romantic Problem of Consciousness," 49–50.
  23. U. C. Knoepflmacher, "Hardy Ruins: Female Spaces and Male Designs" in *PMLA* 105/5 (October 1990, 1055–70), 1064–65.
  24. According to Susan Miller, "The Self-Unseeing" finds its lyric emotion "not in the energy of recognition, but rather in the pathos of the logic that insists we remain ignorant just when meaning would seem to matter most, or that proves the knowledge one would wish for to be unattainable." She regards this as an underlying principle of many of Hardy's poems. See Miller's "Thomas Hardy and the Impersonal Lyric" in *Journal of Modern Literature* 30/3 (Spring 2007, 95–115), 98.
  25. Peter Simpson cites this line as an example of the "disconcerting mixture of tenses" that often occurs in Hardy's verse and that serves as a powerful effect of "Hardy's bifocalism with respect to time" ("Hardy's 'The Self-Unseeing' and the Romantic Problem of Consciousness," 47).
  26. Marjorie Levinson, "Object-Loss and Object-Bondage: Economies of Representation in Hardy's Poetry" in *ELH* 73/2 (2006, 549–80), 572.
  27. Jill Richards observes the linguistic interplay of the poem as, "sliding into the highly wrought 'emblazoned,' the colloquial 'higher and higher' is belatedly set gleaming as it lands upon a word that is at once out of place and irreplaceable." Jill Richards, "'The History of Error': Hardy's Critics and the Self Unseen" in *Victorian Poetry* 45/2 (Summer 2007, 117–33), 121. Yet Richards does not point out the age aspect of the inconsistent linguistic register; the high "emblazoned" marks a shift to strikingly elevated adult diction.

Works Cited

Bloom, Harold (1973), *The Anxiety of Influence: A Theory of Poetry*. London: Oxford University Press.
Bromwich, David (1987), "Poetic Invention and the Self-Unseeing" in *Grand Street*, 7/1, 115–29.
Casagrande, Peter J. (1977), "Hardy's Wordsworth: A Record and a Commentary," in *English Literature in Transition*, 20/4, 210–37.
Friedman, Susan Stanford (1989), "Lyric subversions of Narrative in Women's Writing: Virginia Woolf and the Tyranny of Plot" in *Reading Narrative: Form, Ethics, Ideology*. Ed. James Phelan. Columbus: Ohio State University Press, 162–85.
Hardy, Florence Emily (1962), *The Life of Thomas Hardy, 1840–1928*. London: Macmillan.
Hardy, Thomas (1976), *The Complete Poems*. Ed. James Gibson. London: Macmillan.
_____ (1999), *Jude the Obscure*. New York: W. W. Norton.
Jones, Bernard (1999), "1798–1898: Wordsworth, Hardy, and 'The Real Language of Men': A Centenary Note" in *English Studies: A Journal of English Language and Literature*, 80/6, 509–17.

Kamijima, Kenkichi (1998), "The Terrestrial Imagination: The Poet Hardy in the Romantic Tradition" in *The Wordsworth Circle*, 29/1, 79–84.

Knoepflmacher, U. C. (1990), "Hardy Ruins: Female Spaces and Male Designs" in *PMLA*, 105/5, 1055–70.

Levinson, Marjorie (2006), "Object-Loss and Object-Bondage: Economies of Representation in Hardy's Poetry" in *ELH*, 73/2, 549–80.

Miller, Susan (2007), "Thomas Hardy and the Impersonal Lyric" in *Journal of Modern Literature*, 30/3, 95–115.

Nishimura, Satoshi (2003), "Thomas Hardy and the Language of the Inanimate" in *SEL*, 43/4, 897–912.

Richards, Jill (2007), "'The History of Error': Hardy's Critics and the Self Unseen" in *Victorian Poetry*, 45/2, 117–33.

Simpson, Peter (1979), "Hardy's 'The Self-Unseeing' and the Romantic Problem of Consciousness" in *Victorian Poetry*, 17/1–2, 45–50.

Taylor, Dennis (1999), "The Chronology of Hardy's Poetry" in *Victorian Poetry*, 37/1, 1–58.

―――. (1986), "Hardy and Wordsworth," in *Victorian Poetry*, 24/4, 441–54.

Tillman-Hill, Iris (1972), "Hardy's Skylark and Shelley's" in *Victorian Poetry*, 10/1, 79–83.

Wright, Walter (1967), *The Shaping of* The Dynasts. Lincoln: University of Nebraska Press.

2. Hardy's Cunning in Form and Diction

Emilie Loriaux

In one great act of resistance, following a scandal around his novel *Jude the Obscure* in 1896, Hardy deliberately gave up prose fiction for poetry, his first love. It was an act of resistance to his critics, and to a form the practice of which had always been a means of responding to financial pressure, which he had by now in any case doubtless outgrown. This enigmatic countryman always claimed to be a poet before being a novelist. This essay will mainly focus on Hardy's *Poems of the Past and the Present* (1901), and more specifically on three poems. The success of the volume won him recognition as a poet in his own right, and not merely as a novelist turned poet, something he disliked being seen as.[1] In a letter of October 22nd 1900, Hardy hinted at his reservations concerning the publication of various poems within the collection:

> I am puzzled what to do with some poems, written at various dates, a few lately, some long ago. If I print them I know exactly what will be said about them: "You hold opinions which we don't hold: therefore shut up." Not that there are any opinions in the verses; but English reviewers go behind the book & review the man.[2]

It would perhaps have been easier for Hardy not to publish these poems and passively "shut up." However, he chose to over-ride resentment; in 1901 his *Poems of the Past and the Present* collection became available to the public. Moreover, as Hardy claimed in his preface to this collection in August 1901:

> that portion which may be regarded as individual comprises a series of feelings and fancies written down in widely differing moods and circumstances, and at various dates. It will probably be found, therefore, to possess little cohesion of thought or harmony of coloring. I do not greatly regret this. Unadjusted impressions have their value, and the road to a true philosophy of life seems to lie in humbly recording diverse readings of its phenomena as they are forced upon us by chance and change.[3]

Therefore, diversity does not seem to bother Hardy, and his words above seem to pre-empt any possible criticism; his writing has to be judged as a path towards a particular and "true philosophy of life." Deliberately choosing his own philosophy, Hardy cunningly makes his own way through the creation of diverse poetic works in which chaos and randomness are among the ruling principles. The three main selected poems discussed in this article all bear on the poet's reluctance to enter or fathom a place somehow alien to him — at the core of these poems, there is a contradiction between the proximity of harmless creatures or elements of nature and a deliberate wish on the poet's part to resist the world to which they belong. "An August Midnight" (1899) refers to the animal microcosm, which Hardy is both true to and amazed by, yet which remains inaccessible. "The Darkling Thrush," initially entitled "By the Century's Deathbed" (1900), deals with a grey thrush, seemingly celebrating the new century; yet it was the time of the Boer War (1899–1902) and the poet is unable to enter or fully perceive the thrush's joyful world. These two poems take nature as their starting-point. The third chosen poem, "Drummer Hodge" (1899), alludes to the Boer War and the feelings of an anonymous Dorset soldier killed in battle, the parts of whose body — "His homely Northern breast and brain" (l. 15) — turn into "some Southern tree" (l. 16) in this "unknown," alien landscape. These poems were written at or around the turn of the century, an ambiguous, difficult time for the British nation. A poem like "Drummer Hodge" may run counter to the notion of British Imperial order. Tensions are always perceptible in Hardy's poetry due to the uncertain position of the poet, which up to point reflected the late nineteenth century's own uncertainties. Yet Hardy perceives the world in a still more complex way by resisting the "good and evil (...) philosophy that permeated Victorian literature."[4]

Apart from such general considerations, Hardy resisted certain conventions of written English in his poems, and some of his effects are achieved by the ways in which he brings a prosaic sense into his poetry; he thus opposed standard notions of what was poetic and what was not. Hardy's poetry is known for what Andrew Motion calls its "cunning irregularity"[5] — a term loosely linked to the experimental forms and structures he encountered when he was an apprentice architect. He was a poet who liked coining words. At the same time, nostalgia sometimes shows in his choice of foreign, Anglo-Norman words, dialect words and sounds, Anglo-Saxon or compound words. His "resistance to [the] sense of inevitable loss," in Catherine Lanone's phrase, appears in the choice of poetical structures which contribute to his poems' "unlulling metrical irregularity."[6] Yet a paradox can be underlined between conservatism and innovation. Hardy defies rigid poetics and diction and sets up resistance, as it were, between the nineteenth century and the beginning of the twentieth century. Then, the tensions stemming from what one might call the in-between or interstitial position of the poet reveal other types of resistance specific to Hardy. When his tone is humorous it can be indicative of resistance. Diction — defined as "the manner of enunciation in speech and singing; choice of words or phrases in speech or writing" (OED) — can be both odd and provocative in Hardy's poetry.

"The Darkling Thrush," dated 31 December 1900, and first published beneath a different title two days earlier, stages the turn of the century. In this poem, the wind's moan is a "death-lament" (1. 12) while the solitary thrush carols joyfully: this epitomizes both the dawn of the century and the doubtful feelings of an in-between time. This paradox is evident throughout the poem where Hardy juxtaposes the coldness of the compound adjective "spectre-gray" (1. 2) and the noun phrase "the growing gloom" (1. 24) with the warmth conjured up by "their household fires" (1. 8) and "his happy good-night air" (1. 30). The presence of the possessive adjectives "their" and "his" provides a comforting sense of familiarity. Likewise, the strange atmosphere, with its hint of the *unheimlich*, conjured up by the compound adjectives "spectre-gray" (1. 2), "blast-beruffled" (1. 22) and "death-lament" (1. 12) can be contrasted with the compound adjective "full-hearted" in a "full-hearted evensong" (1. 19). Such a representation of reality through a certain joy in life, almost forgetting the pains of real life and taking pleasure in "the poetic vision"— or, one might say, the poetic audition — is a testimony to Hardy's opposition to a "certain genre of poetry."[7] He is very good at this sort of writing, which Michael Edwards describes as "prosaic."[8] In fact, he paradoxically achieves his effects by a certain prosaicness in his poetry, and this in part embodies his opposition to Romanticism. By describing the thrush as "frail, gaunt and small / In blast-beruffled plume" (1. 21–22) before celebrating the beauty of its voice "caroling" (1. 25), Hardy takes care not to romanticize the bird. At the same time, "there is delicacy and beauty in his realism," even if nature itself can at times be merciless.[9] This type of poetry conveys a blurred image of the world depicted by the poet: a constant restraint seems to be placed on total quietness or happiness.

The world Hardy describes, then, can be dark, without outlandish ornament; yet there are often hints of light or color. The latter are not always obvious at first reading. Hardy subtly disguises the positive attributes of nature, possibly to give his poems more mystery and artistry, as a painter might add a hidden light color to a dark painting. "An August Midnight" focuses on the microcosmic animal world, which is almost baffling for human beings who cannot access its meaning. On the one hand, animals interfere in human life, as they enter the poet's working place and intimacy: "Thus meet we five, in this still place" (l. 7) and these animals are "guests [who] besmear [the poet's] new-penned line / Or bang at the lamp and fall supine" (l. 9). Their gentle intrusion seems to bear fruit as the poet cannot but marvel at their sight: "God's humblest, they!" (l. 11). On the other hand, this gathering is disturbing because, at the end, their realm remains inaccessible to the poet: "They know Earth-secrets that know not I" (l. 12). Some kind of impediment quite often appears in Hardy's poetry, even if at first there is no apparent obstacle to harmony. There is still a suggestion of optimism and hope through the presence of the "lamp" (l. 1), though it is "shaded," and despite his bemusement the poet welcomes the "guests" (l. 9) from the natural world. Tension is conveyed through small constraining details. Thus, the "shaded lamp" resists full brightness, the fly is impeding his work but is described in gently humorous terms as being "idle" and "sleepy" (l. 6); the lamp makes the animals "fall supine" (l. 10), leaving them in a latent state teetering between death and life. One interpretation could be that man-made objects, like the "lamp," can be harmful to nature. These objects have a potentially destructive effect on nature. Through such means, Hardy might be perceived as expressing disapproval of modernity and by extension mechanization at the dawn of the 20th century.

In "The Darkling Thrush," Hardy reverses this perspective — in the apparent opposition between humankind and the natural world reveals the poet's wish to add a touch of human warmth to nature. Thus the "household fires" (l. 8), man-made as they are, stand for human warmth as against the dreariness of nature outside. Hardy breaks down the frontier between the two worlds. However, even if fire adds a touch of coziness to the scene, mystery still permeates the scene, previously "haunted" by "all mankind." As in "An August Midnight," although the two worlds might seem to be meshing, something always interferes. Here, the verb "haunted" adds mystery to the scene. Once more, Hardy resists total darkness or total light in his poetic microcosm. For Hardy, this instability reflects the wealth of impressions afforded by life. His poetic craft may be a product of his skeptical state of mind, at the turn of the century: an in-between period he does not want to leave behind and yet tends to resist through poetry neither black nor white. As Michael Edwards explains: "The prosaic act performed by English poets enables [...] a return to poetry's aspiration to recreate positive reality."[10] What Hardy is offering his readers is as closely authentic and realistic an image of the life of his time as possible.

In "The Darkling Thrush," negative words outnumber the positive ones. "[S]pirits" are "feverless" (l. 15–16), "twigs" are "bleak" (l. 18), the thrush is "aged," "frail, gaunt, and small" (l. 21) and its "plume" is "blast-beruffled" (l.

22). Even positive and optimistic nouns are attenuated by negative adjectives such as "The ancient pulse of germ and birth / Was shrunken hard and dry" (1. 13–14). Yet typically for Hardy, a hint of tenacious and underlying hope is still present through three positive terms: "household fires" (1. 8), "ecstatic sound" (1. 26) and "happy good-night air" (1. 30). The scenes in Hardy's poetry are therefore less contrasted than in Romantic poetry, or indeed in writings by naïve or pessimistic authors. Hardy is not afraid of reaching a state of confusion — his own, unconventional way of perceiving reality. Hardy is a skilful observer and technician:

> I take a keen pleasure in war strategy & tactics, following it as if it were a game of chess; but all the while I am obliged to blind myself to the human side of the matter: directly I think of that, the romance looks somewhat tawdry, & worse. I do not, of course, refer to this particular war, & the precise shade of blame or otherwise which attaches to us.[11]

Fascinated by strategies and "tactics," Hardy seems to learn from them as his way of writing provides different methods such as his technique of concealing "ecstatic"[12] and mysterious details to temper the dark vision of the poem. The world he pictures might appear to be black and white, but as in a "game of chess," rules and "tactics" make it more complex, allowing for cunning strategies within the game, which are a form of resistance to the rules and a way of pre-empting criticism. Therefore, Hardy resists conventions and plays his own poetical game. In order to draw the readers' attention to his words of resistance, Thomas Hardy also resorts to music.

The musicality of Hardy's poetry is another form of tactical resistance to the apparently simplistic black-and-white vision afforded by the poems for which he was reproached. In "The Darkling Thrush," the poet intertwines musical touches with the dark and gloomy atmosphere of the wintry countryside. Music brings the poem to life, breaking up the dreary monotony of the thrush's existence — and the poet's. This is pure resistance to passivity and it disrupts the apparent brooding scene. The thrush's song seems to mend the "broken lyres" (1. 6), as the "ecstatic sound" (1. 26) of his "full-hearted evensong" (1. 19) echoes in the bleak countryside.

Hardy's poetry also reveals resistance to preconceptions, such as animals being worth less than human beings — hence, for example, the gentle personification of the fly in "An August Midnight." He continues with the personification in the second stanza: "My guests besmear my new-penned line, / Or bang at the lamp and fall supine" (1. 9–10). The ridiculousness of the action is conveyed through the rhyme. The humor here arises from the word "guests," the behavior of whom is far from exemplary, as well as from the over-insistent rhyme and the fact that the rhyme jars as natural word-stress—"*Supine*"—clashes with meter here, which in theory would require "*suPine.*" The sound of the rhyme, then, imitates in sound the insects' clumsiness. There is something close to absurdity here; the rational poet is associated with insects. Therefore, as John Paul Riquelme notes "Hardy's humor" can cause "dislocation[s]," since the insect implication turns the poet "back into something less than human."[13] In addition, by "besmearing" the poet's writing, the natural creatures imperil the poet's creation, making it unreadable, and thus poetic composition becomes resistance to the destructive power of nature, though here on a laughably small scale. Hardy on the one hand stands up to the apparent insignificance of life on earth, but he also makes this natural microcosm more vivid than it appears at first sight.

Dennis Taylor's viewpoint is not so far removed from Michael Edwards's conception of the "prosaic" mentioned above. Hardy's poems can be read in the light of Robert Penn Warren's New Critical approach: "Poetry wants to be pure, but poems do not.... They mar themselves with cacophonies, jagged rhythms, ugly words and ugly thoughts, colloquialisms, clichés, sterile technical terms, head work and argument, self-contradictions, clevernesses, irony, realism—all things which call us back to the world of prose and imperfection...."[14] Hardy is therefore a poet, who resists both poetry—or rather a certain kind of "poetry"—and prose, through the creation of a personal form of poetry. Yet, according to Taylor, "the difficulty with the New Critical approach is that it groups Hardy too easily with other modern poets who seem to have much more control over their ironic anomalies of diction; it makes Hardy a less conscious artist than them and ends up supporting the "good little Thomas Hardy" theory."[15] Hardy is different from Modernists and mainly resists any modern form of "cacophonies" as he creates his own cacophonic oddities. Indeed, to return to "The Darkling Thrush," Hardy uses coinages like the compound adjective "blast-beruffled" (1. 22), with its slightly heavy, stuttering alliteration and hint of archaism, to depict the thrush, and perhaps the speaker himself. Oddities may also come from weird associations of nouns and adjectives, as when the thrush sings with "such ecstatic sound" (1. 26).

Beyond musicality, coinages, and contrastive associations of words, Hardy's own mode of poetic resistance is reflected in word choice. The name "Hodge" in the eponymous poem "Drummer Hodge," originally published as "The Dead Drummer" in 1899, is a pejorative nickname attributed to country folk by city dwellers. This term is deliberately chosen to point to, and counter, the scornful behavior of urban inhabitants towards country people and correct their false image. In "Drummer Hodge," a poem of protest and therefore of resistance, the prefix "un-" seems to be significant because it links the words "Uncoffined" (l. 2; although the affirmative verb form "coffined" would in itself be unusual) and "unknown" (l. 13). The prefix "un-" is a marker of absence. "Unknown plain" (l. 13) could be interpreted not only as unknown to the soldier but as a place unfamiliar to the reader; Hardy does not want to mention any place in particular. The poem could almost be any poem dealing with a non-place or anonymous place. Hardy seems to be underlining the sensation of loss and anonymity of soldiers, who are nothing but pawns — almost as "if it were a game of chess" — serving England in the middle of nowhere. Likewise, the "Uncoffined" soldier reveals that he dies with his humanity unacknowledged. Hardy's choice of word is also noteworthy because, etymologically, the prefix "un-" is "often euphemistic."[16] "Uncoffined" (l. 2) implies that the Drummer's life has been literally thrown away at the front line. He is without "coffin" — but he is directly sent forth to the "coffin." A hint of pathos is suggested in protest at the lack of humanity and cruelty towards the "Wessex" crowd (l. 8), even though they served the British nation in wartime. Furthermore, the word "Uncoffined" is not the poet's invention but an archaic word, whose origin goes back to the 1640–1650s.[17] Hardy unearths or literally "uncoffins" the word, suggesting perhaps that leaving a corpse uncoffined is barbaric whatever the historical period, and that the passage of the centuries and progress of civilization have not diminished such barbarity. Such linguistic exploration is, in the context of "Drummer Hodge," an act of resistance to the deceitful reality of war. Besides, the double dashes around "—/ Fresh from his Wessex home —" enclose the Drummer in the past and in rural time, and perhaps imply rejection of the new century. While perpetuating his nostalgia for the drummer's (recent) past, Hardy symbolically and "eternally" (l. 18) sidesteps the Boer War and its horrors. What is more, those dashes might also represent the uncertainties at the turn of the century. James Gibson stresses Hardy's mixed feelings: "Hardy's attitude to war was a strange mixture of horror and sadness, fascination and repulsion."[18] Hardy resists any fixed position towards war, and perhaps any fixed position at all.

The poet here attempts to juxtapose past and present, Wessex and South Africa. Yet he doesn't merely juxtapose them: he plays them off against one other. The term "kopje-crest" (l. 3) begins with a word of Afrikaans origin meaning a small hill, followed by an English word; but each keep their own identity. Taylor states that "the artistic norm of a work's internal coherence is a model of the linguistic norm of a naturalized language. Hardy's awkwardness is interesting because it challenges both these norms of coherence and of naturalized language."[19] The apparent confusions in the poetic writing might hence come from an elusive association and contrast of ideas, meters and sounds. For instance, in "Drummer Hodge," Hardy reiterates the idea of the "constellations" in the first and third stanzas: "And foreign constellations west" (1. 5), "And strange-eyed constellations reign" (1. 17). The adjective "foreign" gives the poem an exotic and unfamiliar mood. This atmosphere is even more outlandish when the constellations are collocated with the compound "strange-eyed." Hardy pushes the reader to the limits of his imagination. These obscure, "typical Hardyisms"[20] keep at bay any possible conclusion concerning the poems. It is as if the poet never wants the poem to end. Uncertainties and indeterminacy linger in Hardy's poems, enacting resistance to any permanent statement. Hardy's poetry incessantly resists closure.

In addition, Hardy's method tends to eschew too much detail. Samuel Hynes, in his comparison of two versions of another poem: "The Caged Goldfinch," which appeared in *Moments of Vision*, notes that the poet's revision and dropping of the last stanza in *The Collected Poems* allows "a juxtaposition of disparate images (...) to produce a kind of minor chord of emotions. To specify details is to destroy this chord."[21] Likewise, in the final line of "The Darkling Thrush" and "An August Midnight," Hardy leaves us as it were in the dark: the poems respectively end on "And I was unaware" (1. 32) and "They know Earth-secrets that know not I" (1. 12). These lines open up the poem to another world, of which the speaker is paradoxically "unaware." The poet purposefully places himself in the margin.

This marginalization is reflected in Hardy's language as well. If we consider Taylor's remark that "the standard language is a sign of deracination,[22]" this Dorset writer, who brings together bits of Standard English with other forms such as occasional dialect words–"Dumbledore" (1. 4) (August Midnight), "kopje-crest" (1. 3), "the veldt" (1. 4), or "Karoo" (1. 9) (Drummer Hodge), nonce words — "stranged-eyed" (1. 17) ("Drummer Hodge) or "ecstatic sound" (1. 26) ("The Darkling Thrush"), and archaisms like "blast-beruffled" (1. 22) ("The Darkling Thrush"), in his poems — is even more than a "déraciné." He is an in-between poet, capable of combining different registers of language within a very personal style. This association of various words helps provide his poetry with a touch of pleasant awkwardness and originality. He refuses to fit in with the expectations of the elite of his time. He deliberately distinguishes himself from them. This could be perceived as a form of protest against the literary circles of his period and might also explain why Hardy was disgusted by the London upper middle-classes. James Gibson says that in the 1890s Hardy was divided between "the artificial gaieties of a London season and the quaintnesses of a primitive rustic life."[23] Hardy had to come to terms with his own ambivalent position, half-rural, half-urban; and he conveys this feeling through his word-choices. His approach was partly intended to counteract metropolitan expectations and reinforce a sense of regionalism — or perhaps, even, attempt to shift the center to the region — through his occasional choice of dialect words. Taylor emphasizes such ambivalence in diction in these terms: "The fun of the literary tradition is how the revolutionaries reveal possibilities in poetic diction and meter not seen before, and how these possibilities come to be accepted. (...) Not only does [Hardy] challenge the conservative ideal of decorum represented in eighteenth-century theory, but he challenges the fundamental bases of taste and choice in word and idiom."[24] Yet Hardy refuses to impose his ideas. Andrew Motion asserts in his selection of Hardy's poems in 1994: "At moments when other writers might feel compromised he is secure; when others might be overwhelmed his imagination discovers its greatest freedom."[25] His poetic irregularity means that his style is not standard resistance but an in-between state between opposition and convention, given how he exploits the standard devices of meter, rhythm and rhyme, not to mention long-established forms like the ballad.

Indeed, a careful look at "Drummer Hodge" will show how Hardy defies canonical word order in poetry. The syntax in the third stanza syntax:

> Yet portion of that unknown plain
> Will Hodge for ever be;
> His homely Northern breast and brain
> Grow to some Southern tree,
> And strange-eyed constellations reign
> His stars eternally.

Instead of: "Will Hodge for ever be;" (1. 14), in prose this might have read: "Hodge will be for ever." The first two lines here might read: "Yet Hodge will forever be a portion of that unknown plain." The inversions show Hardy's resistance to what is traditionally expected. A comparison can be drawn with Milton's style in *Paradise Lost* (1667), which was criticized as "a Northern dialect which adapts to inversions and intonations of Greek and Latin, and despite its magnificence," and which represented "the corruption of the English language."[26] In Hardy's poetry, the breaking of classical and poetic form is also reinforced through the particular structure of the following lines: "And foreign constellations west / Each night above his mound." (1. 5–6) and "And strange-eyed constellations reign / His stars eternally." (1. 17–18). The reader is first disturbed by the apparent lack of verb in ll. 5–6, as "west" is normally a noun or an adjective. Here, "west" is used as a verb. This verb echoes "reign," which is apparently used in a non-standard way, besides conjuring up a vision of the homophonic "rain." Moreover, the noun "stars" stands in apposition to "constellations," and the canonical syntax would commonly have been: "And his stars, strange-eyed constellations, reign eternally." Likewise, in "An August Midnight," the last line: "They know Earth-secrets that know not I" shows a non-canonical order. The usual order might be: "I know not." The slightly archaic diction suggests that the poet repeats the verb "to know"; he might have merely written in Standard English: "They know secrets that I don't." This disruption of the expected order in poetry is in its own right a form of provocation of the literary circles of the time. As Dennis Taylor writes: compared to "many creative writers," Hardy is different; "the difference is that in other writers the sense of deviation from the expected norm is replaced by a new norm within the creative work, a new coherence, a new idiom. But Hardy never arrives at this creation of a new norm; he calls norms themselves into question."[27]

However, Hardy's poetry is in some ways traditional in its form. Indeed, "An August Midnight" presents two stanzas which are headed by the Roman numerals I and II, lending the poem a certain classical *gravitas* perhaps belied by its brevity and informal tone. "An August Midnight" and "Drummer Hodge" also have a strict rhyme pattern. In "An August Midnight," the first stanza is made up of alternate rhymes, and the second of couplet rhymes. In "Drummer Hodge" the regularity of the alternate rhymes evokes the funeral march, as a solemn tribute to the Drummer. On October 12, 1899, the Boer War broke out and threw the English world into chaos. As Morgan says: "Most of the press was urging poets and journalists alike to be martial and patriotic."[28] "Drummer Hodge" can be perceived as a small poetic rebellion against the events and as "Hardy's characteristic political voice, murmuring his dissent from violent and oppressive policies, and calling his readers back to basic issues of human decency."[29]

Consequently, Hardy's work appears to be more complex than merely resisting conventional or classical forms and diction or a mainstream view of life. His poetic oddities show him to be an intuitive thinker who tries to find his own path through emotional dramas and disasters and through the chaotic times of the turn of the century. He stands out by his delicate balance between conservatism and innovation, which tends to create paradoxes in his poetry. Alternations between continuity and rupture, through a variety of poetic form and content, act as opposition to the age, with its wars and sometimes harsh post-industrial change. Consequently, sounds, words and structures appear to be carefully chosen by Hardy in order to create imbalances and to resist a single predetermined structure in poetry. Hardy's resistance is therefore always tested by the poet himself and might be seen as internal resistance or resistance to himself.

Notes

1. A point made by Robert Gittings, *The Older Hardy* (London: Penguin, 1980 [1978]), 146.
2. Michael Millgate, *Selected Letters* (Oxford: Clarendon Press, 1990), 138.
3. Thomas Hardy, *Thomas Hardy: The Complete Poems,* Ed. James Gibson (Basingstoke, Hampshire: Palgrave: 2001), 84.
4. William W. Morgan, "Hardy's Return to Verse: Part 2 — Some Critical Explorations." (2010) http://www.st-andrews.ac.uk/~ttha/Journal/Rethink.2.htm>, accessed 25 May 2010.
5. Thomas Hardy, *Selected Poems,* Ed. Andrew Motion (London: The Everyman Library, 1994), xxvii.
6. Catherine Lanone, "Division and Revision: Thomas Hardy's Poetics of Nostalgia" in *Etudes britanniques contemporaines* 27 (December 2004, 19–36), 33; the phrase "unlulling metrical irregularity" is quoted from Linda Shires, "Hardy and Nineteenth Century Poetry and Poetics" in *Palgrave Advances in Thomas Hardy Studies,* Ed. Philip Mallett (London: Palgrave MacMillan, 2004, 255–278), 272.
7. Michael Edwards, *Le Génie de la poésie anglaise* (Paris : Le Livre de poche, 2006), 313 (all translations mine).
8. Edwards, 313.
9. Whitfield Stanton, "A lecture delivered before La société internationale de philologie, science et Beaux-Arts" (1921) <http://www.archive.org/stream/thomas hardyartis00 whitrich/thomashadyartis00whitrich_djvu.txt> accessed 15 Sept 2009.
10. Edwards, 313.
11. Michael Millgate, *Selected Letters* (Oxford: Clarendon Press, 1990), 135–136.
12. See l. 26 "The Darkling Thrush."
13. John Paul Riquelme, "The modernity of Thomas Hardy's poetry" in *The Cambridge companion to Thomas Hardy,* Ed. Dale Kramer (Cambridge: Cambridge University Press, 1999), 206.
14. Dennis Taylor, *Hardy's Literary Language and Victorian Philology* (Oxford: Clarendon Press, 1993), 37–38.
15. Taylor, 38.
16. Douglas Harper, *Online Etymology Dictionary* (2001–2010) <http://www.etymonline.com/index.php?search=un&searchmode=none>, accessed 25 May 2010.
17. Dictionary.com (2010) < http://dictionary.reference.com/browse/uncoffined>, accessed 25 May 2010.
18. James Gibson, *Thomas Hardy: A Literary Life* (London: Macmillan: 1996), 144.
19. Taylor, 58.
20. Samuel Hynes, *The Pattern of Hardy's Poetry* (London: Oxford University Press, 1961), 147.
21. Hynes, 144.
22. Taylor, 83.
23. James Gibson, *Thomas Hardy: A Literary Life* (London: Macmillan: 1996), 118.
24. Taylor, 69.
25. Thomas Hardy, *Selected Poems,* Ed. Andrew Motion (London: The Everyman Library, 1994), xxxiii.
26. Edwards, 170.
27. Taylor, 7.
28. Morgan.
29. Morgan.

Works Cited

Davie, Donald (1972), *Thomas Hardy and British Poetry.* London: Routledge & Kegan Paul.
_____ (2006), *Purity of Diction in English verse: and, Articulate energy.* Manchester: Carcanet.
Edwards, Michael (2006), *Le Génie de la poésie anglaise.* Paris: Le Livre de poche.
Gibson, James (1996), *Thomas Hardy: A Literary Life.* London: Macmillan.
Gittings, Robert (1980), *The Older Hardy.* London: Penguin.
Hardy, Thomas, (2001), *The Complete Poems.* Ed. James Gibson. Basingstoke: Palgrave.
_____ (1994), *Selected Poems.* Ed. Andrew Motion. London: The Everyman library.
_____ (1979), *The Variorum Edition of the Complete Poems of Thomas Hardy.* Ed. James Gibson. London: Macmillan.
Harper, Douglas (2001–2010), "Online Etymology Dictionary" <http://www.etymonline.com>. Accessed 25 May 2010.
Hynes, Samuel (1961), *The Pattern of Hardy's Poetry.* London: Oxford University Press.
Kermode, Frank (1972), *English Pastoral Poetry from the Beginnings to Marvell: An Anthology.* New York: W.W. Norton.
Lanone, Catherine (Dec. 2004), "Division and Revision: Thomas Hardy's Poetics of Nostalgia" in *Etudes britanniques contemporaines*, 27, 19–36.
Morgan, William W. (2010), "Hardy's Return to Verse: Part 2 — Some Critical Explorations." <*http://www.st-andrews.ac.uk/~ttha/Journal/Rethink.2.htm*>. Accessed 25 May 2010.
Page, Norman (2001), *Thomas Hardy The Novels.* London: Palgrave.
Riquelme, John Paul (1999), "The modernity of Thomas Hardy's poetry," in *The Cambridge companion to Thomas Hardy.* Ed. Dale Kramer. Cambridge: Cambridge University Press, 204–223.
Stanton, Whitfield (April, II, 1921), "A lecture delivered before La société internationale de philology, science et Beaux-Arts" <*http://www.archive.org/stream/thomashardyartis00whitrich/thomashadyartis00whitrich_djvu.txt*>. Accessed 15 Sept 2009.
Taylor, Dennis (1993), *Hardy's Literary Language and Victorian Philology.* Oxford: Clarendon Press.
Tomalin, Claire (2006), *Thomas Hardy: The Time-Torn Man.* London: Penguin Group.
Turner, Paul (1998), *The Life of Thomas Hardy: A Critical Biography.* Oxford: Blackwell.

3. "Minds" and "Manacles" in Late Lawrence

Elise Brault-Dreux

Many readers have resisted D.H. Lawrence's poetry, frequently considering its poetic substance as not resistant enough, slightly too accessible or overly in touch with the poet's unmediated emotions. Straying from his Modernist contemporaries' creation of more resistant poems, Lawrence nonetheless happened to use poetry as a means to resist the ideals of his time ("money, hypocrisy, greed, machines."[1]) Deeply alarmed by the latter, Lawrence, in two heterogeneous collections of poems, *Pansies* and *More Pansies*,[2] formulated infuriated calls for resistance to mechanization and to the exacerbation of the powers of the mind which, he argued, were interrelated and annihilating man's vital being.

Lawrence wrote these poetic apostrophes after he returned from a long stay in New Mexico. And his re-acquaintance with old Europe, just when he was going through the final stages of tuberculosis, renewed in him feelings of intense exasperation. *Pansies* was published in 1928, towards the end of the poet's life, and the publication was an act of resistance in itself: indeed, several poems were seized for obscenity.[3]

One of the particularities of *Pansies* and *More Pansies* (posthumously published in 1932) is that some poems are hardly poetry at all. In his first preface to *Pansies*, Lawrence writes:

> This little bunch of fragments is offered as a bunch of *pensées*, anglicé pansies; a handful of thoughts. Or, if you will have the other derivation of pansy, from *panser*, to dress or soothe a wound; these are my tender administrations to the mental and emotional wounds we suffer from [...]. Each little piece is a thought; [...] they do not pretend to be half-baked lyrics....[4]

As M.J. Lockwood points out in his study of Lawrence's poems, Lawrence here ascribes an as it were medicinal power to his *Pansies*.[5] With the metaphor of the physical cure, he endeavors to show that his poems are meant to resist modern evil, or even to resist the virus of modern civilization, to prevent it from spreading to men's beings. Wounds will be soothed by his poetic *pensées*. In the second preface he declares: "Pascal and La Bruyère wrote their *Pensées* in prose, but it has always seemed to me that a real thought, a single thought, not an argument, can only exist easily in verse, or in some poetic form."[6]

Despite his determination to use verse form, Lawrence keeps insisting that these pieces make "a bunch of scraps of sort of poetry,"[7] and explains to Aldous Huxley that Frieda, his wife, defines them as "real doggerel."[8] But to Martin Secker, his editor, he writes: "before I sign an agreement I want to know exactly what you are omitting from the *complete* MS [...]. I simply don't want to come with a bourgeois "inoffensive" *Pansies*."[9] Lawrence here makes it plain that he wants his "doggerel" to be offensive and to resist the principles he abhors.

In one category of poems (not published together as a group, but spread throughout the collections), the poetic voice articulates urgent calls for resistance to a society that is being ground by the mills of the machine. In these poems Lawrence urges "young men" to fight *for* their physical vitality: this type of resistance is, to a certain extent, political on the surface, and deep down more ontologically oriented. However, while this passionate advocate of Whitmanian free verse voices his irritated appeals to resistance, the form of his poetry tends to be quite stiff and unexpectedly mechanical as it somewhat adheres to the rhythm of the very machine Lawrence urges modern men to resist. The aesthetic form he uses seems weaker than the mechanicity he condemns: the form itself proves unable to resist mechanical modernity. This discrepancy between message and form, however, does not lessen the power of the prophet-like discourse of another type of poems (likewise spread through the collections and mingled with those of the other type) which, as will be pointed out, reveals a deep faith in the *natural* resistance of organic and human nature, an inherent resistance which calls into question the necessity of a more political, or at least ideological, resistance.

In December 1928, D.H. Lawrence wrote to Charles Wilson: "We want a revolution not in the name of money or work or any of that, but of life."[10] This same rebellious desire is expressed in a poem entitled "Let the Dead Bury their Dead"[11] where the "dead" are those who have forsaken their vitality and have espoused a system by embracing a mechanical form of death in life, and who are guided by the lure of money. The title phrase recurs throughout the poem, as the poetic voice urges its readers to resist the desire both to rescue these "dead" and join them in their grinding capitalistic system. In the first stanza, elements such as the negative injunctions "don't help" and "don't serve" which open the second and fifth lines respectively, the repetition of "they" and "them" to define the dead (a mass of non-beings plainly set against "you") and the reiteration of "dead" which ends up sounding performative as Lawrence condemns them to death, all turn Lawrence's poem into a call for resistance – resistance not so much to the dead as to the desire or impulse to espouse their form of death in life.

The "dead" are a malignant threat to living men. In incessantly operating the "mills of industry" and other kinds of machines, they thwart the Heraclitean flow of life: Lawrence perceived existence as a constant state of *becoming*. He hence compares and contrasts these pivotal mills, operated by men, with the mills of God which grind naturally with "the winds of life." If one may yield to the mills of God in whose flow man is then caught, those of industry must be resisted (though the reader is not told how). Lawrence's explicit call to resist is intensified by his appeal to the reader's senses as he draws attention to disgusting aspects of the dead whose eyes are "phosphorescent" and whose wisdom is paradoxically "putrescent." In lines 10–11, the [s] alliteration and the successive polysyllabic words draw attention to the dead's rotting wisdom; the decay is rendered all the more palpable through the sense of smell. Their souls are hence made obnoxiously tangible to the reader. The poem concludes with the oxymoronic reference to "the repulsive, living fat dead."[12] Lawrence distorts the usual semantic coherence of language and thus brings to the surface of the poem the alteration of the modernity the poem depicts – or is it the lethal alteration of modernity that contaminates the semantics? Once again, in hearing (or reading) such distortion, the reader might feel the awkward and even grotesque nature of the dead. This appeal to the senses combined with threatening remarks and images reveals Lawrence's reliance on pathos. He wants his readers to *feel*, with him, the frighteningly immediate reality of things, and thus to strengthen the readers' desire to resist the fall into the mechanical pivotal movement. In thus foreseeing the imminent decay of modernity, this somewhat prophetic voice characterizes a significant number of poems of *Pansies*, where Lawrence repeatedly seems to "behold the future in the present,"[13] often schematically and with apocalyptic undertones, and preaches — sometimes subtly, often awkwardly.

"Fight! O my Young Men"[14] reiterates the same motifs and gathers the two aspects of the poetic-prophetic voice, both foreseeing and above all preaching, in a highly marked apostrophe. His bellicose call develops into an attempt to rescue "his" young men from falling into the same pivotal grinding mills. For they are on the verge of falling, "half-alive," with "half-dead eyes" and "enfeebled vitality" – already seduced by the putrescent lure of "money-muck-worms." The only means to stay alive, Lawrence suggests, is to resist: he urges his men to "rise at" the alluring nastiness of the "worms." In "rise at them," "at" suggests the intensity of the force opposing the young men in their resistance and rebellion against the subspecies.

Through such politically oriented calls for resistance, Lawrence does not exactly parody but to some extent subversively echoes the artists and poets who, around the same period, glorified the machine – among them, the Italian Futurists. The poem "Wonderful Machine"[15] is blatantly ironical in that sense, as Lawrence glorifies the self-sufficiency of the machine. The interjections and hyperboles are deflated at the end of the poem when the voice asserts that the machine is entirely dependent on men — hence reminding us that the ultimate target is man, the originator of the machine. However, though here resisting an artistic trend of his own time, Lawrence's perception of Marinetti's ideology is quite complex. He admired the energy of Futurism and the Futurists' will to free themselves from the stiffness of the immediate past. Yet, he fiercely rejected the Futurist mechanization of the *élan vital*.[16] In a letter addressed to Arthur McLoed in June 1914, he summarizes his position:

> I like it [Futurism] because it is the applying to emotions of the purging of the old forms and sentimentalities [...]. I agree with them about the weary sickness of pedantry and tradition and inertness, but I don't agree with them as to the cure and the escape.[17]

And he adds that their work is "ultra scientific attempts to make diagrams of certain physic or mental states."[18] Like the Futurists, Lawrence glorified the necessity of dismantling the crystallized traditional patterns, but he thought the machine, so glorified by the Futurists, should not be used as the primary tool to resist the pressure of traditions and the past. Lawrence, rather, promoted the smashing of the machine which makes him something of a Luddite poet. As Jeffrey Wallace rightly points out though, if the Luddite movement (started in 1811 in Nottinghamshire) was initially designed to smash the machine, it was not primarily because it mechanized and replaced man, but because it ruined the market.[19] This economic approach is in fact what Lawrence develops in his poems, though differently – his main target has more to do with the capitalist lure of profit and the system it begets, resting on the machine, than the machine as such, which, he confesses, he in part honors:

> I do honor to the machine and its inventor. It will [...] save us the necessity of much labor. [...] But to what pitiable misuse is it put! Do we use the machine to produce goods for our need, or is it used as a muck-rake for raking together heaps of money?[20]

So what Lawrence seeks in fact, both in *Pansies* (in "Let the Dead Bury their Dead" and "Fight! O My Young Men" for instance) and elsewhere in his essays, is not to oppose the machine, but to resist the damage it produces to the functioning of society and, more importantly, to the individual human being.

This more ontological concern is not conveyed through the motif of the machine only, but also through what Lawrence sees as its human equivalents – the mind and the ego which are almost human incarnations of the machine and which have supreme authority over the consequently devitalized body. The modern mind and ego have not been strong enough to resist their mechanical surroundings and have let themselves be contaminated. If Lawrence formulates political prophetic calls, his purpose is in fact not fundamentally political. He actually proposes no alternative political or social system with which he could resist modern mechanic trends. Deep down, his aim is to retrieve man's ontological essence. The nature of Lawrence's attempts to rescue man's fundamental being varied throughout his oeuvre. For instance, in his essay *Apocalypse*, Lawrence blames Christianity for having covered the body with a veil of shame.[21] In *Pansies*, he raises his voice in defense of physical freedom (which is the prelude to ontological freedom, the freedom of being), this time picturing the mind as the originator of the mechanical industry which captured man's body. He means to resist not just the "manacles" but the minds which "forged" them.[22] As early as 1916, Lawrence wrote to Bertrand Russell:

> The whole of the consciousness and the conscious content is old hat — the mill-stone round your neck. [...]
> Do stop working and writing altogether and become a creature instead of a mechanical instrument.[23]

Lawrence here insists on the essential value of spontaneity both in life and in the writing process. Only a *living* natural creature can produce good things: vital life – neither thought nor mechanical formulae – is the prelude to creation.

But the mind has literally turned man – body and soul – into an egoistic machine. And this irrepressible transformation is evoked in the poem "The Gulf,"[24] where the gulf is what lies between the "sons of the earth" and "the hordes of the ego-centric, the robots." Everything from the "robot" to the human "slave" of the machine is an incarnation of the machine. And with the repeated arresting oxymoronic juxtaposition of "machine incarnate" in the fourth stanza, Lawrence once again distorts the reader's expectations. Man does not merely imitate the machine: tyrannized by his mind, his very flesh and blood have become a machine. And even poetry, especially in this fourth stanza, with its repetitive pattern and the anaphoric "and," is the incarnation of the gears of the machine.

Towards the end of the poem, the poetic voice betrays the pessimistic intuition of an upcoming invasion of "egocentric motions" when it addresses the "sons of the earth" who stand on the other side of the gulf. Again the poetic voice raises the question of the possible disentanglement from the machine network. But he gives no clue as to how men could resist the tendency. And if for Lawrence the sons of the earth are "men still unmechanized," the very phrase sounds doubly pessimistic – first with the adverb "still" which renders the process unavoidable, and "unmechanized" which makes "men" the negation of mechanicity, so that the machine becomes a central notional reference. The same device appears at the end of the poem with a reference to the motion of the limbs of sons of men, limbs that are "never mechanical" – while Lawrence could have used a positive adjective: "natural," "vital," "instinctive," etc. These two negatives ("unmechanized" and "never mechanical") pessimistically evoke a form of resistance – the "sons of the earth" survive and evolve by resisting this mechanism, which is the central core *against* which they live. They can only exist in their resisting opposition to/negation of this mechanical system.

This subtle form of pessimism arises from the fact that man is condemned to resist. It appears again in the poem "Nemesis"[25] where Lawrence even adds an expressive sense of fear. In this poem the poetic voice again prophesies, with a sense of urgency. With a prophetic and didactic voice, Lawrence seeks to shock his readers, to make them aware of the risks they will run if they do not open up the stifling idiot space of half-consciousness: they have lost their "whole" consciousness (that is both mental and physical), and by "half-consciousness" Lawrence means mind-consciousness exclusively, that is to say, a consciousness which has completely suppressed the other half-consciousness which is what Lawrence calls the blood-consciousness. He thus urges men to resist the surrounding narrow-mindedness, and to exert physical pressure so as to enlarge and open the consciousness.

In his *Pensées* Lawrence urges his readers to resist social and capitalist constraints, in order for them to recover their spontaneity and freedom of being. Such politically and, indirectly, ontologically oriented resistance, was expressed by Lawrence ten years earlier in his essay "Poetry of the Present," but, at the time, on an aesthetic level, as he applied it to poetry writing.

Lawrence's central idea in "Poetry of the Present"[26] is that poetic rhythm should not be dictated by any formal pattern. Following Walt Whitman who, for him, paved the way for free verse, Lawrence promotes the poetic expression of "the insurgent naked throb of the instant moment." The only source of poetry is "the living plasm" which, in the process of creation, must resist the security of "restricted, limited unfree verse" and "measured symmetry." The kind of poetry Lawrence advocates is thus based on disobedience to the mechanical workings and the mental elaboration of formal poetry. His "plasmic" poetry originates in and conveys "the pulsating, carnal self, mysterious and palpable." This aesthetic resistance to a formal dogma is analogous to the resistance, advocated in *Pansies* (and also sometimes in *More Pansies*) to the dogma of modern times. The poet must disobey the rules which, in the end, will constrain his words within measures and laws. Disobedience, then, on the levels of poetry and existence, is the means to avoid the fall into a world of mental mechanical industry. Poetry must *be* resistant, in its very nature and form, even beyond the message it delivers. It must resist so as not to be curbed to fit a predetermined pattern.

And yet, the poems cited so far hardly put forth any of these living spontaneous pulsations nor any innate aesthetic resistance to patterns. If this sense of a Heraclitean free verse is undoubtedly central in the two collections of poems preceding *Pansies* (*Look! We've Come Through*[27] in 1917 and *Birds, Beasts and Flowers*[28] in 1923) or even following it (*Last Poems*,[29] posthumously published in 1932, like *More Pansies*), Lawrence's *pensées* lack the "creative spark"[30] which is at the heart of his poetic conception. Yet Lawrence, aware of the disjunction between what one might call his theory of poetry and the prosodic features of *Pansies*, fully admitted that these were not poems,[31] *but*, in the meantime, that his *pensées* could only be expressed in verse. David Ellis, one of Lawrence's biographers, accounts for this contradiction between Lawrence's awareness of the quality of his work and his irrepressible desire to write poetry, with the poet's weakening physical condition in 1928: shorter forms of poems were for him both a way to preserve his health and to find an outlet to give vent to his rage.[32] This interpretation reveals Lawrence's yearning to make his voice heard, to resist with his poetic prophetic voice, be it at times unprosodic. Another interpretation, which does not contradict this first hypothesis, would be that Lawrence's rage was so intense that he could hardly give expression to such ideas with a more spontaneous form of poetry.

Indeed, in "Fight! O My Young Men,"[33] the use of an almost perfect rhyming pattern is quite surprising at that stage of Lawrence's oeuvre, for he had hardly used rhyming patterns since 1912, clearly shunning the stiffness they imposed on poetry. In "Let the Dead Bury their Dead," the repetitions sound somewhat excessive, and the anaphoric "don't" is so emphatic that it works as the pivot around which the poem turns. Likewise, with the beginning of "Nemesis," where the succession of definitions sounds slightly systematic. Though the prosody of "The Gulf" is more heterogeneous, the repetition of "incarnate" in a succession of short lines, turns into a stammering enumeration, and sounds like a speech that cannot unfold and keeps returning to the same words, as each line is enclosed by "and" and "incarnate." The prosodic mechanicity mimetically renders the mechanical movement that the poem rejects.

This mimetic closeness of form and content reveals a slight formal weakness. While Lawrence, in "Poetry of the Present," promotes the effulgence of form, in *Pansies* and *More Pansies*, the form tends to be caught in the mesh of the poetic machines whose extra-textual equivalents Lawrence fiercely condemns. The form seems to have fought with the content, but the mechanical, stammering and pivotal aspects of the poetry suggest that the form could, eventually, not resist the content. The poetic images and ideas have, like a virus, contaminated the unresisting form, as though Lawrence had for a while let his poetry, supposedly incarnation of flesh and blood, incarnate the machine. His formal poetry seems to have been caught in the mesh of its own time. Had Lawrence not commented upon – and hence come close to apologizing for – the "doggerel" quality of the pieces, one might have surmised that such mechanical prosody was consciously sought: the prosody would thus let the reader hear and feel the damaged existence. However, Lawrence's remarks suggest some sort of formal failure, where the "living plasm" resists neither the poet's nerves nor his mind. Lawrence, therefore, resists the flaws of society with a poetry whose form does not resist these flaws' poetic equivalents. The tools of poetry too have become the "machine incarnate": in a society driven by the machine and the human mind, verbal messages are themselves reduced to mechanical successions of words.

Another discrepancy surfaces in *Pansies* and *More Pansies* as the voice at times sounds obsolete. In a tone blending rage and threat, the voice entreats the reader to resist, in 1928 and 1929, what in fact took place in the 18th–19th centuries – that is, the industrial revolution and the birth of capitalism; and the resorting to pathos and to prophetic undertones is more in keeping with a 19th–century type of speech than a 20th–century one. In *Pansies* and *More Pansies*, Lawrence does not urge his readers to resist new sciences, new technologies, the X-ray (1895), the theory of relativity, for instance – though they were revolutions of his time. Rather, he rails against the tangible effects in his own life of what, in 1928, was, in fact, well and truly part of the nineteenth–century past.

It may partly be because of this temporal discrepancy that in these poems the potential visionary aspect of the prophetic voice subsides slightly in favor of its more preaching aspect – as though the vision were articulated too late, after the event. And the weakened aesthetic resistance does not contribute to the elevation of the message of such poems which remain for the reader relatively didactic, delivered with irritated and threatening speeches whose purpose is to resist a system, but without offering any clue to the reader as to how to resist it, besides a sort of side-stepping, or disobedience triggered by disgust and fear.

However, in another category of poems in *Pansies* and *More Pansies*, D.H. Lawrence evokes the idea of a type of resistance, different in nature and more positively introduced, through which he questions the necessity of the conscious act of resistance he calls for in the poems mentioned above. In *Pansies* and *More Pansies*, Lawrence's voice is not merely pessimistic or threatening. It now and then happens to express, if not a genuine confidence about man's fate, at least a hesitation regarding the true necessity of the act of resistance. The pessimistic image of men "still unmechanised" coexists with much more positive undertones. The voice of the enraged preacher then subsides and that of the visionary prophet takes over.

The central concern in "To Let Go or to Hold On —?"[34] is: should we resist our civilization or should we let go? The recurrence of the inclusive pronoun "we" ascribes a kinder prophetic tone to the voice, and contrasts with the more didactic use of the exclusive "you" of poems quoted earlier. The questions then sound neither challenging nor threatening, but rather sincere. Moreover, the preoccupation is broadened beyond the narrow concern for the social capitalist mechanized system – it now deals with civilization. This widened scope tends to ascribe a timeless dimension to the poem. Besides, unlike poems cited earlier, the prosody is freer, the aesthetic resistance to formal patterns strengthened.

The two alternatives of "holding on" and "letting go" are developed in turn. With "holding on" Lawrence, in the second stanza, suggests the possibility of a form of active resistance which, he insists, would require the whole individual's physical energy and multiplied efforts. Man then would be resisting his collapsing civilization by launching into an intense physical battle against the flaws of his man-made surroundings in order to give a new life to the human race. Later, the voice asks again, "Must we hold on,"[35] possibly in order to change the course of the human world in bringing human nature further. "Letting go," on the other hand, means drowning with the debris of our civilization, disappearing ("shall we be lost"[36]) and eventually going through the process of rebirth of an entirely new race, in order to find a new form of energy in a transient passage through a state of oblivion which must be accepted rather than resisted. And with "shall we" the value of the modal conveys the poet's half-voiced enthusiastic desire to unify men and encourage them to let go. The rebirth would actually follow a passage through oblivion, and the resurgence resulting from essential resistance would be experienced as a sort of physical salvation. This alternative would lead to a new race thriving from the fertile, potent debris of the human race, to a living nature that derives, precisely, from human nature. After this natural selection, the new species would be fitter; they would be, Lawrence says with Darwinian echoes, "an improvement on humans."[37] In this case, relinquishing corresponds to a form of disobedient resistance: Lawrence defends the idea that living nature is to experience rebirth (therefore is to be resistant throughout time), by going through a transient state of complete oblivious non-resistance – or a passive form of resistance where resistant nature goes along with non-resistant action.

Till the end of the poem, the poetic voice chooses not to choose between "holding on" and "letting go." Though not obviously given, an answer seems to surface in the ultimate stanza, which is a succession of three interrogations, and where "hold on" is preceded by "must" while "let go" is introduced by "can." With the first interrogative "must we," the speaker submits to the co-speaker's will, and "hold on" thus prospectively sounds like an injunction. The act of resistance would then be imposed by the co-speaker. With "can we," the speaker either requires the co-speaker's permission to "let go" or, more probably, questions our innate capability to do so. The potential validation of the predicate < we now / LET GO > is introduced more leniently than that of < we / HOLD ON > – and it also seems temporally closer to the subject with "now." "To let go" hence sounds more obvious, because easier and more immediate, than to "hold on." However the final line of the poem blurs this distinction as the epistemic "is it possible," which questions the chances of occurrence of both holding on and letting go, co-exists with the deontic modality of "must" ("is it possible we must..."). Will and destiny merge, and no answer is given to the Hamlet-like question: "to resist or not to resist?"

Lawrence in fact indirectly provides an answer to this question in poems cited earlier: man must resist the machine and the lure of money in order to stay alive, though Lawrence never explains how. However, on several occasions, the answer is not that obviously positive, as in the ironically entitled poem, "The Triumph of the Machine."[38]

In the first two lines, the poetic voice sets itself against the discourse of an undefined "they" who foresee the ultimate triumph of the machine. He immediately announces its ultimate failure with prophetic determinacy. The poem then pictures the inner natural rebellion of the man who is operating the machine and whose heart is animated with creative energy. Imaginary animals are lodged in his heart, loins, breast and brain, and eventually wildly give vent to their despair. Their rebellion, whose depiction, by bringing in images of havoc in an intensified rhythm, is redolent of the Book of Revelation, announces the defeat of the machine, with the insistent use of the modal "will"[39] which, unlike "shall," denotes the individual will of the subjects beyond a potential external form of destiny. Nature will rebel. This apocalyptic scene triggers another, where machines, engines, and traffic run amok, collide and smash. They end up in "ruins," extinct, lying just like a scar upon the surface of the earth. And among the devastated shambles, nature awakes again. Machines have not resisted the creative power of natural life which lies within each living element and "cannot die." And each vital being preserves this constantly renewed creative energy that no machine can destroy for "the depths of man" are too remote from the reach of the engine. Besides, the prosody is, this time, not mechanical. The apocalyptic images are coupled with an irregular and at times chaotic cadence which powerfully conveys the intensity of Nature's rebellion. If the first two lines are stiff, echoing the didactic or preaching speech of the other type of resistant poems, the rhythm then yields, "lets go," and in so doing aesthetically resists the pressure of traditional forms, as in the ultimate scene of chaos, crashing and colliding machines, depicted in the single sentence which forms the penultimate stanza. This long sentence, made up of short words together with the accretive use of the conjunction "and" repeated four times and creating a Biblical resonance, conveys the endless, accelerated rhythm of the scene it describes: neither form nor content seem to be repressible, as though nothing could resist the poeticity as well as the extra-textual drive. The alliterative [k] in the second part supersedes the softer [m] in the first, and hence enhances the intensity of the final "shock."

Lawrence's prophetic vision in this poem partly resolves the dilemma of "To Let Go or to Hold on – ?" as resistance is pictured as a natural process, which can therefore not be consciously decided. In "letting go" – that is to say in not abandoning one's self but being in touch with human, organic and cosmic nature – one will naturally resist. One will be selected, for one's resistance is not related to one's actions but to the acceptance of one's innate nature – an acceptance, an awareness even, that, Lawrence complains, the machine has smashed. This optimistic version implies that human, animal, and organic nature is naturally fitter and more resistant than the man-made machine and the machine-made self. Essentially resistant, and even resilient, Nature will thrive and triumph.

In other words, resisting a system is meaningless compared with one's being resistant, not *to* something specifically, but just resistant. As early as 1914, in his essay *Study of Thomas Hardy*, Lawrence points out the distinction between two different forms of struggle:

> We must always hold that life is the great struggle for self-preservation; that this struggle for the means of life is the essence and whole of life. [...] Yet we ding-dong at it, always hammering out the same phrase about the struggle for existence, the right to work, the right to the vote, the right to this and the

> right to that, all in the struggle for existence, as if any external power could give us the right to ourselves. That we have within ourselves. And if we have it not, then the remainder that we do possess will be taken away from us.[40]

And it is this idea of inherent struggle for life that Lawrence again imparts fourteen years later in *Pansies*. Resistance is like "the great struggle for self-preservation": one should *be* resistant, "within" oneself, rather than try to resist the menial noxious events and trends of one's immediate social system. And the poetic quality of "The Triumph of the Machine" and other such optimistic pieces, which sets the poems outside temporality, conveys this very message about natural innate resistance; while the other types of more politically oriented poems, through which Lawrence nonetheless wishes to call for resistance, are much less credible and poignant.

The discussion of a selection of poems from *Pansies* and *More Pansies* reveals that, for Lawrence, when one fully embraces one's flesh-and-blood humanity, beyond all forms of stifling constraints, one is essentially resistant to the machine, the mind and the lure of profit. Only then will living nature be the fittest and survive the man-made material ideological systems and the "money-muck worms."[41] The act of resistance is much weaker than the acceptance and assertion of one's innate resistance; and therefore, what surfaces in all these poems is an encouragement for individual rather than collective resistance – "we" therefore refers more to a collection of individuals than to a mass. For Lawrence then, when he fully accepts it, man is by nature resistant. In the previous consideration of such poems as "Fight! O my Young Men," it was argued that, for D.H. Lawrence, the only means of staying alive was to resist. However the logic is much more cogent and closer to the Lawrentian creed when it is reversed: for Lawrence, the only means of resisting is to stay fully, physically alive, to accept one's life, therefore to accept change and sometimes a transient passage through oblivion, a state in which the self lets go and does not actively resist, a state at the heart of which resilience lies. One's being lives, dies, emerges again, consequently resists neither life nor oblivion, but fully accepts them and hence can *be* resistant to external noxious forces. In other words, political and ideological resistance is only the outcome, the materialization, or the consequential expression, of an ontological and natural innate form of resistance, which is the essential, primary source of all.

This aspect of Lawrence's thought is inscribed in the 20th century. If his calls happen to sound slightly dated, pertaining more to the 19th than the 20th century, his means of resistance can also be modern and sound much more convincing than his more politically oriented prophetic appeals. Such calls for innate powerful resistance are a great deal nourished by the combination of a modern and idiosyncratic understanding of Nietzsche, with

Bergson's *élan vital* and a return to primitive vital forces, characteristic of an early 20th-century interest in ethnology and anthropology (especially through Frazer's *The Golden Bough*). The Dionysian assertion of the self against its definitive loss is, in itself, the most powerful form of resistance that underlies the enraged discourse of *Pansies* and *More Pansies*.

Notes

1. "Fight! O My Young Men," D. H. Lawrence, *Complete Poems*, Eds. Vivian de Sola Pinto and Warren Roberts (NY, London: Penguin, 1993), 457.
2. Lawrence, *Complete Poems*, 415–564, 599–684.
3. In his second preface, written in March 1929, D.H. Lawrence explains: "Some of the poems are perforce omitted – about a dozen from the bunch. When Scotland Yard seized the MS. in the post, at the order of the Home Secretary, no doubt, there was a rush of detectives, postmen, and Home Office clerks and heads, to pick out the most lurid blossoms. They must have been very disappointed. When I now read down the list of the omitted poems, and recall the dozen amusing, not terribly important bits of pansies which have had to stay out of print for fear a policeman might put his foot on them, I can only grin once more to think of the nanny-goat, nanny-goat-in-a-white-petticoat silliness of it all." (*Complete Poems*, 423).
4. Lawrence, *Complete Poems*, 417.
5. M.J. Lockwood, *A Study of the Poems of D.H. Lawrence – Thinking in Poetry* (Basingstoke: Macmillan Press, 1987), 147.
6. Lawrence, *Complete Poems*, 423.
7. *The Letters of D. H. Lawrence Volume VII: November 1928–February 1930*, Eds. Keith Sagar and James T. Boulton (Cambridge: Cambridge University Press, 1993), 80.
8. *The Letters of D. H. Lawrence Vol. VII*, 64.
9. *The Letters of D. H. Lawrence Vol. VII*, 241–2.
10. *The Letters of D. H. Lawrence Vol. VII*, 99.
11. Lawrence, *Complete Poems*, 440–1.
12. Lawrence, *Complete Poems*, 440–1.
13. P.B. Shelley, *A Defence of Poetry*, *The Complete Works of Percy Bysshe Shelley Vol. VII* (New York: Gordian Press, 1965), 112.
14. Lawrence, *Complete Poems*, 456–7.
15. Lawrence, *Complete Poems*, 643.
16. In *Les Clôtures de la modernité* (Paris : Armand Colin, 2007), Michel Blay brings together Bergson's concept of the *élan vital* and its appropriation by the Futurists, who literally transferred the *élan vital* from humanity to the machine.
17. *The Letters of D. H. Lawrence Volume II: June 1913–October 1916*, Eds. George J. Zytaruk and James T. Boulton (Cambridge: Cambridge UP, 1981), 180.
18. Lawrence, *The Letters of D. H. Lawrence Volume II*, 181.
19. Jeffrey Wallace, *D.H. Lawrence, Science and the Posthuman* (Basingstoke, Palgrave Macmillan, 2005), 202–4.
20. D.H. Lawrence, *Study of Thomas Hardy* and *Introduction to These Paintings*, Ed. J.V. Davies (London: Heinemann, 1973), 38.
21. D.H. Lawrence, *Apocalypse* (NY, London: Penguin Books, 1995).

22. "mind-forged manacles" in William Blake's poem, "London," *Songs of Experience* (1794).
23. Lawrence, *The Letters of D. H. Lawrence Volume II*, 547.
24. Lawrence, *Complete Poems*, 635.
25. Lawrence, *Complete Poems*, 514–5.
26. Lawrence, *Complete Poems*, 181–6.
27. Lawrence, *Complete Poems*, 189–274.
28. Lawrence, *Complete Poems*, 275–414.
29. Lawrence, *Complete Poems*, 685–728.
30. Lawrence, "Poetry of the Present," *Complete Poems*, 182.
31. Lawrence, *Complete Poems*, 417.
32. David Ellis. *D.H., Lawrence – Dying Game 1922–1930* (Cambridge: Cambridge University Press, 1998), 452–3.
33. And also in "Beware the Unhappy Dead," *Complete Poems*, 722.
34. Lawrence, *Complete Poems*, 428–9.
35. Lawrence, *Complete Poems*, 428–9.
36. Lawrence, *Complete Poems*, 428–9.
37. Lawrence, *Complete Poems*, 428–9.
38. Lawrence, *Complete Poems*, 623–5.
39. Lawrence, *Complete Poems*, 623–5.
40. Lawrence, *Study of Thomas Hardy*, 16.
41. Lawrence, "Fight ! O My Young Men," *Complete Poems*, 456.

Works Cited

Blay, Michel (2007), *Les Clôtures de la modernité*. Paris : Armand Colin.
Ellis, David (1998), *D.H. Lawrence – Dying Game 1922–1930*. Cambridge: Cambridge University Press.
Lawrence, D.H. (1993), *Complete Poems*. Eds. Vivian de Sola Pinto and Warren Roberts, London: Penguin.
____(1981), *The Letters of D. H. Lawrence Volume II: June 1913–October 1916*. Eds. George J. Zytaruk and James T. Boulton. Cambridge: Cambridge University Press.
____(1993), *The Letters of D. H. Lawrence Volume VII: November 1928–February 1930*. Eds.
Keith Sagar and James T. Boulton. Cambridge: Cambridge UP.
____(1973), *Study of Thomas Hardy and Introduction to These Paintings*. Ed. J.V. Davies. London: Heinemann Educational Books.
Lockwood, M.J. (1987), *A Study of the Poems of D.H. Lawrence – Thinking in Poetry*. Basingstoke: Macmillan Press.
Shelley, P.B. (1965), *The Complete Works of Percy Bysshe Shelley, Vol. VII*. Eds. Roger Ingpen and Walter E. Peck. New York: Gordian Press.
Wallace, Jeffrey (2005), *D.H. Lawrence, Science and the Posthuman*. Basingstoke, Palgrave Macmillan.

4. Lawrence Between Resistance and Dissolution

Sarah Bouttier

In the physical sciences, resistance is defined as the opposition offered by one body to the pressure or movement of another. Resistance is based on the concepts of matter and energy. Throughout the nineteenth century, these two concepts were considered as distinct from one another, and the opposition between them implied a certain definition of life, and of living matter: life was defined as energy, and matter was inert until it was animated by energy. Of course, as a transition took place during the nineteenth century from a "matter-based" physics to an "energy-based" physics, this conception of life was questioned. John Tyndall, in his 1874 Belfast address, argued that life was inherent to matter, that matter contained in itself "the promise and potency" of life.[1] As a movement involving matter and energy, as an image representing either the opposition of matter and energy or a conflict between different energies within matter, resistance taken in its literal meaning was still at the heart of any conception of life at the turn of the twentieth century, when D. H. Lawrence (1885–1930) began his poetic career. Later on, Lawrence's perception of living matter changed. How do images of physical resistance and opposite images of dissolution work as prisms through which Lawrence's evolving conception of living matter is revealed? This not only informs the imagery but also the structure of his poems, as he considers his poetry as the poetry of the incarnate "Now," and of the "living plasm,"[2] and his poems purportedly aim at giving a sense of "living tissue" in all its complexity and mutability:

> The seething poetry of the incarnate Now is supreme, beyond even the everlasting gems of the before and after. In its quivering momentaneity it surpasses the crystalline, pearl-hard jewels, the poems of the eternities.[3]

Here, the words themselves are seen as throbbing living matter when they achieve their aim, and inert minerals when they are not. Therefore, the formal consequences of the different statuses Lawrence attributes to physical resistance throughout his poetic career, must also be traced.

Lawrence often uses images of physical resistance — to a strong wind, to a flow, etc. — in order to assert the vitality of his creatures[4]; and yet, his vision of life is essentially that of a flow, to which all creatures must yield:

> Life is not a question of points, but a question of flow. It's the *flow* that matters. If you come to think of it, a daisy even is like a little river flowing, that never for an instant stops. From the time when a tiny knob of a bud appears down among the leaves, during the slow rising up a stem, the slow swelling and pushing out the white petal-tips from the green, to the full-round daisy, white and gold and gay, that opens and shuts through a few dawns, a few nights, poised on the summit of her stem, that silently shrivels and mysteriously disappears — there is no stop, no halt, it is a perpetual little streaming of a gay little life out into full radiance and delicate shriveling, like a perfect little fountain that flows and flows, and shoots away at last into the invisible, even then without any stop.[5]

This undifferentiated principle of life is frequently represented in the poems by the very wave, or strong wind, the creatures resist. How does Lawrence combine a belief in resistance as a mode of being with his vitalist imperative of dissolution?

A possible answer lies in a clear distinction, in most of Lawrence's works, between what one must resist and what one must yield to. In "Fish," the creature resists social bonds:

> Admitted, they swarm in companies,
> [...]
> But soundless, and out of contact.
> They exchange no word, no spasm, not even anger.[6]

Paradoxically, this resistant singleness allows the fish to live in perfect osmosis with the water, which stands as the nourishing flow of life. The water becomes the substance of his body and actions: his eyes are "fixed water-eyes," his whispers are "wavelets" ("to speak endless inaudible wavelets into the waves"), his tail is a "whorl."[7] Allying resistance to social bonds with osmosis with the flow of life ensures the fish a fullness of being almost inaccessible to humans. Wrapped within epanalepses ("Himself all silvery himself / in the element"[8]), the fish is miraculously self-contained, a dense figure of independence.

Colin Clarke's *River of Dissolution* offers an explanation for this twofold condition. In his chapter on *Women in Love*, Clarke establishes different forms of singleness and belonging: in order to truly belong to the cosmos or the great flow of life, a creature must sever its social, sentimental bonds which would dissolve its true self. Resistance to social relationships is necessary in order to be able to yield to the great flow of life, and that is how we may understand Colin Clarke's statement: "The truly integral spirit then preserves its integrity both by its resistance to dissolution and by its aptness to dissolve; and true individuality is a matter of belonging."[9]

However, what Colin Clark does not address, perhaps because he does not focus on Lawrence's poetry, is that, even when the environment of the creature is exclusively elemental, and not in the least social or human, Lawrence often insists on the necessity of the creature's resistance, which, then, is only physical. Then, in the poems, the combination of Lawrence's belief in resistance as a mode of being with a vitalist imperative of dissolution into the great flow of life is most of the time not resolved by the distinction between a social surface environment to which one must resist and a living depth to which one must surrender: instead, it is the poet's evolving conception of living matter that informs the different images conjured up by this tension.

In his early poems, the perceptible shapes of living things are borne out of the resistance of inert matter to the flow of life. "Corot" features the vital flow as a wind blowing through a country landscape. It seems the trees and leaves tend to resist this vital flow:

> For the trailing, leisurely rapture of life
> Drifts dimly forward, easily hidden
> By bright leaves uttered aloud; and strife
> Of shapes by a hard wind ridden.[10]

For a living thing to become perceptible it must apparently behave as an obstacle to "the luminous purpose of life" to which the "rapture of life" here mentioned is later equated: in particular, it is in their attempt to "hide" the vital flow that the leaves are given perceptible life, as they are "uttered aloud"— utterance, for Lawrence, being as Diane Bonds argues, the activity which expresses the life force of individual organisms.[11] By the end of the poem, Lawrence acknowledges that revealing life by resisting it is the only activity matter is capable of, as if its only strength derived from its inertia:

> For what can all sharp-rimmed substance but catch
> In a backward ripple, the wave-length, reveal
> For a moment the mighty direction, snatch
> A spark beneath the wheel![12]

Such images echo Henri Bergson's description of the flow of life or *élan vital* in *Creative Evolution* (1907) which Lawrence read about in 1911, the very year "Corot" was written.[13] Bergson distinguishes the *élan vital* from inert matter. In order to prove his point, he depicts the *élan vital* as an invisible hand, and matter as iron filings. Bergson insists that it is through the resistance of the iron filings to the *élan vital*, and not through any active strength on their part, that things are shaped and that life is revealed:

> But the truth is that there has been merely one indivisible act, that of the hand passing through the filings: the inexhaustible detail of the movement of the grains, as well as the order of their final arrangement, expresses negatively, in a way, this undivided movement, being the unitary form of a resistance, and not a synthesis of positive elementary actions.[14]

In Bergson, resistance as a shaping force amounts to a mere force of inertia, a passive property by virtue of which a body opposes any agency that attempts to put it in motion. It seems that Lawrence did embrace such ideas early in his literary career, as the poem just after "Corot," "Michael Angelo," features an artist-deity blowing life into the nostrils of an inert body:

> Who, crouching, put his mouth down in a kiss
> And kissed thee to a passion of life, and left
> Life in thy mouth, and dim breath's hastening hiss?
> Whence cometh this, that thou must guard from theft?[15]

This poem, intentionally following "Corot," shows how close Lawrence's early vitalism is to a biblical conception of the soul as the breath of God: "And the Lord God formed man of the dust of the ground, and breathed into his nostrils the breath of life; and man became a living soul."[16]

Even though, when these poems were written (their manuscript is dated April 1911), Lawrence already claimed to have abandoned Christianity, it is easy to see how this early vitalism, by replacing God with Life or the living flow, provided a reassuring compromise between what was then called a "materialist" conception of life (evolutionary theory and its vulgarized avatars) and a religious one.

This poem not only reflects Lawrence's conception of living matter at an early stage: since the body he mentions is that of a painted figure, that is to say an artistic object, the conception he subscribes to as regards life is also valid for poetic objects. The artist-deity may well be a mirror image of the poet itself, who, at this stage of his career, may have believed that words were in most cases inert (in the essay quoted earlier, Lawrence also mentions his will to "break the stiff neck of habits"[17]) and must therefore be given life.

And indeed, Lawrence himself uses the term "inertia" in order to refer to the difficulties he finds in dealing with rhymed poetry: "The very adherence to rhyme and regular rhythm is a concession to the Law, a concession to the body, to the being and requirements of the body. They are an admission of the living, positive inertia which is the other half of life, other than the pure will-to-motion."[18]

This may explain why Lawrence clung to rhymes and regular rhythm in his early poems: what we would naturally consider as opposed to the flux and vibration of the body was still seen as the most faithful representation of it. Lawrence may have believed that the tension engendered in his poems by the constraint of metrics reflected the resistance of inert matter when a life force shaped it. In the stanza of "Michael Angelo" quoted earlier, the sibilant endings and the artificial separation of the verb from its object ("and left / life in thy mouth"[19]) resulting from the rhyming nature of the poem convey a sense of struggle not only between life and inert matter but also between the poet and his textual material. Then, perhaps because such rhyming verse expressed tension more than harmony, even as late as 1918, Lawrence prefaced an earlier book of rhyming poems, *New Poems*, some of which obey metrical regularity, with the essay, "Poetry of the Present," claiming that his poetry was the poetry of living matter.

Bergson only uses a life/matter dualism as an "ideal limit," a first step to think the *élan vital*, since he then claims that the *élan vital* is always already in every living thing. In Lawrence, it seems that such a distinction is not to last either. Already in *A Study of Thomas Hardy*, published in 1914, the concept of a "living, positive inertia" is problematical: it stands more as a pole that both attracts and repels what Lawrence calls "the pure will-to-motion," than as its opposite. The very epithet "pure" shows how this dualism, like Bergson's, is more of an "ideal limit" than a realistic statement. Lawrence's refusal to simplify the complexities of the "living tissue" in his poetry, together with his reverence for matter, made him unable to maintain that it was inert, even "positively" inert: in later poems, resistance as the shaping force of living things ceases to be associated with inertia, and metrical regularity is abandoned.

Indeed, later poems picture a living impulse inside the creatures as well as outside them. It seems life and matter are no longer distinct; therefore, the living impulse inside the material creatures commands them to snatch some matter away from the material living flow represented outside them, in an active movement which we may identify as analogous to the chemical process of condensation. Indeed, as the act of changing from a gas or a solid to a liquid state, condensation seems to be the phenomenon at stake here. Many of Lawrence's later poems depict a transfer of matter from a shapeless body in which its components are loosely connected, to a denser and more visible body as when, in the poems, creatures take shape and gain materiality. As a result, the resistance inherent in matter is no longer a force of inertia: it is now represented as a positive movement aiming to retain enough density of matter within an individual organism.

Such a conflict over density between matter and the living flow appears between the "Almond Blossom" and a strong wind:

In long-nighted January,
In the long dark nights of the evening star, and Sirius, and the Etna snow-wind
   through the long night.
[...]
Think, to stand there in full-unfolded nudity, smiling,
With all the snow-wind, and the sun-glare, and the dog-star baying epithalamion.[20]

The almond blossom resists the wind with a miraculous strength, yet the mystery of this resistance might lie in the nature of the strong wind shaking the almond tree: "Something must be reassuring to the almond, in the evening star, and the snow-wind, and the long, long nights."[21] Rhythmically, the paratactic juxtaposition of complements, each of them giving a new impulse to the line, accounts for a sense of abundance and renewal which contrasts with the supposed bareness of the tree and its environment. Besides, as far as imagery is concerned, the almond blossom being metaphorically made of snow (it is pictured as "odd bits of snow"[22] earlier in the poem), the wind, as it carries snow itself ("snow-wind") appears as a stock of matter for the flower. Both the wind and the flower are driven by a life impulse, and therefore come into conflict with each other: the wind tries to dissolve the flower in order to gain matter, and the flower resists and tries to grow by condensing the wind's matter — the snowflakes. The word "reassuring" takes on a new meaning, as the miracle of the almond blossom's existence is due precisely to its *assurance*, the flower being described "with such insuperable, subtly-smiling *assurance*"[23] (my italics).

The fight for density and materiality is even more explicit in "Humming-Bird," which sets the newborn humming bird against undifferentiated matter:

> I can imagine, in some otherworld
> Primeval-dumb, far back
> In that most awful stillness, that only gasped and hummed,
> Humming-birds raced down the avenues.
>
> Before anything had a soul,
> While life was a heave of Matter, half inanimate,
> This little bit chipped off in brilliance
> And went whizzing through the slow, vast, succulent stems.[24]

The bird is somehow made of the same stuff as the "Matter" it comes from: it shares its defining feature, its humming, with this matter. Undifferentiated matter being still "half inanimate," it has not yet taken the form of a flow, but it stands, in this prehistoric setting, as the life principle. The creature resists the all-engulfing life principle by opposing a centripetal force of condensation to it in order to detach itself and live a separate existence. The confrontation of both entities (undifferentiated living matter and emerging living creature) over the amount of substance needed for the creation of the humming bird results in a violent antagonism, as the main action of the humming-bird, once created, is to tear apart other bits of this living matter ("And went whizzing through the slow, vast, succulent stems").

In those poems, conflict and resistance are borne out of life's propensity to gather and condense as much matter as possible, both in its differentiated forms (the individual organisms) and undifferentiated forms (namely, the vital flow). Matter is no longer celebrated as an inert body shaped by its resistance to the flow of life, but as the dense, palpable result of the vital impulse of condensation understood as a process of gathering the material living flow, leading to differentiation.

This conception is based on the idea of the indestructibility of matter, widespread in the nineteenth century:

> The comet which is suddenly discovered and nightly waxes larger is proved not to be a newly-created body, but a body which was until lately beyond the range of vision. The cloud formed a few minutes ago in the sky consists not of substance that has just begun to be, but of substance that previously existed in a transparent form.[25]

The dynamics of condensation to be found in some of Lawrence's poems fits this conceptual frame, as the almond blossom, for instance, may be interpreted as the condensation of the snow carried by the wind instead of the appearance of a flower out of thin air. Yet most of all, this vision recalls the colorful monism of the German biologist Ernst Haeckel, whom Lawrence had read by 1908. In his bestseller, *The Riddle of the Universe*, Haeckel links his popular "law of substance" (all is substance — and therefore substance must be revered) with a polar conception of the world. Matter is everywhere, yet in very different densities, and conflicting energies are employed to condense it:

> The positive ponderable matter, the element with the feeling of like or desire, is continually striving to complete the process of condensation, and thus collecting an enormous amount of potential energy; the negative, imponderable matter, on the other hand, offers a perpetual and equal resistance to the further increase of its strain and of the feeling of dislike connected therewith, and thus gathers the utmost amount of actual energy.[26]

Even though Haeckel's ether ("the imponderable matter" referred to here) is by no means a life principle, such a conception may well have influenced Lawrence. The idea of a desiring matter and of everlasting confrontation of ether and positive matter over density is visual enough to be translated into a poetic image. More importantly, Lawrence may have combined this vision with his sense of a vital flow, when soon after reading Haeckel, he discovered Nietzsche, who turned out to be his strongest philosophical influence.[27] The will to power, a life-impulse at the root of every being and thing in the world, driven by self-preservation and imperialism rather than Christian altruism, may have enriched and complicated Lawrence's notion of the flow of life.[28] Since everything is will to power, the impulse is endlessly confronting and resisting itself: with his images of condensation, Lawrence depicts precisely that type of resistance.

Those conflicts and resistances over density have a formal counterpart, mostly visible in *Birds, Beasts and Flowers*. It is a stylistic pattern that lists various descriptions of the creature or object and then identifies it by its name, thereby creating a surprise effect:

> Pure blood, and noble blood, in the fine and rose-red veins;
> Small, interspersed with jewels of white gold
> Frail-filigreed among the rest;
> Rose of the oldest races of princesses, Polynesian
> Hibiscus.[29]

Or, in a less lyrical piece:

> Creatures that hang themselves up like an old rag, to sleep;
> And disgustingly upside down.
> Hanging upside down like rows of disgusting old rags
> And grinning in their sleep.
> Bats![30]

The naming of the creature (hibiscus, bat) is utterly distinct from but also enriched by the endless variations preceding it. The objectivity of the species name comes clashing against the extended imaginary vision, made up of variations — here, mainly alliterations and echoes — upon the nobility of the hibiscus or the disgust inspired by the bat, as if the reality and density of matter resisted its dissolution into a poetic vision. On the other hand, when the creature is named, the abstract species name is enriched by the various images and sensations conveyed in the preceding stanza. Here, therefore, Lawrence concentrates the conflict at stake in his creatures' living matter within this poetic technique: as the process of emerging amounts for a creature both to condensing the living flow and to resisting it, the emergence of the name of a creature entails both encapsulating the essence of the poetic vision introducing it and clashing against it. The poet is no longer struggling against the inert matter of words. Rather, he is playing off the different tendencies of words against each other, in order to create the new kind of tension out of which he believes living matter now emerges.

This vision of a dynamic monism where all is matter and where the flow of life and substance resist each other in order to gain density was not to last long: as the years went by, Lawrence was more and more tempted by a phantasm of pure physical dissolution, implying the end of all resistance. The main event in later poems is no longer the creature's resistance and condensation, but its dissolution into the flow of life. Matter is then celebrated in its ability to dissolve, because if dissolution amounts to a loss of matter for the creature, it also amounts to a gain in matter for the flow of life, which gradually becomes more important to Lawrence than any individual creature.

The first hints of such a shift in perspective already appear in some poems in *Birds, Beasts and Flowers*. Creatures resisting dissolution are then not considered as more alive, but rather as creatures through which life has not passed yet. Such is the case of the "Turkey-Cock":

> Your brittle, super-sensual arrogance
> Tosses the crape of red across your brow and down your breast
> As you draw yourself upon yourself in insistence.
>
> It is a declaration of such tension in will
> As time has not dared to avouch, nor eternity been able to unbend
> Do what it may.
> A raw American will, that has never been tempered by life,
> You brittle, will-tense bird with a foolish eye.[31]

The insistence with which the bird asserts its presence reminds us of the assurance and resistance of the almond blossom: however, here, instead of being a sign of vitality, the bird's resistance amounts to a lack of life, "a raw American will, that has never been tempered by life." Later in the poem, the turkey-cock is said to be "unfinished." Paradoxically, it is now by yielding, by accepting dissolution, that material creatures show their vitality.

This tendency becomes very visible in *More Pansies* and *Last Poems*, two books of poems written in 1929, the year preceding Lawrence's death. From his sick room in Baden Baden, Lawrence watches the "Trees in the Garden" shaken by the wind. Once more, the wind stands as an image of the "great flow of life" to which the creature returns when it disappears. At first, Lawrence celebrates the resistance of the frail trees in the wind:

> Ah in the thunder air
> how still the trees are!
>
> And the lime-trees, lovely and tall, every leaf silent
> hardly looses even a last breath of perfume.[32]

However, the revisions of the second stanza, visible in the manuscript, show that Lawrence mitigated this image of resistance in order to lay a greater emphasis on the imminent surrender of the tree to the wind. While, in the first version, the poet exclaims: "how exquisite it stands alone on the green grass,"³³ the final version reads:

> And the ghostly, creamy colored little tree of leaves
> white, ivory white among the rambling greens
> how evanescent, variegated elder, she hesitates on the green grass
> as if, in another moment, she would disappear
> with all her grace of foam!³⁴

In the final version, dissolution, which may have appeared as weakness in preceding poems, such as "Almond Blossom" in which the frail flowers are celebrated for resisting the Sicilian wind, becomes a source of aesthetic emotion, and even gives the trees a form of aura ("with all her grace of foam!").

Lawrence's health, which declined as tuberculosis wore him down, may account for this shift of focus from dense, resistant material bodies, to a more ethereal form of living: from 1925, when he was diagnosed with tuberculosis, to his death in 1930, his material body, his own resistance, kept failing him, and he might have taken refuge in an aesthetics of thinness, thus sublimating his own weakening body into a long-awaited dissolution of matter. Indeed, as Noëlle Cuny shows in *D. H. Lawrence: le corps en devenir*, from 1922 onwards, Lawrence's prose (apart from the celebration of the body in *Lady Chatterley's Lover*) features the exceedingly material bodies of the obese eponymous character of *Kangaroo* and of the thick-blooded Mexicans in *The Plumed Serpent* as repulsive.³⁵ Interestingly, this excess of materiality is due to their will to dissolve their selves within the mass of humanity, as if the dissolution of one's social and emotional self coincided with a reinforcement of one's materiality. For example, Kangaroo, the Australian leader of a secret fascist organization, has as his main project to sympathize with all of Australia, and he refers to his immensely fat belly as a pouch in which he could carry all the citizens of the young country. Kangaroo may be seen as the exact opposite of the "loveless" fish in the eponymous poem, which resists all social bonds and dissolves into the vital flow: the mass of people Kangaroo claims to love nourishes and expands his pouch, his material body, yet it dissolves his central selfhood, and its physical connection with the living flow. Thus, Kangaroo's misplaced dissolution, into the social order instead of the physical one, gives way to a form of material resistance, as if the obese body were an obstacle to the proper dissolution into the vital flow. While the resistance of sheer matter was still celebrated in *Birds, Beasts and Flowers*, it is now seen as an obstacle to the proper way of living, which consists in yielding to the great flow of life.

Linked to this disgust for material bodies, another factor may be that Lawrence carried the vision of life at stake in the previous poems (living forms and the flow of life fighting for material density) to its logical extreme: if all is matter, and the conflict is over density, then it means that the flow of life is not an abstract entity, and may be in need of density itself. As a result, going back to the flow actually means nourishing it as much as it had nourished one when one resisted it. Consequently, in the last poems, material bodies remain important only as sources of matter which will ultimately, by their dissolution, nourish the flow of life.

In "Butterfly," the resistance of the butterfly to a strong wind is at first deemed almost unnatural: "Butterfly, the wind blows sea-ward, [...] why do you settle on my shoe [...]?"[36] The material kinship between butterfly and wind is then revealed: both are made of snow, as the wind "polished with snow" echoes the whiteness of the butterfly. The poem celebrates wind as a life-flow into which things must return, while the butterfly is allowed attention only inasmuch as the poet imagines its dissolution:

> Will you go, will you go from my warm house?
> Will you climb on your big soft wings, black-dotted,
> as up an invisible rainbow, an arch
> till the wind slides you sheer from the arch-crest
> and in a strange level fluttering you go out to sea-ward, white speck![37]

The dissolution of the butterfly's body into the wind appears as the resolution of a tension, a return to the natural order of things: "You have melted in the crystalline distance."[38]

The literal snow that comes from the hills seems to have been symbolically condensed in the butterfly which is called a "white speck": in order for the vital flow to be redeemed, a certain materiality — the white speck — must go back to the wind, and thus make the sky "crystalline." More than the butterfly, what is at stake in such poems is the permanence and materiality of the vital flow.

Besides, as the main object of focus is no longer a perceptible creature made of "ponderable matter,"[39] but the vital flow where all things return, Lawrence's visions no longer confront the resistance that material things offer to understanding and representation. In terms of contents and structure, in Lawrence's last poems, the new situation has two almost opposite consequences. On the one hand, Lawrence's thinking is no longer constrained by any care for material reality and becomes so abstract and ideological that many poems in *Pansies*, *Nettles* and *More Pansies* hardly differ from pamphlets or essays:

> Only the best matters, in man especially.
> True, you can't produce the best without attending to the whole
> but that which is secondary is only important
> in so far as it goes to the bringing forth of the best.[40]

On the other hand, it allows Lawrence to develop rich poetic visions which expand without being constrained by any resistance on the part of a material poetic object. The poems do not obsessively return to the naming of a creature; instead, they are concerned with extending the presence of the poetic object and the amplitude of the vision, as is the case in "Lucifer":

> Angels are bright still, though the brightest fell.
> But tell me, tell me, how do you know
> he lost any of his brightness in the falling?
> In the dark-blue depths, under layers and layers of darkness.
> I see him more like the ruby, a gleam from within of his own magnificence
> coming like the ruby in the invisible dark, glowing
> with his own annunciation, towards us.[41]

Here "Lucifer" is not even named inside the poem; as a pure product of Lawrence's imagination, he is able to take on as many poetic qualities as Lawrence wishes to give him. Besides, as opposed to the creatures described in *Birds, Beasts and Flowers*, he seems open to manifestation ("glowing with his own annunciation"), and ready to move forward: the end of the line opens the poem to a universal meaning, characteristic of the *Last Poems*. At a time when Lawrence no longer seeks vitality in resistance but in dissolution, words, whose fate parallels that of living matter, seem to flow without resistance. In "Lucifer"— and in "Only the Best Matters"— the enjambments, such as "how do you know / he lost any of his brightness" seem natural, more balanced than in "Angelo," as if words were no longer at odds with the structure of the poems, or with each other in a struggle to name a creature into presence.

Resistance takes on different shapes as it works its way through D. H. Lawrence's poems: unsatisfactory inertia, a state in which matter is perceived as lifeless, gives rise to poetic expression held in check by metrical regularity. It then becomes the expression of a living force in a polar world where everything is both matter and life. This form of resistance by condensation has an aesthetic counterpart, a technique which consists of bringing together creatures' names and long descriptive variations. As Lawrence takes this dynamic conception of resistance and matter to its logical extreme, resistance becomes unnecessary, so that abandon and dissolution prevail completely in his last poems, bringing forth both the worst sort of abstract, ideological poems and expansive poetic visions, no longer constrained by any resistance on the part of external, material reality. In that sense, Lawrence's poetical trajectory, and the fact that the resistance of material living things becomes less and less important to him, show his gradual rejection of realism. Lawrence becomes increasingly convinced that whatever resists his poetic enterprise has nothing to do with real life as he feels it, and that any creature worth describing must be able to dissolve into the great flow of life, his ultimate poetic object.

Notes

1. John Tyndall, *Address Delivered Before the British Association Assembled at Belfast*, With Additions. (1874), http://www.victorianweb.org/science/science_texts/belfast.html, accessed 22 Aug. 2010.
2. "Poetry of the Present," *CP* 182.
3. *CP* 183.
4. This term will be used to mention living beings in Lawrence's poetry. Not only is it a generic word Lawrence uses himself, for example in the extract from "Bat" below, but it also emphasizes both the continuity existing between divine, human, animal, and vegetal beings and their materiality in the poems, which is all the more crucial here as we are dealing with resistance as a scientific concept.
5. D. H. Lawrence, "Do Women Change?" in *Phoenix II Uncollected, Unpublished and Other Prose Works,* Eds. Warren Roberts and Harry T. Moore (London: Heinemann, 1968), 542.
6. *CP* 337.
7. *CP* 334.
8. *CP* 336.
9. Colin Clarke, *River of Dissolution: D. H. Lawrence and English Romanticism* (London: Routledge, 1969), 91.
10. *CP* 68.
11. Diane S. Bonds, *Language and the Self in D. H. Lawrence* (Ann Arbor: UMI Research Press, 1978), 8.
12. *CP* 68.
13. In D. H. Lawrence, *Sons and Lovers,* Eds. Helen Baron and Carl Baron, (Cambridge University Press, 1992), 576, Helen Baron mentions that in 1911, Lawrence read an article by A. J. Balfour on Bergson's *Creative Evolution.*
14. Henri Bergson, *Creative Evolution*, Transl. Arthur Mitchell (New York: Henry Holt and Co., 1911), 94.
15. *CP* 69.
16. *The Authorized King James Version of The Bible* (Oxford: Oxford University Press, 1997). Genesis II, 7.
17. *CP* 184.
18. D. H. Lawrence, *A Study of Thomas Hardy and Other Essays,* Ed. Bruce Steele (Cambridge: Cambridge University Press, 1985; first edition, 1914), 91.
19. *CP* 69.
20. *CP* 305–306.
21. *CP* 305.
22. *CP* 304.
23. *CP* 306.
24. *CP* 372.
25. Herbert Spencer, *First Principles* (London: Williams and Norgate, 1909), 135.
26. Ernst Haëckel, *The Riddle of the Universe,* Trans. Joseph McCabe (New York: Harper and Brothers, 1901), 179.

27. Cf. Robert Montgomery, *The Visionary D. H. Lawrence, Beyond Philosophy and Art*, (Cambridge: Cambridge University Press, 1994), 74: "We know from Jessie Chambers that Lawrence discovered Nietzsche at Croydon [1908–1911]. (...) During his years at Croydon Lawrence was immersed in the most modern thought and could not have escaped at least the indirect influence of the philosopher whose name was on everyone's lips. The influence was deepened when he visited Germany with Frieda and was exposed to the highly intellectual circle surrounding the von Richtofen sisters."

28. In *The Visionary D. H. Lawrence*, 28–34, Robert Montgomery claims that Haeckel's philosophy was too naïve to have a lasting influence on his mind, while he considers Nietzsche as one of his strongest influences.

29. *CP* 314.
30. *CP* 342.
31. *CP* 370.
32. *CP* 646.
33. D. H. Lawrence, "Trees in the Garden" in the D. H. Lawrence Collection, Department of Manuscripts and Special Collections, The University of Nottingham, UK. Ref. 154/2.
34. *CP* 646.
35. Noëlle Cuny, *D. H. Lawrence: Le corps en devenir* (Paris: Presses de la Sorbonne Nouvelle, 2008), 101–155.
36. *CP* 696.
37. *CP*.
38. *CP* 696.
39. Haëckel, *The Riddle of the Universe*, 179.
40. *CP* 668.
41. *CP* 697.

Works Cited

The Authorized King James Version of The Bible (1997).Oxford: Oxford University Press.
Bergson, Henri (1911), *Creative Evolution*. Trans. Arthur Mitchell. New York: Henry Holt and Co.
Bonds, Diane (1978), *Language and the Self in D. H. Lawrence*, Studies in Modern Literatures 68. Ann Arbor: UMI Research Press.
Clarke, Colin (1969), *River of Dissolution: D. H. Lawrence and English Romanticism*. London: Routledge.
Cuny, Noëlle (2008), *D. H. Lawrence : Le corps en devenir*. Paris: Presses de la Sorbonne Nouvelle.
Haëckel, Ernst (1901), *The Riddle of the* Universe. Trans. Joseph McCabe. New York: Harper and Brothers.
Lawrence, David Herbert (1964), *The Complete Poems*. Eds. Vivian de Sola Pinto and Warren Roberts. Harmondsworth: Penguin. (In endnotes: *CP*).
———— (1968), *Phoenix II Uncollected, Unpublished and Other Prose Works*. Eds. Warren Roberts et Harry T. Moore. London: Heinemann.
———— (1992; first edition, 1913), *Sons and Lovers*. Eds. Helen Baron and Carl Baron. Cambridge: Cambridge University Press.

_____ (1985; first edition, 1914), *A Study of Thomas Hardy and Other Essays*. Ed. Bruce Steele. Cambridge University Press.
Montgomery, Robert (1994), *The Visionary D. H. Lawrence: Beyond Philosophy and Art*. Cambridge: Cambridge University Press.
Spencer, Herbert (1909), *First Principles*. London: Williams and Norgate.
Tyndall, John (1874), *Address Delivered Before the British Association Assembled at Belfast, With Additions*. http://www.victorianweb.org/science/science_texts/belfast.html. Accessed 22 Aug. 2010.

PART II: AGAINST THE ODDS

5. The Poem or the "Fierce Desire" to Live
Isaac Rosenberg and Robert Graves

Anne Mounic

Isaac Rosenberg (1890–1918) and Robert Graves (1895–1985) were both involved in the Great War, the latter as officer, the former as private, and resisted through writing poems and resorting to myth. What the soldiers had to face in the trenches was not only the enemy, death, and warfare, but also boredom since they were deprived of any individual prerogative — "we get no private time," Rosenberg wrote in 1915.[1] And Graves, who denounced the "sacrifice of the idealistic younger generation to the stupidity and self-protective alarm of the elder,"[2] spoke of the "impermanence of trench life and the sordidness of life in the billets"[3] and said that what he "most disliked in the Army was never being alone, forced to live and sleep with men whose company, in many cases, I would have run miles to avoid."[4] He insisted on the feeling of boredom and the neurasthenia which took hold of the men after nine or ten months[5]: "a black depression held me."[6] The issue of time was essential since the soldiers were denied any kind of personal life, which meant absolute individual alienation — as Eugène Minkowsky pointed out in the book he wrote after the war, *Le Temps vécu*.[7] Boredom was part of the impression of utter dissolution they felt.

Rosenberg, the painter and poet, who died in 1918, planned to write a play on Judas Maccabee, or Maccabaeus, a victorious resistant to Antiochus IV, but he dropped the project for a play on Lilith. He had written one on Moses, who "symbolizes the fierce desire for virility, and original action in contrast to slavery of the most abject kind."[8]

For Robert Graves, who survived the war, the trauma he experienced in the trenches oriented all his poetic work and myth-making afterwards. Just as he wrote the poem "Escape" about his wound in 1916, poetry and myth helped him to apprehend the specter of death and resist it throughout his life.

In that poem, he told the story of how he had managed to defeat Cerberus's guard and to escape from Hell: "Too late! for I've sped through. / O Life! O Sun!"[9] Then, when he wrote *The White Goddess* during the Second World War, he elaborated on the trauma and developed the figure of the poet, half resistant, half submitting to fate. Poetry helped him to overcome his war neurasthenia without forgetting his dead comrades:

> Show me the two so closely bound
> As we, by the wet bond of blood,
> By friendship blossoming from mud,
> By Death: we faced him, and we found
> Beauty in Death,
> In dead men, breath.[10]

With both poets, the Bible is a key reference. With Robert Graves, the figure of Jacob, withstanding the angel and negative forces, is central. He refers to it in *The White* Goddess (1948) and in *The Hebrew* Myths (1963). In both cases, the figure of the individual resisting fate emerges. Yet it would not be accurate to think of these poets as "war poets" only, since it would mean paying more attention to facts, to the fascination violence exerts on our minds, than to the depth of being. Even if the Great War had a considerable significance for both their works and their lives (a life interrupted on April 1st, 1918, as far as Rosenberg was concerned), being a poet meant resisting the fatality of facts and of history, and giving precedence to the individual human being. Poets should endeavor not to be the non-entities George Orwell described when denouncing totalitarian states. Emmanuel Levinas remarks at the end of an essay about Franz Rosenzweig, who wrote *Der Stern der Erlösung*, (published in 1921), in the Balkan trenches in 1917 and 1918: "Independence as regards history asserts the right possessed by human conscience to judge a world that is ready for Judgement at any moment, before the end of History and not taking it into account, i.e. a world peopled with persons."[11] In his Foreword to the *Collected Works of Isaac Rosenberg*, Siegfried Sassoon wrote: "Rosenberg was not consciously a 'war poet.' But the war destroyed him and his few but impressive 'Trench Poems' are a central point in this book."[12]

Dealing with poets means dealing with persons, through what remains of their personal experience as expressed in their work. Rosenberg wrote, around 1911: "They only live who have not lived in vain, / For in their works their life returns again."[13] A poem is an instance of what Kierkegaard called "repetition," which means that the mind is able to retrieve what is transient and ephemeral, thus connecting the present moment to eternity. "Job is blessed and has received everything *double*.— This is called a *repetition*."[14] Kierkegaard refers to the end of the Book of Job: "also the Lord gave Job twice as much as he had before."[15] However, those poets were not quite like Job, as described by Kierkegaard — "a man who holds a trump card such as a thunderstorm in his hand."[16] It would mean giving way to the idealistic view of war as held by Ernst Jünger, Pierre Teilhard de Chardin or Jan Patočka.[17] What is the significance of Biblical and mythical figures in their resistance to history?

Two Different Personalities

Born in 1890, Isaac Rosenberg had already published two collections of poetry when he was sent to France with the 11th Battalion of the King's Own Royal Lancaster Regiment at the beginning of June 1916. These two collections were *Night and Day*, published in London in 1912, and *Youth*, in 1915. In the poems of this period, the Biblical elements are numerous. It is important to know that Dovber Rosenberg, Isaac's father, who was born in Lithuania, decided to emigrate in order to avoid being conscripted into the Russian army, which was contrary to his principles as a student of the Torah and as a Tolstoyan. "Thou shalt not commit murder" is one of the Ten Commandments and, as Deuteronomy says: "I have set before you life and death, blessing and cursing: therefore choose life, that both you and thy seed may live."[18] In his political writings, Tolstoy denounced political and economic violence and in his *Confession*, he wrote, in echo of Deuteronomy: "Faith is a knowledge of the meaning of human life, the consequence of which is that man does not kill himself but lives. Faith is the force of life."[19] Tolstoy denied science the power of accounting for life and disagreed with the definition of the individual as "a temporary, incidental accumulation of particles."[20] He overcame Schopenhauerian pessimism, insisting on the inability of philosophical knowledge to answer the question of life. "Strictly expressed, as it is by the Brahmins, Solomon, and Schopenhauer, the answer is but a vague one, an identity: 0 equals 0, life presented to me as nothing is nothing."[21]

With this Biblical and Tolstoyan background, Rosenberg should never have joined the army, but he could not find a job; Ezra Pound had suggested to Rosenberg that he enlist. In 1915, in an unfinished letter, Rosenberg wrote to Pound: "As to your suggestion about the army I think the world has been terribly damaged by certain poets (in fact any poet) being sacrificed in this stupid business. There is certainly a strong temptation to join when you are making no money."[22] In June 1915 Rosenberg wrote to Sydney Schiff: "I am thinking of enlisting if they will have me, though it is against all my principles of justice — though I would be doing the most criminal thing a man can do —

I am so sure my mother would not stand the shock that I don't know what to do."[23] Then, when in the barracks, he wrote: "Believe me the army is the most detestable invention on this earth and nobody but a private in the army knows what it is to be a slave."[24]

His Biblical outlook gave Rosenberg a sense of becoming — becoming is at the core of Biblical tradition. It helped him develop an approach to the ambivalence of life, and a reliance on joy which recalls Spinoza's philosophy. All these elements appear clearly in a poem called "Creation":

> Love, joy, dwell in infinity.
> Love begets love; reaching highest
> We find a higher still, unseen
> From where we stood to reach the first.
> Moses must die to live in Christ.
> The seed be buried to live to green.
> Perfection must begin from worst.
> Christ perceives a larger reachless love
> More full, and grows to reach thereof.
> The green plant yearns for its yellow fruit.
> Perfection always is a root,
> And joy, a motion that doth feed
> Itself on light of its own speed,
> And round its radiant circles runs,
> Creating and devouring suns.
>
> Thus human hunger nourisheth
> The plan terrific,— true design–
> Makes music with the bones of death,
> And soul knows how to shine.
>
> What foolish lips first framed "I sin?"[25]

"God Made Blind," a poem written in 1914 or 1915, develops the conceit of how we can cheat God. In an undated letter, the poet explained to Edward Marsh: "The idea in the poem I like best I should think is very clear. That we can cheat our malignant fate who has devised a perfect evil for us, by pretending to have as much misery as we can bear, so that it withholds its greater evil, while under that guise of misery there is secret joy."[26] This is the first stanza. In the second, the poet suggests how love, in "gleeful secrecy," reaches the outskirts of "Eternity without us, heaven's heat." In the third stanza, it is no longer with "gloom" that we are to cheat God but with Joy itself:

> For say! what can God do
> To us to Love, whom we have grown into?
> Love! the poured rays of God's Eternity!
> We are grown God — and shall His self-hate be?[27]

The poem plays on the two faces of God, grace and rigor, and is based upon the assumption of Man's freedom, which means that he can reach infinity through his relationship with others. The second person of the subjective dialogue, I and You, is the other, and then God, as Martin Buber showed in a book he wrote approximately at the same period as Rosenzweig's *Stern der Erlösung, Ich und Du* (1923).

As for Robert Graves (1895–1985), he published poems in *The Carthusian*, the school magazine in Charterhouse, and was noticed by Edward Marsh, who took some of his poems for the 1916–17, 1918–1919, and 1920–1922 volumes of *Georgian Poetry*.[28] In 1916 he published his first collection, *Over the Brazier*, which included war poems as well as earlier verse such as "Youth and Folly," a poem he thought of during a Charterhouse sermon. The poet's ironical tone, his rejection of Protestant dogma and his taste for ancient mythic figures are already present:

> In Chapel often when I bawl
> The hymns, to show I'm musical,
> With bright eye and cheery voice
> Bidding Christian folk rejoice,
> Shame be it said, I've not a thought
> Of the One Being whom I ought
> To worship: with unwitting roar
> Other Godheads I adore.
> I celebrate the Gods of Mirth
> And Love and Youth and Springing Earth.[29]

He also mentions Bacchus, Pan, Apollo, and Atlas. Yet, as he stated in *Goodbye to All That* (1929): "The last thing that Protestants lose when they cease to believe is a vision of Christ as the perfect man. That persisted with me, sentimentally, for years."[30] "In the Wilderness," which was first published in *Over the Brazier*, alludes to Jesus' stay in the wilderness after His baptism (*Matt.* 4). Graves describes Him as followed by the scapegoat (*Leviticus*, 16, 20–22), which already suggests a refusal of idealistic duality of good and evil and a realization of the ambivalence of life:

> He, of his gentleness,
> Thirsting and hungering
> Walked in the wilderness;
> Soft words of grace he spoke
> Unto lost desert-folk
> That listened wondering.
> He heard the bittern call
> From ruined palace-wall,
> Answered him brotherly;
> He held communion

> With the she-pelican
> Of lonely piety.
> [...]
> Then ever with him went,
> Of all his wanderings
> Comrade, with ragged coat,
> Gaunt ribs — poor innocent–
> Bleeding foot, burning throat,
> The guileless young scapegoat:
> For forty nights and forty days
> Followed in Jesus' ways,
> Sure guard behind him kept,
> Tears like a lover wept.[31]

The war confirmed his distrust of dogmatic religion: "I went on leave in April 1916. That Good Friday was the last occasion on which I ever attended a church service, apart from subsequent weddings, church parades, and so on."[32] He particularly resented sermons about the soldiers' "Divine Sacrifice": "To please my mother I took the sacrament, though by no means in the required mood of spiritual resignation."[33] The poet also had to resist the universal idealistic philosophy of self-sacrifice. In the war, he first perceived a reversal of values: as Simone Weil was to argue in *The Iliad or the Poem of Force*, written in 1938 and published in 1941, force had come to prevail over ethical values, and notably over the choice of life. David could no longer win against Goliath. On the death of his friend David Thomas, Graves wrote a poem called "Goliath and David" which ends with the following lines:

> "I'm hit! I'm killed!" young David cries,
> Throws blindly forward, chokes ... and dies.
> Steel-helmeted and grey and grim
> Goliath straddles over him.[34]

To his friend Robert Nichols, he dedicated a poem in which he said that "the Gods of Mirth" were "out of season" in the trenches.[35] Therefore poetic diction as it stood prior to the Great War was no longer valid; poetic language had to change. Graves said so to Siegfried Sassoon, who thought that "war should not be written about in such a realistic way": "Siegfried had not yet been in the trenches. I told him, in my old-soldier manner, that he would soon change his style."[36]

More than a simple reversal of values, Graves perceives chaos and dissolution. Even the mythical figures which symbolize life lose all reality:

> Here now is chaos once again,
> Primaeval mud, cold stones and rain.
> Here flesh decays and blood drips red
> And the Cow's dead, the old Cow's dead.[37]

The point is that both Graves and Rosenberg see the war as a process of dissolution. Moreover the soldiers are haunted by the faces of their dead comrades:

> Stare! Killed last month at Festubert,
> Caught on patrol near the Boche wire,
> Torn horribly by machine-gun fire!
> He paused, saluted smartly, grinned,
> Then passed away like a puff of wind,
> Leaving us in blank astonishment.[38]

The question then is: how is it possible to remain an individual when thus alienated from oneself through violence and terror? In her essay, Simone Weil shows how people subjected to force and violence are transformed into mere things: "It is a very strange being, that thing which has a soul; a strange state for the soul. Who will say how it has to twist and bend double to keep adapting? It has not been made to inhabit a thing; when it has to, all of it suffers violence."[39]

Moreover, as mentioned previously, the soldiers were deprived of any privacy; they had no time to themselves, no life of their own. Graves writes about "The Assault Heroic":

> Today we've killed your pride;
> Today your ardour ends.
> We've murdered all your friends;
> We've undermined by stealth
> Your happiness and your health?
> We've taken away your hope;
> Now you may droop and mope
> To misery and to death.
> But with my spear of faith,
> Stout as an oaken rafter,
> With my round shield of laughter,
> With my shard, tongue-like sword
> That speaks a bitter word,
> I stood beneath the wall
> And there defied them all.[40]

Those voices are those of "My foes that lay within" (line 11 of the same poem), the voices of war neurasthenia. Resisting the tragic imposition of self-sacrifice, the individual discovers his soul's inner depth.

In "Escape," a poem written after he had been wounded on July 20th 1916 and reported as dead in *The Times* on the 24th, his own birthday, we can already see how the "spear of faith" worked. In his mind, and in the poem, he reconstructed the scene of his wounding as a struggle to escape from Hades through wrestling with Cerberus ("Good Cerberus!... Good dog!... but stop!"[41]) and coming out alive:

> Then swift Cerberus' wide moths I cram
> With army biscuit smeared with ration jam;
> And sleep lurks in the luscious plum and apple.
> He crunches, swallows, stiffens, seems to grapple
> With the all-powerful poppy ... then a snore,
> A crash; the beast blocks up the corridor
> With monstrous hairy carcase, red and dun–
> Too late! for I've sped through.
>   O Life! O Sun!

This poem is quite significant because it shows the poet's need for exemplary figures to help him weather and spiritually overcome his neurasthenia. In *The White Goddess*, written during the Second World War and published in 1948, Graves fought against the abstraction of the ideal (Apollo) and promoted the figure of the limping poet submitting to real-life experience — birth, love, and death as embodied by the Goddess. The poet is like Dionysos or Jacob, the latter described by Graves as another instance of the dying king, the figure discovered by Frazer in his studies of myth and primitive kingship in *The Golden Bough*. Graves seeks figures to represent his own experience; the "I" is predominant in his poems while Rosenberg mainly uses the first person plural "we," and chooses figures with a collective impact. Yet in both cases we can speak of individual resistance against oppression.

Later, when middle-aged, Graves called himself, using a Greek word, *deuteropotmos*, or "second-fated." He meant he had achieved his descent into hell during the war, and now wished to choose life:

> Fortune enrolled me among the second-fated
> Who have read their own obituaries in *The Times*,
> Have heard "Where, death, is thy sting? Where, grave, thy victory?"
> [...]
> We were then shot through by merciful lunar shafts
> Until hearts tingled, heads sang, and praises flowed;
> And learned to scorn your factitious universe
> Ruled by the death which we had flouted;
> Acknowledging only from the Dove's egg hatched
> Before aught was, but wind — unpredictable
> As our second birth would be, or our second love:
> A moon-warmed world of discontinuance.[42]

Graves's exile to Deyà in 1929, after publishing, significantly, *Goodbye to All That*, expressed a wish to live in a real universe, endowed with substance and rhythm by the cycle of the seasons and a rural way of life. "I am nobody's servant and have chosen to live on the outskirts of a Majorcan mountain-village, Catholic but anti-ecclesiastical, where life is ruled by the old agricultural cycle."[43]

Against Slavery and the Functional World

Moses was Rosenberg's response to life in the barracks from his enlistment to his departure for France. The poet was filled with a desire for renewal. In November 1915, he wrote to Sidney Schiff: "One might succumb[,] be destroyed — but one might also (and the chances are even greater for it) be renewed, made larger, healthier."[44] It is worth remembering here what Lawrence wrote in his novel published in 1915, *The Rainbow*: "God burned no more in that bush. It was dead matter lying there."[45] And he too, especially with his idea of a small community called *Rananim*, hoped some regeneration would come out of the war. However, when Rosenberg went into the trenches, he changed his mind. At the beginning of *Lady Chatterley's Lover*, Lawrence, who was aware of the chaos created by the war, wrote: "Ours is essentially a tragic age, so we refuse to take it tragically. The cataclysm has happened, we are among the ruins, we start to build up new little habitats, to have new little hopes. It is rather hard work: there is no smooth road into the future: but we go round, or scramble over the obstacles."[46] His description of the new Clifford Chatterley gives a clue as to the sort of danger the war survivors might have to resist: "But he had been so much hurt that something inside him had perished, some of his feelings had gone. There was a blank of insentience."[47] Indifference certainly fits the status of mere things.

Nevertheless, although the poet had to endure hardships in the barracks, Rosenberg's Moses is a strong character, some sort of leopard, who dreams in apocalyptic terms, and proclaims:

> I am sick of priests and forms,
> The rigid dry-bones refinement.
> As ladies' perfumes are
> Obnoxious to stern natures,
> This miasma of a rotting god
> Is to me.
> Who has made of the forest a park?
> Who has changed the wolf to a dog?
> And put the horse in harness?
> And man's mind in a groove?[48]

At the end, Moses kills the Egyptian overseer Abinoah, saying:

> So grandly fashion these rude elements
> Into some newer nature, a consciousness
> Like naked light seizing the all-eyed soul,
> Oppressing with its gorgeous tyranny
> Until they take it thus — or die.[49]

Moses is a "rebel," who wants to achieve "a nation's harmony."[50] In a letter to Sidney Schiff, Rosenberg says: "Besides my being a Jew makes it bad among these wretches."[51] He wrote a poem entitled "The Jew":

> Moses, from whose loins I sprung,
> Lit by a lamp in his blood
> Ten innumerable rules, a moon
> For mutable lampless men.
>
> The blonde, the bronze, the ruddy,
> With the same heaving blood,
> Keep tide to the moon of Moses,
> Then why do they sneer at me?[52]

At the beginning of his stay in France, Rosenberg contemplated the idea of "a Jewish play with Judas Maccabeas for hero."[53] In the autumn, he mentioned the project again: "I have thoughts of a play round our Jewish hero, Judas Maccabeus. I have much real material here, and also there is some parallel in the savagery of the invaders then to this war."[54]

Certainly, the "savagery" was such that the poet substituted the "spirit of dissolution,"[55] Lilith, for the victorious hero. He wrote two sketches, *The Amulet* and *The Unicorn*. Lilith is a female demon, often thought to have been Adam's first wife in post–Biblical tradition. She is mentioned in *Isaiah*[56]: "Wildcats shall meet hyenas, / Goat-demons shall greet each other; / There too lilith shall repose / And find herself a resting place."[57] Here "Lilith" with a lower-case "l" refers to a group of female demons in ancient Semitic folklore. In the Authorized Version a "screech owl" is to be found instead. In *The White Goddess*, Graves refers to "the same owl [Athene's] that gave its name to Adam's first wife Lilith.[58] In *The Hebrew Myths* he explains that the name "Lilith" derives from the Babylonian word "lilitu," a female demon, or spirit of the wind.[59] In the French Jewish translation of *Isaiah* (1899), Lilith is written with a capital "L."

The atmosphere, in *The Amulet*, is apocalyptic; it is even more so in *The Unicorn*:

> But God's unthinkable imagination
> Invents new tortures for nature
> Whose wisdom falters here.
> No used experience can break, make aware

> The imminent unknowable.
> Sullen destruction
> Till the stricken soul wails in anguish
> Torn here and there.[60]

Lilith is kidnapped on the unicorn by Tel, the chief of a declining race in need of women: "Saul and Lilith are ordinary folk into whose ordinary lives the Unicorn bursts."[61] The play should be read in tandem with one of Rosenberg's war poems, "Daughters of War." We can compare Rosenberg's outlook with Graves's. In *The White Goddess*, the latter wrote about the poet: "No poet can hope to understand the nature of poetry unless he has had a vision of the Naked King crucified to the lopped oak, an watched the dancers, red-eyed from the acrid smoke of the sacrificial fires, stamping out the measure of the dance, their bodies bent uncouthly forward, with a monotonous chant of: 'Kill! kill! kill!' and 'Blood! blood! blood!'"[62] It means that poetry has nothing to do with philosophical idealism, or the "emancipated reason."[63] Its theme is the substance of life, a combination of joy and suffering. Rosenberg's first stanza is the following:

> Space beats the ruddy freedom of their limbs—
> Their naked dances with man's spirit naked
> By the root side of the tree of life
> (The underside of things
> And shut from earth's profoundest eyes.)[64]

Both poets have discovered the "root side" of individual life — what Goethe called the "demonic," the ambivalent force of life which inspires the poem.

> I saw in prophetic gleams
> These mighty daughters in their dances
> Beckon each soul aghast from its crimson corpse
> To mix in their glittering dances.[65]

The poet goes beyond the aesthetic field usually allotted to poetry, and his vision becomes "prophetic." The term is Biblical. A prophet has the intuition of the future through his ethical viewpoint, since it is a question of choice. In his 1937 Foreword mentioned above, Siegfried Sassoon wrote: "I have recognized in Rosenberg a fruitful fusion between English and Hebrew culture. Behind all his poetry there is a racial quality — Biblical and prophetic. Scriptural and sculptural are the epithets I would apply to him."[66] It is worth noting what Siegfried Sassoon, who was himself involved in the Great War and whom Graves ironically called "heroic"[67] when he became a pacifist, felt about Isaac Rosenberg's poems: "They are all of them fine poems, but 'Break of Day in the Trenches' has for me a poignant and nostalgic quality which eliminates critical analysis. Sensuous frontline existence is there, hateful and repellent, unforgettable and inescapable."[68] Considering Sassoon, Graves evinced his dislike of idealism: "In fact, Siegfried's unconquerable idealism changed direction with his environment: he varied between happy warrior and bitter pacifist."[69] Graves's conclusion —"I was both more consistent and less heroic than Siegfried"— is reminiscent of his famous poem "In Broken Images": "He becomes dull, trusting to his clear images; / I become sharp, mistrusting my broken images."[70]

Between October 1916 and June 1917, the period during which Rosenberg wrote "Daughters of War," he perceived what was at stake in history:

> Tho' there are human faces
> Best sculptures of Deity,
> And sinews lusted after
> By the Archangels tall,
> Even these must leap to the love-heat of these maidens
> From the flame of terrene days,
> Leaving grey ashes to the wind — to the wind.

The demonic, apocalyptic force has taken hold of the universe, providing deeper clues to the nature of human life.

Like Blake, Graves rejects the exclusive rule of "emancipated reason," which banishes the rest of life into the realm of the abject, or the devilish. In "Nine Hundred Iron Chariots," he quotes his son asking him in a plane from London to Geneva: "Why is there only one propeller going round?"[71] One propeller means reason only, the "male principle" only while the whole of the poet's person is involved in the creative act: "In a poetic trance, which happens no more predictably than a migraine or an epileptic fit, this power is traditionally identified with the ancient Moon-Goddess. All poems, it seems, grow from a small verbal nucleus gradually assuming an individual rhythm and verse form."[72] The Moon-Goddess is the figure of resistance not only against what destroys man but also against what would corrode his spirit from the inside (remember the "Assault Heroic") if he refused to take it into account. This is the poet as described by Graves: "The poet is, on the whole, anti-authoritarian, agoraphobic and intuitive rather than intellectual; but his judgments are coherent."[73] In "In Broken Images," mentioned above, the intellectual type and the poet are opposed, starting with: "He is quick, thinking in clear images; / I am slow, thinking in broken images,"[74] and ending with:

> He continues quick and dull in his clear images;
> I continue slow and sharp in my broken images.

> He in a new confusion of his understanding;
> I in a new understanding of my confusion.

Poetry comes from the "root side of the tree of life," to use Rosenberg's expression. What makes the originality of a poem is the depth of the poet's creative leap: "True originality implies a leap taken by the mind across a dark gulf of nothingness into new regions of scientific thought, and the establishing of a bridgehead on the far side to help routine scientists across."[75] True originality is the same for scientists and poets — the plane should work on two propellers in each case. Originality is not aesthetic but ethical: "Nowadays, however, poetic originality is insisted upon, and the routineers must pretend to possess it, by embellishing their poems with rhetorical tropes borrowed from abstractionism, psycho-analysis, and undigested foreign literature."[76] What counts is the quality of the inner leap, the human insight. In a poem, even a dead face will tell of the human plight. Rosenberg's "Dead Man's Dump" ends:

> Will they come? Will they ever come?
> Even as the mixed hoofs of the mules,
> The quivering-bellied mules,
> And the rushing wheels all mixed
> With his tortured upturned sight,
> So we crashed round the bend,
> We heard his weak scream,
> We heard his very last sound,
> And our wheels grazed his dead face.[77]

The words revealing the "underside of things" resist the destruction of man when they come from a powerful inner impulse and vision. In an essay called "Genius," Graves insists on this inner power of creation, which is very close to sexual power. "But *genius* had a spiritual rather than a physical sense and implied the primitive creative power with which a man is born and which accompanies him throughout life as his highest spiritual self, his protector, his oracle."[78] Unfortunately, Graves was blinded by his historical, positivist outlook as to the poetic significance of Jacob in the Jewish tradition. Commentators on *Genesis* 27, 22 expatiated on the fact that Jacob is the voice — the inner spiritual power. It is through that inner power that he not only resists his brother Esau but also the angel, or rather the other man, on the famous night when they wrestled and which ended in Jacob's being blessed. The word for blessing in Hebrew means a flow of water and has sexual connotations. The poet's resistance is active through his voice and rhythm. Although Rosenberg does not mention Jacob, and Graves did not fully understand the character's significance, both poets understood that poetry comes from the individual's creative depth. Graves thought a poem emerged from the dark and became rhythm. In April 1911, in a story called "Rudolph," Rosenberg wrote: "But it is his imagination, his refinement of sentiment, that only uses the object itself as a basis to give expression to his vision. Why then were we given the creative faculty? What, if not this, is the meaning of God?"[79] Furthermore the creative faculty gives man — even the dead man — a face. As Rosenberg opposes the Amazons and the Deity and Archangels in "Daughters of War," we may oppose the sacred and the holy. The sacred imposes the "Divine Sacrifice" Graves would not accept, and, from 1920 on, nor would he accept the monuments to the war victims. By dint of the unquestioning, even inert, acceptance of necessity, the sacrifice could be demanded over and over again. On the other hand, the meaning of man's life, and the infinite, is to be found within the sphere of what Levinas calls the holy. "The nothingness of death," Emmanuel Levinas writes: "Is the nothingness of death not the very nakedness of the other's face? 'Thou shalt not commit murder' is the nakedness of the face."[80] The "Divine sacrifice" (the sacred) can be rejected on behalf of ethics (the holy), which counteracts the spirit of dissolution, or chaos.

The twentieth century poet had to withstand collective violence as imposed by history and justified by an idealistic philosophy of the universal, as developed by Hegel.[81] In a poem entitled "Soldier: Twentieth Century," Rosenberg wrote:

> Out of unthinkable torture,
> Eyes kissed by death,
> Won back to the world again,
> Lost and won in a breath,
>
> Cruel men are made immortal.
> Out of your pain born.
> They have stolen the sun's power
> With their feet on your shoulders worn.[82]

Another important twentieth-century poet, Benjamin Fondane, murdered in Birkenau in October 1944, remarked: "Human nature has not resisted the inhuman Tower of Babel which we have built and called civilization; we do not notice it because violence increases and the taste for blood is stronger, but because they enter history under the guise of principles and the mask of science."[83]

> "Cruel men are made immortal."

Robert Graves, who was lucky enough to survive the Great War, transformed his own resistance against history and the universal into his individual embrace of man's existential plight. He fully exposed the principles of that quest in *The White Goddess*, who became the Black Goddess[84] in the 1960s, and in a lot of his poems. One of the most significant instances of such principles is "Counting the Beats," in which the present moment, as well as the pair the lovers form, is a paradoxical unit, a dialectical reciprocity of being and non-being, of life and its negation—which may be symbolized by Jacob's wrestling with the Angel. The rhythm of the poem withstands the destructive rhythm of time and implies that life should be preserved within the unity of the two lovers ("we") in that of time and place ("now and here"), the reference to time coming first. Love transcends unrest and is being fed by it.

> You, love, and I,
> (He whispers) you and I,
> And if no more than only you and I
> What care you or I?
>
> Counting the beats,
> Counting the slow heart beats,
> The bleeding to death of time in slow heart beats,
> Wakeful they lie.[85]

Graves claimed that: "Poetry is the profession of private truth, supported by craftsmanship in the use of words; I prefer not to call it an art, because the art or Classical Verse from the time of Virgil onwards allied itself to the art of rhetoric."[86] The "profession of private truth" is resistance, and requires a genuine tongue, not rhetoric—which is what Shakespeare displays in many of his plays: *Hamlet, King Lear, As You Like It*, to mention only those. What is at stake is the individual's embrace of Time and his own power of creation and choice, which we may call freedom. For Graves, the White Goddess or Muse is the existential figure of freedom. This is obvious from the last lines of "On Portents":

> Such portents are not to be wondered at
> Being tourbillions in Time made
> By the strong pulling of her bladed mind
> Through that ever-reluctant element.[87]

The Goddess is not only for Graves the female version of the transcendent principle (Jehovah) but also the presence of the human desire to grasp and undergo life's experience. The "ever-reluctant element" is Time itself, real otherness. Through this spiritual wrestling, the individual mind dilates so as to communicate with the whole of the living universe. Choosing life means resisting—and resisting means choosing life. That is the ethical choice.

Notes

1. *The Collected Works of Isaac Rosenberg*, Foreword by Siegfried Sassoon, Ed. Ian Parsons (London: Chatto & Windus, 1984), 224.
2. Robert Graves, *Goodbye to All That* (London: Penguin, 1957; first edition, 1929), 202.
3. *Goodbye...*,103.
4. *Goodbye...*, 187.
5. *Goodbye...*, 143.
6. *Goodbye...*, 142.
7. Eugène Minkovski, *Le temps vécu* (Brionne: Gérard Monfort, 1988; first edition, 1933), 5.
8. *The Collected Works of Isaac Rosenberg*, 235.
9. Robert Graves, *Complete Poems, Volume 1*, Eds. Beryl Graves and Dunstan Ward (Manchester: Carcanet, 1995), 31.
10. "Two Fusiliers," Robert Graves, *Complete Poems, Volume 1*, 7.
11. Emmanuel Levinas, *Difficile liberté* (Paris: Le Livre de Poche, 1984; first edition, 1963), 281 (my translation).
12. Siegfried Sassoon, Foreword, *The Collected Works of Isaac Rosenberg*, ix.
13. "My Days are But the Tombs of Buried Hours," *The Poems and Plays of Isaac Rosenberg*, Ed. Vivien Noakes (Oxford: Oxford University Press, 2004), 15.
14. Søren Kierkegaard, *Repetition*, Ed. and transl. Howard V. Hong and Edna H. Hong, (Princeton, New Jersey: Princeton University Press, 1983), 212.
15. *Job*, 42, 10 (Authorized Version).
16. Kierkegaard, 216.
17. On this point cf. Anne Mounic, Chapitre 8, *Monde terrible où naître : La voix singulière face à l'Histoire* (Paris: Honoré Champion, 2012).
18. *Deuteronomy* 30, 19.
19. Leo Tolstoy, *A Confession and Other Religious Writings*, Transl. by Jane Kentish (London: Penguin Classics, 1987), 54.
20. *A Confession...*, 39.
21. *A Confession...*, 53. We should add that *Ecclesiastes*, although pessimistic at first, reads as a quest for wisdom in which life is celebrated.
22. *The Collected Works of Isaac Rosenberg*, 214.
23. *The Collected Works of Isaac Rosenberg*, 216.
24. *The Collected Works of Isaac Rosenberg*, 230.
25. *The Poems and Plays of Isaac Rosenberg*, 66.
26. *The Poems and Plays of Isaac Rosenberg,*, 340.
27. *Ibid.*, 98.
28. See Robert Graves, *Complete Poems, Volume 1*, 335.
29. Robert Graves, *Complete Poems, Volume 1*, 8.
30. *Goodbye to All That*, 21.
31. Robert Graves, *Complete Poems, Volume 1*, 11.
32. *Goodbye to All That*, 165.
33. *Goodbye to All That*, 167.
34. Robert Graves, *Complete Poems, Volume 1*, 27.
35. Robert Graves, *Complete Poems, Volume 1*, 38.
36. *Goodbye to All That*, 146.
37. Robert Graves, *Complete Poems*, Volume 1, 39.

38. Robert Graves, *Complete Poems*, 60.
39. Simone Weil, *Œuvres*, Ed. Florence de Lussy (Paris : Gallimard Quarto, 1999), 542 (translation mine).
40. Weil, 61.
41. Weil, 31.
42. Robert Graves, *Complete Poems, Volume 2*, Eds. Beryl Graves and Dunstan Ward (Manchester: Carcanet, 1997), 244.
43. Robert Graves, *The White Goddess* (London: Faber, 1957; first edition, 1948), 14.
44. *The Collected Works of Isaac Rosenberg*, 221-22.
45. D.H. Lawrence, *The Rainbow* (London: Penguin, 1987; first edition, 1915), 203.
46. D.H. Lawrence, *Lady Chatterley's Lover* (London: Penguin, 1984; first edition, 1928), 5.
47. *Lady Chatterly's Lover*, 6.
48. *The Poems and Plays of Isaac Rosenberg*, 192.
49. *The Poems and Plays of Isaac Rosenberg*, 208.
50. *The Poems and Plays of Isaac Rosenberg*, 207.
51. *The Collected Works of Isaac Rosenberg*, 219.
52. *The Poems and Plays of Isaac Rosenberg*, , 126.
53. *The Collected Works of Isaac Rosenberg*, 238.
54. *The Collected Works of Isaac Rosenberg*, 248.
55. *The Poems and Plays of Isaac Rosenberg*, 242.
56. Isaiah 34, 14.
57. *The Jewish Study Bible* (Oxford : Oxford University Press, 1999), 851.
58. *The White Goddess*, 315.
59. Robert Graves, Raphael Patai, *Les Mythes hébreux* (Paris: Fayard, 1987; first English edition, 1963), 85.
60. *The Poems and Plays of Isaac Rosenberg*, 250.
61. *The Collected Works of Isaac Rosenberg*, 257.
62. Robert Graves, *The White Goddess*, 448.
63. Robert Graves, "The Philosopher," *Complete Poems, Volume 2*, 69.
64. "Daughters of War," *The Poems and Plays of Isaac Rosenberg*, 142.
65. *The Poems and Plays of Isaac Rosenberg*, 142.
66. Siegfried Sassoon, Foreword, *The Collected Works of Isaac Rosenberg*, IX.
67. Robert Graves, *Goodbye to All That*, 226.
68. Siegfried Sassoon, Foreword, *The Collected Works of Isaac Rosenberg*, IX.
69. Robert Graves, *Goodbye to All That*, 226.
70. Robert Graves, *Complete Poems, Volume 2*, 14.
71. Robert Graves, *Some Speculations on Literature, History and Religion* (Manchester: Carcanet, 2000), 118.
72. Robert Graves, *Some Speculations...*, 118.
73. Robert Graves, *Some Speculations...*, 118.
74. Robert Graves, *Complete Poems, Volume 2*, 14.
75. Robert Graves, *Some Speculations...*, 117.
76. Robert Graves, *Some Speculations...*, 117-8.
77. *The Poems and Plays of Isaac Rosenberg*, 142.
78. Robert Graves, *Some Speculations...*, 269.
79. *The Collected Works of Isaac Rosenberg*, 276.
80. Emmanuel Levinas, *Dieu, la mort et le temps* (Paris: Le Livre de Poche, 1997; first edition, 1993), 132.

81. See Anne Mounic, *Monde terrible où naître : La voix singulière face à l'Histoire* (Paris: Honoré Champion, 2012). See also Anne Mounic, *Counting the Beats : Robert Graves' Poetry of Unrest* (Amsterdam: Rodopi, 2011).
82. *The Poems and Plays of Isaac Rosenberg*, 146.
83. Benjamin Fondane, "L'homme devant l'histoire ou le bruit et la fureur," *Le Lundi existentiel et le dimanche de l'histoire* suivi de *La philosophie vivante* (Monaco : Editions du Rocher, 1990), 139. See Anne Mounic, Chapitre 10, *Monde terrible où naître...*
84. Robert Graves, *Mammon and the Black Goddess* (New York: Doubleday, 1965).
85. Robert Graves, *Complete Poems, Volume 2*, 180.
86. Robert Graves, *Poetic Craft and Principles* (London: Cassell, 1967), 26.
87. Robert Graves, *The White Goddess*, 343; *The Complete Poems, Volume 2*, 63.

Works Cited

The Jewish Study Bible (1999), Oxford: Oxford University Press.
Fondane, Benjamin (1990), *Le Lundi existentiel et le dimanche de l'histoire* suivi de *La philosophie vivante*. Monaco: Editions du Rocher.
Graves, Robert (1995), *Complete Poems, Volume 1*. Eds Beryl Graves and Dunstan Ward. Manchester: Carcanet.
_____ (1997), *Complete Poems, Volume 2*. Eds Beryl Graves and Dunstan Ward. Manchester: Carcanet.
_____ (1957; first edition, 1948), *The White Goddess*. London: Faber.
_____ (1957; first edition, 1929), *Goodbye to All That*. London: Penguin.
_____, Patai, Raphael (1987; first English edition, 1963), *Les Mythes hébreux*. Paris: Fayard.
_____ (1965), *Mammon and the Black Goddess*. New York: Doubleday.
_____ (1967), *Poetic Craft and Principles*. London: Cassell.
_____ (2000), *Some Speculations on Literature, History and Religion*. Manchester: Carcanet.
Kierkegaard, Søren, (1983), *Repetition*. Ed. and transl. Howard V. Hong and Edna H. Hong. Princeton, New Jersey: Princeton University Press.
Lawrence, D. H. (1984; first edition, 1928), *Lady Chatterley's Lover*. London: Penguin.
_____ (1987; first edition, 1915), *The Rainbow*. London: Penguin.
Levinas, Emmanuel (1997; first edition, 1993), *Dieu, la mort et le temps*. Paris: Le Livre de Poche.
_____ (1984; first edition, 1963), *Difficile liberté*. Paris: Le Livre de Poche.
Minkovski, Eugène (1988; first edition,1933), *Le temps vécu*. Brionne: Gérard Monfort.
Mounic, Anne (2011), *Counting the Beats : Robert Graves' Poetry of Unrest*. Amsterdam: Rodopi.
_____ (2012), *Monde terrible où naître: La voix singulière face à l'Histoire*. Paris: Honoré Champion.
Rosenberg, Isaac (1984), *Collected Works*. Foreword by Siegfried Sassoon, Ed. Ian Parsons. London: Chatto & Windus.
_____ (2004), *The Poems and Plays*. Ed. Vivien Noakes. Oxford: Oxford University Press.
Tolstoy, Leo (1987), *A Confession and Other Religious Writings*. Transl. Jane Kentish. London: Penguin Classics.
Weil, Simone (1999), *Œuvres*. Ed. Florence de Lussy. Paris: Gallimard Quarto.

6. Resisting Theological Error as a Means of Political Salvation
Charles Williams' and Dorothy L. Sayers' Second World War Poetry
Suzanne Bray

In the period up to and during the Second World War, many Christian writers in Britain found themselves to be in a difficult position. The beginning of the twentieth century had been a period of spiritual penury in literary production. When choosing poems for the section 1900–1925 of *The Oxford Book of Christian Verse*, Lord David Cecil stated: "It is an age of doubt, especially among poets. Not many of them write about religion. During the first twenty years of the century little beyond some verses of Mr. Chesterton and Mr. Belloc remains in the memory."[1]

The situation improved after the conversion of T.S. Eliot in 1927 and the 1930s saw a dramatic increase in the publication of quality works by authors with a clearly Christian world view. However such writers found themselves part of a minority whose theological convictions led them to be severely critical of the spirit of the age and of the political implications of the majority ideologies. In the turbulent international and economic situation of the time, this could present difficulties.

Charles Williams and Dorothy L. Sayers, who had been friends since the early 1930s, were among those who believed that the general abandonment of the doctrines of original sin and of the existential solidarity of the whole human race had led to errors with serious consequences for the world. With the development of the international crisis which led to the outbreak of the Second World War, they both started to express this in various literary forms, including in their poetry. As the war continued with both sides experiencing the horrors of saturation bombing in addition to numerous military casualties, the continued habit of ignoring these doctrines started, in their opinion, to present problems for the future of Europe.

In this context, we shall examine four very different poems and their religious and political implications: Dorothy L. Sayers' "The English War" (1940) and "Target Area" (1944), followed by a brief look at Charles Williams' "Percivale at Carbonek" (1938) and a more detailed study of "The Prayers of the Pope" (1944).

Sayers' "The English War" first appeared in the special export number of *The Times Literary Supplement* on 7th September 1940, shortly after both the fall of France and the symbolic resurrection of Dunkirk.[2] This number was "specially directed to strengthening the export of British ideas in British books" and to "passing on the torch of the humane ideal ... during the darkness of war."[3] The editorial with the poem was entitled "The Heroic Theme" and claimed "a wartime poetic renaissance."[4] The poem was very popular, probably because, as Nick Hayes has stated, Sayers' words "typically capture that moment of splendid isolation [...] of the summer of 1940."[5] It was anthologized several times, first in *The Best Poems of 1941*,[6] then in Lord Wavell's *Other Men's Flowers*[7] and, later, *The Terrible Rain: The War Poets 1939–45*.[8] Lord Wavell, who was Viceroy of India from 1943–47, was particularly attached to "The English War" and his private secretary later informed Sayers that he had heard the Viceroy recite it from memory.[9] It was in Wavell's residence in New Delhi that Noel Coward first encountered the poem and "was so attracted by it"[10] that he introduced it into his programme of literary recitals when entertaining the troops. In this way several thousand soldiers came to know it. More recently five stanzas were published in the "Fifty Years On" column of *The Times* on 7th September 1990 and a current GSCE English Literature guide suggests that students compare it with Tennyson's "The Charge of the Light Brigade"[11] for the assignment they have to submit on war poetry.

The poem as first published was preceded by a quotation from a radio broadcast by Philip Jordan, war correspondent for the *News Chronicle* and, after the war, press officer for the Prime Minister: "What other race on earth, well aware of its danger, isolated to fight, would utter a great sign of relief that all had abandoned it, and say to itself: 'Well, thank goodness for that; now we know where we are?'"[12]

For Sayers, the relief came from the fact that England could return at last to her traditional values with "no more advice to listen to"[13] from "the Voice of the Enlightenment,"[14] which had for twenty years "never ceased dinning into her ears that everything she had believed in, everything she had been accustomed to do, everything that for her own sake and for the world's she needed to do, was *naughty*"—a point of view which Sayers could not accept. This voice, which she also referred to as Progressive Humanism, denied the doctrine of original sin.[15] It "had been proclaiming for years" that "There were no sinful men; indeed, there was no such thing as sin [...] Take away the unfavorable environment and everyone would at once be good and cooperate for the happiness of all."[16] It also meant that totalitarian regimes were perceived as misguided rather than evil and had trouble accepting that the human race was not inevitably evolving towards a greater and greater moral perfection.

In Sayers' opinion, this had led to a certain naivety in international affairs, with some people "supposing we could abolish wars merely by disapproving of them"[17] and the peoples of Europe in general having the tendency to "consider peace, conceived as the immediate good-in-itself— not as a spiritual condition, but as a political aim, and consisting in the bare absence of bloodshed."[18] These ideological errors were, from her point of view, not only unrealistic because "nobody can abolish the consequences of sin and error merely by cutting them in the street."[19] They were also liable to produce."
...on the one hand, sloth, timidity, reluctance to interfere with persecution and injustice; on the other hand, the triumph of force by way of threats, blackmail, perjury, and the whole "sickening technique" of oppression, till [...] the logical result of total peace is seen to be total war."[20]

Britain had gone to war still influenced by this progressive mentality until what Sayers called "the miracle"[21] happened: "Hitler scooped up Norway, swallowed Denmark alive, bombed and blazed his way across Holland, battered Belgium to a mummy, tossed the British army into the sea, blew France to fragments and smashed through to the Channel Ports."[22] At this point, with England "ringed with an angry host" when "no allies are left," the occupied countries of Europe, persecuted by the Nazis, "love [England] not" but still "look to [her] for liberty" as her victory is their only hope for liberation.[23] The ethical questions the English had faced for a generation were clear at last. As Sayers wrote to an exiled German, opponent of the Nazi regime, Helmut Kuhn: "We feel pretty sure there's a moral justification for staying alive if possible."[24] What was more, Britain had a new leader, Winston Churchill, whose theology, according to Sayers, "was coarse and Christian enough to allow for sin and the devil."[25] There was also no difficulty in explaining Britain's determined resistance to the rest of the world. Hitler, by his invasion of Czechoslovakia and Poland, had proved he was a tyrant in the tradition of "King Philip of the galleons" and his supposedly invincible Armada, or the French Louis XIV "whose light outshone the sun's" or even Napoleon, "the conquering Corsican"; Sayers even evokes the legend of Francis Drake's drum.[26] He had used this drum in the battle against Philip's Armada:

> Whilst on his deathbed [Drake] ordered that his drum be taken and hung in Buckland Abbey near Plymouth, where it hangs today. He vowed that if

England should ever again be in danger from an unjust foe and someone were to beat upon the drum he would return to defend her shores.[27]

This drum had apparently been heard during the retreat from Dunkirk.[28]

Although Sayers' poem includes a prayer that God will send "the will and power"[29] to enable the Englishmen of her generation to fight as their ancestors had done before them, Sayers neither assumes that England is or always will be in the right, nor that the English will inevitably be victorious. As Paul Volsik has pointed out, "the stark nature of the tragedy in which [England] found itself might have encouraged an emphatic rhetoric. But Sayers does not enter this space."[30] Stanzas 10 and 11 evoke Sayers' hopes for the future: "an English peace — / Some sense, some decency, perhaps / Some justice too,"[31] and also express misgivings about the past, and in particular about the aftermath of the First World War. Lines 49 to 55 almost certainly refer to the negotiations around the Treaty of Versailles, which Sayers considered to be "a scandalous and oppressive Peace Treaty,"[32] as it both assigned "absolute value" to the "dogma of race" on which Hitler would later base his claims for expansion and, through the reparations clauses, inflicted "an almost limitless punishment on generations unborn."[33] If the "sly jackals" refer to those delegates who insisted on making Germany pay beyond its means, the "wishful men"[34] make us think of both American idealists, like President Wilson, whose fourteen points provided an unrealistic vision which his own countrymen would, in the end, be unwilling to endorse, and the British non-combatant politicians who, from their comfortable country estates, promised and failed to deliver either "a land fit for heroes" or "abiding peace and lasting security."[35]

While Sayers supported Churchill's leadership, thoroughly condemned the Nazi ideology in Germany and committed herself wholeheartedly to the war effort, she continued to worry about many prevalent attitudes among her contemporaries and, in particular, about the continued lack of understanding of the nature of sin, which she defined elsewhere as "a kind of inner dislocation" in the will of man, making him "not really free to do, in his own strength, the good he chooses" and therefore needing help from God if he is to avoid disaster.[36] One specific area of concern was the moral debate over saturation bombing of German towns by the RAF's Bomber Command. Mark Connelly has convincingly demonstrated that "as the German Blitz of British cities began in the autumn of 1940, so too did the desire for retribution"[37] and that, probably as a result, "Bomber Command became the darling of the British People."[38] Some British Christians, the best known being George Bell, the Bishop of Chichester, and the writer Vera Brittain, energetically opposed all bombing of civilians. Sayers could not share their viewpoint. As she wrote to the editor of *The News Chronicle*, the bombing of cities, while it is "a painful business in one sense" is not "painful in the sense that the shooting of hostages and the torture of Jews is painful — it's just war."[39] However, she was concerned by and determined to resist the hatred of the enemy, the pseudo-righteous indignation and the desire for revenge which had clearly taken told of a part of the British population. These attitudes were particularly obvious in the media. Numerous members of the public wrote to the editors of major newspapers, as did one J.M.L. Service in April 1941, "to advocate bombing of Berlin and all Germany's regional capitals to teach the Germans a lesson."[40] Winston Churchill himself publicly encouraged reprisals and a spirit of revenge, while the cinema news expressed glee at the thought of the death and destruction inflicted on German civilians. For example, British Movietone in March 1944 "trumpeted a new record of tonnage dropped in one night,"[41] while British Paramount News, after the bombing of Cologne, declared: "This once proud city [...] lies today as a symbol of the all-but divine anger of free men, slow to wrath, terrible in vengeance."[42]

For Sayers, such sentiments were neither Christian nor acceptable, and when the editor of *The News Chronicle* invited comment on reprisals for the use of the German V1 pilotless bombers, she made her position clear. Her letter was published together with one from Lord Vansittart, who favored reprisals. Sayers wrote:

> If by "reprisals" is meant doing something savage merely in order to "pay the other fellow out," without improving one's own situation, then all reprisal is not only a crime, but a first-class military blunder.... The use of a weapon of war is to destroy a) as many as possible b) of the *right* people and c) the *right* material objects d) as expeditiously and e) as inexpensively as possible without f) more cruelty than is necessary to attain that end.[43]

It was, however, in March 1944, just after the British bombing of Frankfurt, that Sayers found the most effective way of expressing her convictions about saturation bombing, by writing "Target Area," which has been described as "a poem which speaks eloquently about humanity's essential sinfulness"[44] and which transforms the victims of war from statistics into tragic human beings. It was first published concurrently in *Fortnightly*[45] in Britain and in *The Atlantic Monthly*[46] in the United States.

On the night of 22nd / 23rd March 1944, 816 British aircraft set out to bomb the city of Frankfurt.[47] The marking and bombing were accurate and large parts of the city center were destroyed. The East Port and almost the entire Old City were reduced to ruins. There were thousands of civilian casualties. Among those who lost their homes that night was an elderly music teacher, Fräulein Cäcilie Fehmer (1867–1949),[48] who had taught German and music to Dorothy L. Sayers at the Godolphin School in Salisbury. Sayers had appreciated her lessons and had particularly admired her as a pianist, writing in her autobiographical novel *Cat O'Mary* that "when she played Chopin, she could magic your soul out of your body."[49] That night in March 1944 Fräulein Fehmer's house in the Escherheimer Landstrasse was bombed and destroyed by the RAF and she lost all her possessions, except two of Dorothy Sayers' novels, which she had lent to a former pupil. Sayers was unaware of this until much later, but in 1947 she wrote to her former teacher that she had thought of her when Frankfurt was bombed.[50]

Sayers introduces the poem with an impersonal quotation from a radio news broadcast on the morning of March 23rd 1944: "OUR bombers were out over Germany last night, in very great strength; their main target was Frankfurt." The capital letters for OUR show her personal identification with the act of war. The poem then starts with the same mix of the calmly neutral: "blue uniforms," "professionally laconic," and the intensely personal, as the deadly bombs become a "basket of eggs"[51] specifically intended for Fräulein Fehmer.

The next twenty-seven lines provide a vivid description of Sayers' former teacher, in terms very similar to those used in *Cat O'Mary*[52]—the "hand of the potter,"[53] a common term for God the creator, has formed her as she is, a gifted musician who could make the piano wires sing "under her touch like bells." At the same time her "eye-glasses" and "shawl" and the fact that she "must be getting an old woman now" accentuate how inoffensive she is; no threat at all to British national security, which makes the reminder of the "grim young men in blue uniforms" from line one, who may or may not have, euphemistically, "cancelled time for her," all the more shocking. The description continues as the reader sees how the English schoolgirls appreciated this German woman's music so much that they "did not grudge seating the hall for Fräulein Fehmer" and that "there is a particular Nocturne" Sayers cannot hear "without thinking of her." These personal recollections become even closer and more vivid as Sayers describes receiving a letter from her former teacher. The "much affection" with which she remembers England and her desire "to read something [Sayers] had written" make Fräulein Fehmer more human and appealing to the reader. This makes the statement in quotation marks, purportedly from Fräulein Fehmer's letter, more surprising: "Of course [...] I am an ardent Nazi." Yet even this is made comprehensible as Sayers reminds her readers that "times were hard" in Germany and that "Hitler rose to power on the despair of the middle classes," suffering to make ends meet in a devastating economic crisis.

Elisabeth Bader has convincingly disputed whether the words "ardent Nazi" were part of a genuine quotation:

She might have told her this in one of her letters, and the quotation marks in *Target Area* give the statement an appearance of authenticity. But if Fräulein Fehmer had really done so, she would never have used the term "Nazi." Supporters of the NS party would call themselves "National Socialists" and not "Nazis" because Nazi was a derogatory term, which was used mainly by left-wing adversaries of the NS and, of course, by the war enemy.[54]

We also know that Fehmer was not a member of the National Socialist party in 1934, although she may have joined it later, and that her maternal grandmother, whose maiden name was Adamsohn, almost certainly had Jewish origins. However, as Sayers was in contact with Fräulein Fehmer at the time of writing "Target Area," continued to write to her until her death in 1949, and knew that other former pupils and colleagues did so as well, it is extremely unlikely that she would have completely misrepresented her in a published work, which the German woman was likely to see. It is more probable that Sayers, unaware of the pejorative nature of the term "Nazi" for a German native speaker, either quoted inaccurately from memory or adapted a statement like "I am an ardent supporter of the NS party" to fit into the verse structure of her poem. It is also possible that Fräulein Fehmer exaggerated her support for the regime knowing that letters abroad were likely to be opened by the authorities. In any case, for the purposes of Sayers' poem, it was important that the author and Fräulein Fehmer should be on different sides in the conflict and that each should voluntarily identify herself with her country's policy.

The poem continues, showing that as Sayers, through giving money and metal and time to the British war effort, has "filled the bombs, loaded the bomb-racks, / built the planes, equipped / the laconic grim young men in blue uniforms"[55] who are going to bring destruction to Frankfurt, so Fräulein Fehmer has contributed out of her "pittance" to the bombs which "went up in reek and smoke behind Paul's Churchyard" in the City of London. Both women are committed to their nation's cause, but also helpless to change anything: "Neither of us can stop what is happening now, / nor would if we could." Despite this, Sayers is distressed by "the personal assault, the particular outrage" which may expose her elderly teacher to the indignity of being seen in public in her nightclothes amidst the ruined contents of her bathroom. She also supposes that Fräulein Fehmer will have been distressed when the German "bombs went down over Warsaw," destroying the homeland of her beloved Chopin, and even suggests that she may not have played "the Nocturne" with which she had entranced her English pupils since "the last night of August" 1939, the eve of the German invasion of Poland. And as the poem reaches its climax, both women are declared "responsible for what we do." They are forever united as "all men," and women, "stand convicted of blood" and "the solidarity of mankind is a solidarity in guilt." As Sayers would write elsewhere: "Every human soul carries within it that seed of corruption and that will to death which is technically called 'original sin,' and ... this corruption is manifest not simply in our vices, but also in our virtues and our ideals."[56]

This highly personal poem presents a potential, and in fact actual, victim of Bomber Command's activities, not as a wicked enemy, but as a frail and vulnerable old woman and as a gifted pianist who loved playing the works of a Polish composer and felt affection for England and those she had known there. But she is also "an ardent Nazi,"[57] and Sayers was known to deplore and condemn the Nazi ideology. The poem was an attempt to resist the stereotyping which removes the horror from acts of war, which in any other context would be unthinkable, and leads to hatred and unjustifiable self-righteousness. Sayers explained the problem to her German friend, Helmut Kuhn:

> We have a sort of top compartment of consciousness in which we keep the feelings of exaltation and revenge and the awful thrill of large-scale destruction; and we are very careful to hang there only caricatures of objectionable storm-troopers and Gestapo agents and what I call "bogey–Germans," we avoid going down into the basement where we keep the blood and terror and the real people (victims of air raids), because it wouldn't do right now.[58]

By presenting a real person, Fräulein Fehmer, in "Target Area," Sayers made her compatriots face the real ethical dilemmas and the inevitable guilt shared by all participants in the "cataract of calamity" of the Second World War. At around the same time she would start work on her play *The Just Vengeance*, which developed the theme further and make the shared, mandatory guilt even clearer:

> ....We try to do right
> And someone is hurt — very likely the wrong person;
> And if we do wrong, or even if we do nothing,
> It comes to the same in the end. We drop a bomb
> And condemn a thousand people to sudden death,
> The guiltless along with the guilty. Or we refuse
> To drop a bomb, and condemn a thousand people
> To a lingering death in a concentration camp
> As surely as if we had set our hands to the warrant.[59]

Charles Williams shared many of Dorothy Sayers' concerns about the international situation and about the beliefs of his compatriots. Like her, he thought that the Allies had missed an opportunity after the First World War, remarking that: "the experience of the Versailles Treaty ... in which the Germans were compelled to admit their guilt in 1914, was not encouraging, nor, obviously, can be. It is [...] too much like confession extracted under torture."[60]

He also shared her profound belief in the doctrine of original sin and in the heavy, but inevitable, burden of guilt borne by all mankind. Like Sayers, he agreed that acceptance of the fact that we are all sinners and all guilty, but all called to fight to the best of our ability against evil, led to difficult ethical dilemmas. However, Williams also had no doubt that as an English Christian, opposed to Hitler's ideology, his duty was clear:

> Must we, for example, consent that other men shall be maimed and killed? The answer to that is simple — we must. We may do it by ourselves inflicting death or torment on others (by bombs or however), or we may do it by abandoning others to death and torment (in concentration camps or wherever), but one way or another we have to consent by our mere acts. To call the one war and the other peace does not help.[61]

The reason for this certainty was based on Williams' awareness that human solidarity in guilt was not limited to the sins and crimes of war, but was part of the natural condition of fallen men living in society:

> Capital punishment, the whole penal law, the instability of the poor, a hundred social evils are part of it.... While we remain as part of the State we are involved in its life. Disagreeing leaves us where we were; we might as well disagree with the Fall, as no doubt most of us do. We cannot, so far, escape the nature of man, the original and awful coinherence of man with man in which we were created.[62]

Conscious of this problem even before the war, Williams chose to portray it in its most extreme form in one of his Arthurian poems, "Percivale at Carbonek."[63] The three seekers of the Grail, Percivale, Galahad and Bors, have reached the city of Carbonek, where they have to go to the house of the Grail and heal King Pelles, wounded by the Dolorous Blow, which represents the Fall. However, in the forest around the city wanders the wolf-man Lancelot, Galahad's father, who engendered him in morally dubious circumstances.

Galahad himself is as pure and innocent and as dedicated to God and the Grail as it is possible for fallen man to be. In human terms, none of the tragedies occurring around him are his fault. However, by the mere fact of his existence, his father has been driven mad and is experiencing deep suffering. Equally, his prophesied and long-awaited arrival at Arthur's court provides the opportunity for the breaking up of the Round Table and the start of the horrific Wars of Identity. If the direct responsibility for these disasters lies with Lancelot and Guinevere for their adultery, with Arthur and Morgause for their act of incest and with the son of that incest, Mordred, who has deliberately stirred up trouble, Galahad accepts his part of the solidarity in guilt, acknowledging that his birth and life, even in doing nothing but good and the will of God, has caused others to suffer. Before he enters Carbonek, Galahad first kneels and prays, begging forgiveness of the father who did not want him and later abandoned him: "Pardon, Lord Lancelot; pardon and blessing, father."[64] Ken Sears has pointed out the paradox in this act as "Galahad, the sinned-against, to angels' astonishment, begs forgiveness of Lancelot the guilty, the miserable, the joyless."[65] Lancelot, in his wolf form, cannot speak, so Galahad asks Bors, Lancelot's cousin and friend, to speak for him. When asked by Bors to be more explicit, Galahad clarifies what he is asking for:

> "Forgive us," the High Prince said, "for Our existence;
> Forgive the means of grace and the hope of glory.
> In the name of Our father forgive Our mother for Our birth."[66]

Galahad's existence is good. It is good that he is and will be "the means of grace and the hope of glory" for Britain.[67] Yet, it is only when he has received forgiveness for these good things, but which have been tainted with the guilt he inherited from before his birth, that Galahad is free to go forward and fulfill his glorious destiny. In the same way, not even the best of the English can claim to be without guilt or not in need of forgiveness. But this guilt should not stop each individual from seeking to do good and to fulfil their destiny, especially in time of war against an evil enemy.

From Williams' point of view, the solidarity in guilt should be seen in the context of even greater solidarities, the coinherence and interdependence of all men and women and the unity of all Christians within the body of Christ. For this reason, English people and German people, and even more so English Christians and German Christians should acknowledge the links between them:

> What is the duty of church-folk as church-folk? Precisely the opposite of their duty as nationals. Their duty as nationals involves separation from and killing of German nationals. Their duty as church-folk involves union with and spiritual dependence on Germans. Both duties must be fulfilled.[68]

In 1939, Williams founded the Order of the Coinherence, an informal Christian movement committed to this doctrine of supernatural unity and called to pray for and bear the burdens of those whom God should place before them. A literary account of this can be found in the Arthurian poem "The Founding of the Company."[69] Williams hoped, through this, that in the problems of his day "of international and social schism, among the praises of separation here and there, the pattern might be stressed, the image affirmed"[70] and the spiritual unity and interdependence of all humankind declared. In his opinion, although the differences between the Allies and their enemies in the war were numerous, one of the greatest was the Nazi desire to define differences between different groups of people and then "having defined [...] to exclude, and then, so far as it can, to enslave or annihilate."[71] According to his biographer, Alice Mary Hadfield, who knew Williams well, Williams' last published poem, "The Prayers of the Pope" is explicitly "a long poem on the world of Charles [Williams's] time, on the 1939–45 war."[72]

In this poem, as C.S. Lewis noted, when the lights go out all over Europe[73] during the Arthurian Wars of Identity, indicating the death of Christian civilization, "the situation which the young Pope Deodatus [...] contemplates is [...] very like that which Williams contemplated in 1944." This is, in his opinion, the decline of a civilization, according to a pattern seen several times before: "from Augustus to Tiberius, from Arthur to Mordred, from Voltaire to Vichy."[74]

While the poem is extremely complex and several themes are woven together, we can note that the Pope, contemplating Arthur and his knights on the one hand and Mordred and his pagan allies on the other, asks: "Where is the difference between us?"[75] He observes that both sides are alike in weapons, motivation and courage: "Causes and catapults they have and we have, / and the death of a brave beauty is mutual everywhere."[76] However, there is a difference. The Pope notices that: "we declare ... / and they deny ... / that we derive from them and they from us, / and alive are they in us and we in them."[77] The Christian allies acknowledge their unity and solidarity with their enemies, while these enemies refuse to admit that they have anything in common with those they seek to destroy. Lewis explains this in his commentary:

> But if coinherence is the one grand secret, how can the faithful remnant reject even the "puppets of reputation" and "evil wizards" without committing the same sin as they? [...] the difference lies, and must always be made to lie, only in this, that we confess and they deny their coinherence in us.[78]

If this is clearly true of Hitler's Germany, so is the evocation of "race / by sullen marshes separated from race"[79] and a society where "virtue is monopolized and grace prized in schism." The result of all this in the poem is also relevant "as band after band stamped into darkness cities / whose burning had lamped their path" and populations whose "wrath grew / with vengeance and victory" and where, instead of unity, "the miserable conquest of the categories over identity / split all." In this context of decline, destruction and devastation, the young and, humanly-speaking, innocent pope prays, offering "his soul's health," as well as "his guilt" and "his richness of repentance." He identifies himself with those loveless ones "who affirm only vengeance and value of victory," promulgating the "sacred union" of all mankind in Adam and in Christ.

Aware that the civilization he loves is crumbling away, he prays too that God will preserve a remnant of his people: "keep thy word in thine unknown elect," so that love of God and love of man may remain alive in the dark days ahead. There is a definite echo here of the words of T.S. Eliot, a personal friend of both Sayers and Williams, as well as a fellow Anglican Christian, in his essay "Thoughts after Lambeth":

> The Universal Church is today more definitely set against the World than at any other time since pagan Rome. I do not mean that our times are particularly corrupt; all times are corrupt. In spite of certain local appearances, Christianity is not and cannot be within measurable time, "official." The World is trying the experiment of attempting to form a civilised but non–Christian mentality. The experiment will fail; but we must be very patient in awaiting its collapse; meanwhile redeeming the time: so that the Faith may be preserved alive through the dark ages before us; to renew and rebuild civilization and save the world from suicide.[80]

In this hope, both Sayers and Williams wrote their war poems, calling their readers to resist the temptation to refuse forgiveness to the enemy, to take vengeance or to consider themselves and their nation as guiltless and superior. Knowing, as Sayers declared, that "all men stand convicted of blood / in the High Court, the judge with the accused"[81] and that all, English and German together "stand in need of forgiveness,"[82] Williams' Pope cried out to God for the future, political and spiritual, of all the peoples of Europe in the words of the *Magnificat*: "Send not, send not, the rich empty away."[83]

Notes

1. Lord David Cecil, *The Oxford Book of Christian Verse* (London: Oxford University Press, 1940), xxxiii.
2. Dorothy L. Sayers, "The English War," *The Times Literary Supplement* 7th September 1940, 445.
3. See *The Letters of Dorothy L. Sayers vol. 3, 1944–1950: A Noble Daring*, Ed. Barbara Reynolds (Hurstpierpoint: The Dorothy L. Sayers Society, 1998), 121.
4. See Nick Hayes, "An English War," "Wartime Culture" and "Millions like Us'" in *"Millions like us?": British Culture in the Second World War*, Eds. Nick Hayes, Jeff Hill (Liverpool: Liverpool University Press, 1999), 2.
5. Hayes, "An English War," "Wartime Culture" and "Millions like Us'" in *"Millions like us?": British Culture in the Second World War*, Eds. Nick Hayes, Jeff Hill, 1.
6. Thomas Moult (ed.), *The Best Poems of 1941* (London: Jonathan Cape, 1942), 38–40.
7. Lord Wavell, *Other Men's Flowers* (London: Jonathan Cape, 1948).
8. Brian Gardner (ed.), *The Terrible Rain: The War Poets 1939–45* (London: Methuen, 1966), 45–47.

9. See Ralph E. Hone (ed.), *Poetry of Dorothy L. Sayers* (Hurstpierpoint: The Dorothy L. Sayers Society, 1996), 122.
10. *The Letters of Dorothy L. Sayers vol. 3*, 121, n. 2.
11. See *http://www.theanswerbank.co.uk/Media-and-TV/Question409843.html*, accessed 14th April 2010.
12. Hone (ed.), *Poetry of Dorothy L. Sayers*, 120.
13. "The English War," *Poetry of Dorothy L. Sayers*, 120, (1. 19).
14. Dorothy L. Sayers, "They Tried to be Good," *Unpopular Opinions* (London: Methuen, 1946), 98.
15. "They Tried to be Good," 99.
16. "They Tried to be Good," 99.
17. "Letter to Kathleen Penn" in *The Letters of Dorothy L. Sayers vol. 2: from Novelist to Playwright*, Ed. Barbara Reynolds (Hurstpierpoint: The Dorothy L. Sayers Society, 1997), 362.
18. Dorothy L. Sayers, "The Religions behind the Nation" in *The Christ of the Creeds and Other Broadcast Messages to the British People during World War II* (Hurstpierpoint: The Dorothy L. Sayers Society, 2008), 48.
19. "Letter to Kathleen Penn," 15th May 1942 in *The Letters of Dorothy L. Sayers vol. 2*, Ed. Barbara Reynolds, 362.
20. "The Religions behind the Nation," 48.
21. "They Tried to be Good," 103.
22. "They Tried to be Good," 104.
23. "The English War," *Poetry of Dorothy L. Sayers*, 120.
24. "Letter to Helmut Kuhn," 30th August 1943 in *The Letters of Dorothy L. Sayers vol. 3*, Ed. Barbara Reynolds, 423.
25. Sayers, "They Tried to be Good," *Unpopular Opinions*, 103.
26. "The English War," *Poetry of Dorothy L. Sayers*, 120–121.
27. John Mount, "Drake's Drum" (2000), *http://www.paranormality.com/drakes_drum.shtml*, accessed 14th April 2010.
28. J. Mount.
29. "The English War," 121.
30. Paul Volsik, "'But the Happy Future is a thing of the past': Cataclysms, Apocalypses and Impossible Milleniums? British War Poetry in the Early Twentieth Century" in *Études* Anglaises, T. 54, N° 1 (2001), *http://www.cairn.info/article_p.php?ID_ARTICLE=ETAN_541_68*, accessed 14th April 2010.
31. "The English War," 121.
32. Dorothy L. Sayers, "A Woman Looks at the World," Wade Center 17/77-84, quoted in Manfred Siebald, "Dorothy L. Sayers and Germany" in *Proceedings of the Dorothy L. Sayers Society Annual Convention 1996* (Hurstpierpoint: The Dorothy L. Sayers Society, 1997), 24.
33. Sayers, *Begin Here*, (London, Victor Gollancz, 1940),140.
34. "The English War," 121.
35. Letter to Helmut Kuhn, 30 August 1943, in *The Letters of Dorothy L. Sayers vol. 2*, Ed. Barbara Reynolds, 424.
36. Dorothy L. Sayers, "The Man of Men" in *The Christ of the Creeds and Other Broadcast Messages* 57.
37. Mark Connelly, "The British People, the Press and the Strategic Air Campaign against Germany, 1939–45" in *Contemporary British History* 16 (Summer 2002, 39–58), 47.

38. Connelly, "The British People, the Press and the Strategic Air Campaign against Germany, 1939–45" in *Contemporary British History* 16, 41.

39. Letter to Anthony Davies, 23 June 1944, in *The Letters of Dorothy L. Sayers vol. 3*, Ed. Barbara Reynolds, 24.

40. Cf. Connelly, "The British People, the Press and the Strategic Air Campaign against Germany, 1939–45" in *Contemporary British History* 16, 48.

41. Connelly, 51.

42. Connelly, 51.

43. Letter to the Editor of *The News Chronicle*, 27 June 1944, in *The Letters of Dorothy L. Sayers vol. 3*, Ed. Barbara Reynolds, 33–34.

44. Catherine Kenney, *The Remarkable Case of Dorothy L. Sayers* (Kent, Ohio: Kent State University Press, 1991), 289.

45. Dorothy L. Sayers, "Target Area," *Fortnightly*, vol. 155 (March 1944), 181-184.

46. Dorothy L. Sayers, "Target Area," *The Atlantic Monthly* (March 1944), 48–50.

47. See *http://www.raf.mod.uk/bombercommand/mar44.html* (consulted April 14th 2010).

48. See Elisabeth Bader, "Who is Fräulein Fehmer?—An Investigation" in *Proceedings of the Dorothy L. Sayers Society Annual Convention 2009*, (to be published by The Dorothy L. Sayers Society, Summer 2010), 37-51.

49. Dorothy L. Sayers, "Cat O'Mary" in *Child and Woman of her Time* (Hurstpierpoint: The Dorothy L. Sayers Society, 2002), 104.

50. Bader, 50.

51. All quotes in paragraph: "Target Area," Ralph E. Hone (ed), *Poetry of Dorothy L. Sayers*, 140, (1. 4).

52. Sayers, "Cat O'Mary" *in Child and Woman of her Time*, 104.

53. All remaining quotes in paragraph: "Target Area," Ralph E. Hone (ed), *Poetry of Dorothy L. Sayers*, 141.

54. Bader, 46.

55. All quotes in paragraph up to "solidarity in guilt": "Target Area," Ralph E. Hone (ed), *Poetry of Dorothy L. Sayers*, 144.

56. Dorothy L. Sayers, "The Gospel is a Thing of Terror" in *The Christ of the Creeds and Other Broadcast Messages to the British People during World War II* (Hurstpierpoint: The Dorothy L. Sayers Society, 2008), 80.

57. "Target Area," 142.

58. Unpublished letter to Helmut Kuhn, 23rd May 1944, quoted in Manfred Siebald, "Dorothy L. Sayers and Germany" (Hurstpierpoint: *Proceedings of the Dorothy L. Sayers Society Annual Convention 1996*, 1997), 24.

59. Dorothy L. Sayers, *The Just Vengeance* (London: Victor Gollancz, 1946), 17–18.

60. Charles Williams, *He Came Down from Heaven* and *The Forgiveness of Sins* (London: Faber & Faber, 1950), 194.

61. Williams, 172.

62. Williams, 173.

63. Charles Williams, "Percivale at Carbonek" in *Charles Williams,* Ed. David Llewellyn Dodds (Cambridge, The Boydell Press, 1991), 84–85.

64. Williams, "Percivale at Carbonek," 84.

65. Ken Sears, "Unpopular Opinions" in *Proceedings of The Dorothy L. Sayers Society 31st Annual Convention*, University of York, 4–7 August 2007 (Hurstpierpoint : The Dorothy L. Sayers Society, 2008), 25.

66. Williams, "Percivale at Carbonek," 85.

67. Williams is quoting here from the General Thanksgiving in the *Book of Common Prayer*: "We bless thee for our creation, preservation, and all the blessings of this life; but above all for thine inestimable love in the redemption of the world by our Lord Jesus Christ; for the means of grace, and for the hope of glory."

68. Charles Williams, "Church & State" (1938) in *The Image of the City & Other Essays* (London: Oxford University Press, 1958), 116.

69. Charles Williams, "The Founding of the Company" in *The Region of the Summer Stars* (London: Oxford University Press, 1944), 36–41.

70. Charles Williams, "The Order of the Coinherence" in *Essential Writings in Spirituality and Theology* (Boston: Cowley Publications, 1993), 148.

71. Charles Williams, "The Redeemed City" in *Essential Writings in Spirituality and Theology* 156.

72. Alice Mary Hadfield, *Charles Williams: An Exploration of his Life & Work* (London: Oxford University Press, 1983), 219.

73. C.S. Lewis, *Arthurian Torso* (London, Oxford University Press, 1948), 180.

74. Lewis, 180.

75. Williams, "The Prayers of the Pope" in *The Region of the Summer Stars*, 53.

76. "The Prayers of the Pope," 53.

77. "The Prayers of the Pope," 53.

78. Lewis, *Arthurian Torso*, 183.

79. All quotes in paragraph up to "thine unknown elect": Williams, "The Prayers of the Pope," 52.

80. T.S. Eliot, "Thoughts after Lambeth" in *Selected Essays* (London, Faber & Faber, 1932), 387.

81. "Target Area," 144.

82. "Target Area," 144.

83. "The Prayers of the Pope," 61.

Works Cited

Bader, Elisabeth (2010), "Who is Fräulein Fehmer?—An Investigation," in *Proceedings of the Dorothy L. Sayers Society Annual Convention 2009*. Hurstpierpoint: The Dorothy L. Sayers Society, 37–51.

Cecil, Lord David (ed.) (1940), *The Oxford Book of Christian Verse*. London: Oxford University Press.

Connelly, Mark (Summer 2002), "The British People, the Press and the Strategic Air Campaign Against Germany, 1939–45," in *Contemporary British History*, 16, 39–58.

Dodds, David Llewellyn (ed.) (1991), *Charles Williams*, Cambridge, The Boydell Press.

Eliot, T.S. (1932), "Thoughts After Lambeth," in *Selected Essays*. London, Faber & Faber, 363–387.

Gardner Brian (ed.) (1966), *The Terrible Rain: The War Poets 1939–45*. London: Methuen.

Hadfield, Alice Mary (1983), *Charles Williams: An Exploration of his Life and Work*. London: Oxford University Press.

Hayes, Nick and Hill, Jeff (eds.) (1999), *"Millions Like Us?": British Culture in the Second World War*, Liverpool: Liverpool University Press.

Hone, Ralph E. (ed.) (1996), *Poetry of Dorothy L. Sayers*. Hurstpierpoint: The Dorothy L. Sayers Society.
Kenney, Catherine (1991), *The Remarkable Case of Dorothy L. Sayers*. Kent, Ohio: Kent State University Press.
Lewis, C.S. (1948), *Arthurian Torso*. London, Oxford University Press.
Moult, Thomas (ed.) (1942), *The Best Poems of 1941*. London: Jonathan Cape.
Mount, John (2000), "Drake's Drum."
http://www.paranormality.com/drakes_drum.shtml, accessed 14th April 2010.
Reynolds, Barbara (ed.) (1997), *The Letters of Dorothy L. Sayers vol. 2: From Novelist to Playwright*. Hurstpierpoint: The Dorothy L. Sayers Society.
Reynolds, Barbara (ed.) (1998), *The Letters of Dorothy L. Sayers vol. 3, 1944–1950: A Noble Daring*. Hurstpierpoint: The Dorothy L. Sayers Society.
Sears, Ken (2008), "Unpopular Opinions," in *Proceedings of The Dorothy L. Sayers Society 31st Annual Convention*. Hurstpierpoint: The Dorothy L. Sayers Society, 18–29.
Siebald, Manfred (1996), "Dorothy L. Sayers and Germany," in *Proceedings of the Dorothy L. Sayers Society Annual Convention 1996*. Hurstpierpoint: The Dorothy L. Sayers Society, 17–28.
Sayers, Dorothy L. (2002), "Cat O'Mary," in *Child and Woman of her Time*. Hurstpierpoint: The Dorothy L. Sayers Society.
Sayers, Dorothy L. (2008), *The Christ of the Creeds and Other Broadcast Messages to the British People During World War II*. Hurstpierpoint: The Dorothy L. Sayers Society.
Sayers, Dorothy L.(1940), "The English War," *The Times Literary Supplement* (7th September 1940), 445.
Sayers, Dorothy L. (1946), *The Just Vengeance*. London: Victor Gollancz.
_____. (1946), *Unpopular Opinions*. London: Methuen.
Volsik, Paul, "'But the Happy Future is a thing of the past': Cataclysms, Apocalypses and Impossible Milleniums? British War Poetry in the Early Twentieth Century," in *Études Anglaises*.
http://www.cairn.info/article_p.php?ID_ARTICLE=ETAN_541_68, accessed 14th April 2010.
Wavell, Lord (1948), *Other Men's Flowers*. London: Jonathan Cape.
Williams, Charles (1993), *Essential Writings in Spirituality and Theology*. Boston: Cowley Publications.
_____. (1950), *He Came Down from Heaven* and *The Forgiveness of Sins*. London: Faber & Faber.
_____. (1958), *The Image of the City & Other Essays*. London: Oxford University Press.
_____. (1944), *The Region of the Summer Stars*. London: Oxford University Press.

7. Resilience and Regeneration
Four Quartets *in French Translation*
Jessica Stephens

T.S. Eliot began writing "Burnt Norton" in 1935, in the years leading up to World War II, a time that he considered to be a time of spiritual and intellectual decline. He finished his work on "East Coker," "The Dry Salvages" and "Little Gidding" by early 1942. War however is barely touched upon in *Four Quartets*, apart from a few references to an enemy plane dropping bombs on London and the persona's presence in the streets, in the early hours of dawn after an air raid,[1] a scene that can be explained by Eliot's work as an air-raid warden during the war. Something remains unsaid, at the heart of this beautiful composition where various strands of thoughts are woven and gathered like so many musical variations. The poem is organized around the ineffable — the spiritual havoc and emotional stunting wrought by the war. In other words the poet focuses on the consequences of the war on an individual and on society as a whole, but not on the event, the thing itself. Just as in "Little Gidding," the persona, standing in the street after an air raid, observes the dust that lingers in the air and describes the destruction entailed only indirectly.[2] *Four Quartets* does offer solace — this long, intricate poem can be read as a reflection on resilience leading to renewal ... something that the French translators of *Four Quartets*, Pierre Leyris and Claude Vigée, responded to by producing — or generating — two very personal translations..

The "poet as witness"[3] focuses on details, small things that testify to "Meaning," meaning that can only be approached[4] according to French philosopher Philippe Lacoue-Labarthe. And indeed, in *Four Quartets*, the poet does not conjure up, imagine or represent war but attempts to provide an indirect and powerful response to it. George Bataille's own oblique response to the war between Germany and France in *Le coupable* is also very interesting in this respect: "The date when I begin to write (September 5, 1939) is not a coincidence. I begin because of the events, but not to speak about them."[5]

Four Quartets is the end result of Eliot's perception of and response to spiritual and social turmoil. Certainly the Anglo-American poet tries to come up with what Seamus Heaney calls "a 'vision of reality' [...] adequate to [the] time[...],"[6] but his approach is often hesitant, meek even. To respond, to better encompass, to encircle, yes, but not to conjure up and say expressly. What can words say or do at a time when silence prevails? When one is asked not to speak or give information in public lest one be overheard by the enemy? A few years later, survivors were unwilling or unable to relate their experience in the camps, and thus kept silent about the horror. The drying up[7] of the sense of touch, of the material world and of meaning to which language gives access — goes hand in hand with spiritual entropy. In "The Social Function of Poetry," T.S. Eliot notes that daily life and language are intertwined, they interact — decay in one brings about decay in the other:

> For our language goes on changing; our way of life changes, under the pressure of material changes in our environment in all sorts of ways; and unless we have those few men who combine an exceptional sensibility with an exceptional power over words, our own ability, not merely to express, but even to feel any but the crudest emotions, will degenerate.[8]

Language and words also bear the brunt of war and fall apart. And one of the entries by the Romanian-French dramatist Ionesco in his *Journal en miettes* gives us an idea of the challenges that a writer faces, especially in difficult times:

> It is as if, through becoming involved in literature, I had used up all possible symbols, without really penetrating their meaning. They no longer have any vital significance for me....[9]

In *Four Quartets,* the poet's toil with words is mentioned several times. Eliot's endeavor consists in piecing together words, lines, sentences and reviving language, very deliberately, very carefully.[10]

Throughout the poem, a voice speaks, an impersonal voice which is subdued and sometimes falters as it develops a line of thought, grapples with and tries to make sense of such binary notions as time and eternity, experience and awareness, love and desire, incarnation and redemption. To endeavor and try are key notions in *Four Quartets* since the Poet, according to Eliot, can only try to counteract the spiritual decline which he perceives around him and the deepening fault in language. One way of doing this is by giving another impetus to language but without any guarantee of success.[11] Another way of "cushion[ing] the blast,"[12] an expression that Heaney applies to Eliot's enterprise, is to root the long monologue, interspersed with a few ghostly voices, in a literary tradition by using, for instance, the sestina or Saint John of the Cross's near biblical incantatory rhythm. The poet is a link in a chain as, through his craft, he restores and upholds an aesthetic continuity.

How to make sense of decline and havoc? The set of binary notions and elements which are recurrent in the text, but also the strange presence and absence of war all point to the figure of the oxymoron. And this very yoking together of antithetical terms is, according to French neuroscientist, Boris Cyrulnik, at the heart of the concept of resilience. In his book, *Un merveilleux malheur*, he begins by summing up the widely received definition of resilience[13] and then goes on to explain resilience in terms of an oxymoron:

> [...] the oxymoron sets off the contrast in the person who, having been dealt a big blow, adapts to this blow through a process of cleavage — the part which has received the blow suffers and necroses whilst another part, better protected, still sound but more secret, gathers together [...] everything that can still provide a little happiness and meaning in life.[14]

Boris Cyrulnik's preliminary definition tallies with the etymological definition of resilience meaning "to leap back," "to recoil." The neuroscientist then goes on to explain that the oxymoron "points to [...] the break of the link that will have to be restored."[15] Resilience is an impulse, a drive that allows us to assign a restorative meaning to experience as we turn damage into something else by structuring it, by weaving[16] it constantly into the fabric of our lives and into language. Negative experience is constantly reinterpreted, internalized and let go of through the combination of language, action and the presence of another.

In the opening lines of "Burnt Norton" a voice speaks, the voice of a man in the early hours of the morning, in the uneasy dawn. The persona, who can only be sensed as a shape throughout the poem, appears only in the very last poem, "Little Gidding," when he comes face to face with a ghost-like *doppelganger*, and it is this shade, in fact, who turns him into a physical presence. Dawn is a hiatus, a short period conducive to thought, propitious for transformation and the weaving of experience. During this in-between time, meaning is redeemed through the intersection of past experience and present reappraisal, an intersection on which the future is built. Georges Didi-Huberman compares these interstitial times to fireflies whose bodies light up the enveloping darkness.[17] And these moments, which bring light and hope, occur when past experience is re-appropriated either by an individual or by a society.

What Giorgio Agamben has to say about modern man whose experience is in a way inoperative since he feels dispossessed and unable to share it with others also applies here to the persona when the poem opens.[18] Yet the persona does manage to re-appropriate his own experience, first by grounding himself in the innocence and beauty of a closed garden.[19] In this most beautiful and potent scene, the poet describes an ordered and delicately refined place which, like Yeats' Great Houses, testifies to civilization. The memory of the garden is perhaps imagined; this does not make its value less powerful or true for the image is an archetype of innocence. We can all relate to it. What might have been — the past imagined — and what was — actual past experience — are placed on the same level. And the experience is all the more powerful as it is unexpected; the moment, the memory is given like a revelation, a blessing. Innocence and the simplicity of raw desire — in the very broad meaning of the word — are modes of resistance to decline. As Georges Didi-Huberman reminds us in his essay on resistance, based on the Italian director Paolo Pasolini's letter, published in *The Corriere della Sera* on February 1, 1975:

> Pasolini's letter ends and peaks in the violent contrast between the *exception* of innocent joy, which welcomes or radiates the light of desire, and the *rule* of a reality made of guilt.[20]

There are a few other extremely moving in-between moments when the beauty of the natural world is so sharp and vivid that it stands out and is uplifting: the bushes covered in snow[21] but also fleeting evocations of brooks and berries.[22] Desire is not extolled in this particular work, which is quite abstract and intellectual, yet the deeply restorative and assuaging action of touch is suggested in the first poem.[23] Indeed the motion of the flower that may reach towards the passer-by is reminiscent of Coleridge's "To Nature" and conveys the deep joy that contact with another — be it the natural world or a human being — brings. Again the poet endeavors to counteract spiritual decline and give another impetus to spirituality by exploring what Georges Didi-Huberman calls the life-affirming *"resource of desire* and of experience, at the very heart of our most immediate decisions and of our daily lives."[24]

It would be a mistake however to think that these charmed moments during which the poet engages in the world are unmediated. The first image of the garden illustrates this well: at the end of the garden's alley, at the end of his itinerary, the man has a revelation: mesmerized, he sees a lotus ascend from the water.[25] What is striking in these lines, apart from the beauty of the scene, is the fact that the persona is both engrossed in his experience, his vision, but also at one remove from it. He remains lucid and conscious of what is happening throughout: for indeed, though very simple and very simply conveyed through light touches, the experience is structured: it has a beginning, a middle and an end; the process is described, seemingly as it happens. This is what, for Eliot, consciousness consists in: the ability to experience and at the same time step back and be aware of the moment.[26] Then and only then, does time seem to stop and intersect with timelessness. Like a feeling of déjà-vu, the memory stands out of time. Awareness consists in a lucid perception or monitoring of the world by a man who is deeply engaged in it. Awareness as it is conceived by Eliot is closely associated with one of the etymological meanings of resistance: to cause to stand back.

The moments of intense happiness which are alluded to throughout the poem, at regular intervals, like the bell which rings now and then, are deeply connected to light, illumination and resistance in several ways. First because they underpin individual emotions like joy, untrammeled exhilaration and a sense of carefree wholeness, that elude the constraints of society and upset the very notions of time past and time future; and these notions of time and space seem to vanish altogether — the persona is released from his own sense of mortality and the constraints of time. Such privileged moments are also associated with light and resistance because they serve as stepping stones, strengthening man's sense of self, energizing him so that he stands *straight again*—a variation on the etymological meaning of resistance.

Re-appropriation of experience occurs during such intense moments but it can also occur retrospectively through the use of memory. Indeed, through memory — another form of retrospective awareness — man can hope to experience again and revive these moments of joy which he wasn't quite able to fathom.[27] Thus memory is what releases man from the servitudes of the past and of the future, since it allows him to move freely back and forth along the timescale of experience and access experience that is stored more or less deeply in the mind and in the heart.[28] Ordinary and past events can be revisited by consciousness, so that they become meaningful in the present and for the future. By allowing past and present to intersect freely, memory assigns added meaning to the past, fuels life and counteracts — resists — entropy. Here again George Didi-Huberman's concept of resources that are stored in desire, ready to be deployed can also apply to this interaction — a new living impetus is given, a light is kindled when past and present intersect meaningfully. Human and social time can thus be redeemed by memory, that is both dynamic and creative.

Ultimately however, present or retrospective awareness of an event is not enough to bring real meaning and freedom. This first level of awareness is not valid enough.

Regeneration through desire and sexuality is not so present in the poetic text. "East Coker" opens[29] with the Bruegel-like picture of country people meeting and coming together, as was the custom, by leaping through the flames of a summer bonfire, and with the portrayal of the various stages of life in an ordered sequence — love, procreation, work, life, death. "To every *thing, there is* a season"[30]–various agricultural tasks punctuating moments of the calendar. The inexorable passing of time and of generations is what the poet focuses on in these opening lines taken from an account by Thomas Elyot.[31] Time is experienced in a linear fashion from birth to death and the middle-aged poet who stands in a *selva oscura* is a link in the chain; he accepts his place in the scheme of things and the successive (re–) generation(s) of man whose life is prolonged through his children and thus leaves a trace behind him Thus the poet participates in the current of life and in the brotherhood of man.

The persona also awaits and embraces a spiritual form of regeneration, which can come in two ways: through illumination — for example, the experience in the garden — or, through the *via negativa* advocated by the mystic Saint John of the Cross, whose presence can be felt in "East Coker" namely through the incantatory rhythm of lines 136 to 146.[32] The poet also quotes Heraclitus' maxim according to which the way up and the way down are one and the same.[33] Indeed, illumination and the *via negativa* are two sides of the same coin but the *via negativa* is more intrinsically connected with the figure of the oxymoron and the process of change. For instance, in "Burnt Norton," the *via negativa* is exemplified in the description of the haggard men sitting in the tube, shuttling back and forth in London, the city of the seven hills ... but unlike Rome, the Eternal City, London is depleted of its spiritual energy; later in "East Coker," the poet focuses again on people traveling on the underground, perhaps during war time; the train is at a halt; the passengers gradually fall silent and are overwhelmed by the fear of the void within. However, out of no-thing, some-thing comes. Only through acceptance of the night and by letting-go, can the process of spiritual transformation and refinement occur and elevation begin.[34] Not surprisingly, in the following lines, the poet evokes potent images of the natural world associated with innocence. At the end of what is a night for the soul, the perception of life and time is altered and the secret of life, the mystery of the *agon* of life and death, at the heart of our mortal lives is not so much uncovered as made present and accepted.

In this light, the very notion of active resistance becomes meaningless. What the poet advocates, in "East Coker" and throughout the poem, is acceptance. Acceptance of flux, joy, pain and the trials of existence, exacerbated during wartime; but the poet comes up against a fundamental contradiction: since the pattern of our lives is ever-changing, ascribing meaning to experience makes no sense. The construct which consists in weaving pain into the fabric of one's life, into language and with the help of another is not valid ... enough. As stated above, for Eliot, as for the Christian, regeneration can only come through the acceptance of a mystery — the mystery of the Incarnation. The compassion integral to the physician — Christ — solves the puzzling riddle concerning the patient's illness[35]–the pain, suffering and spiritual *accidie*. A mystery, something that exists but resists interpretation and cannot therefore be explained away or revealed. A living secret.

The crucial importance of Incarnation is further developed in "The Dry Salvages" and "Little Gidding." Spiritual regeneration which is brought about by the converting of one's nature to another mode of being comes through participation in the Incarnation, at the intersection of timelessness and time — God who embodies timelessness chooses incarnation; His Son leads an earthly life in time.[36] Through spiritual acknowledgment of the Example of Christ, the Old man can be cast out. Through his Incarnation and Passion, Christ takes on the burden of all men, freely offers himself up to death on the cross, and rises again; his Resurrection offers the possibility of redemption. Man is given an alternative — the possibility of redemption through divine Intercession, the Intercession of another. By aligning himself with the Divine, man constantly has the possibility of converting[37] the passions of life — flux. He is given the possibility of refining his being, coming into his own and joining the brotherhood of man.

Resistance in the usual meaning of the word becomes irrelevant and shades into self-surrender, a state in which submission is deliberately embraced and accepted, in which submission and necessity strangely fuse. For Eliot, only through acceptance of the divine Other, through the leap of faith, can the fabric of life be truly woven. This is the frame of mind which ultimately brings about resistance, the ability to stand up straight, to be upright, to act in the right way. To align oneself with Christ as the Example, to follow Kant's categorical imperative — whose ultimate embodiment is Christ — frees one from the constraints of time. We act in the right way because we have to, which, in turn, frees us.[38] Time is no longer perceived in a linear fashion but in terms of transcendence — a hiatus during which man is engaged in the spiritual moment, where present, past and future fuse.

The voice that speaks throughout the poem is impersonal and detached; however, there are variations in the tone. Initially hesitant, it is puzzled as if the persona were lost in a forest of signs — many adverbs, conjunctions, modal verbs convey hypothesis, conjecture, as do certain expressions or marked hesitations.[39] Gradually however, the persona more grows self-assured and assertive as the man with a hollow voice turns into a new man. Another striking feature is that the voice assumes different cadences and carries other writers' voices: Yeats and the recurrent image of the dance,[40] Mallarmé and his set of binary oppositions[41] or again the reference to Saint John of the Cross,[42] Dame

Julian of Norwich,[43] the Dantean encounter with the ghost-like shade of the master....[44]

The collage of voices, the impersonality of the persona's tone during what amounts to a tribulation, together with the relative opaqueness of the text, which was a huge success when it came out, are puzzling. T.S. Eliot's writing is abstract, a quality that allows him to reach universality, but another explanation for this very impersonal voice, which is his stylistic signature, is that it is also at one remove. In other words, the detachment that is integral to awareness is also palpable in the poet's voice.

Four Quartets has as much to do with spiritual entropy and wartime as with language and the poet's place in society. In the poem, the persona, a mask for Eliot — the poet, reflects on the task that awaits the writer who grapples, sometimes despairingly, with what Mallarmé calls the fault or deficiency in language.[45] After Babel, language becomes opaque, flawed, intractable, it resists. How does a writer express reality and structure it through language? Yet the apt question as regards Eliot's work is the following: how can language and reality intersect since meaning fluctuates constantly and since our perception of the world and our knowledge of the world are ever-changing?

What applies to Eliot's perception of life, also applies to language in *Four Quartets*— a writer must bow down to language. Instead of trying to push back the linguistic boundaries of a language or finding a new form, like Mallarmé or Rimbaud, the poet acknowledges the constraints and inherent failings of language. Obedience to language entails a soothing lifting of the burden. Here too, he accepts to travel along the *via negativa*. Perhaps this is another explanation for the impersonality of the voice — very simple images, exact words, pared-down, simple sentence structures. Eliot's language is abstract because it describes everyday reality but does not enter into play with it. At a grammatical level, his recurrent use of the structure "there is," "this is" thematizes existence and sets it up without any flourish. However, language in *Four Quartets* also enacts a spiritual experience : language thrives — and the exact words flow meaningfully — when it is fully redeemed through the poet's alignment with the Divine....[46] In fact Eliot's poetry springs from language which is transcended as it strives for redemption. Again, resistance in the usual meaning of the word is meaningless, obedience is all. The shifts in the impersonal voice constitute what Umberto Eco calls the extra-linguistic dimension of language[47] — in *Four Quartets* language is a prayer, which rises.

Modern man, according to Agamben, is dispossessed, but language allows him to internalize his experience. Georges Didi-Hubberman argues that experience can be a light for others provided that the narrator finds an adequate form that can convey the story of the experience and contribute to its being handed down.[48] The telling of a story and the structuring of one's experience through words contribute to survival, for instance in the novel *La Peste* by Camus[49] or in Jorge Semprun's autobiographical account of his suffering in a camp.[50] An individual story, but also history, can only survive and resist the test of time when they are put down on paper. George Steiner points out in *After Babel*: "What material reality has history outside language, outside our interpretative belief in essentially linguistic records (silence knows no history)?"[51] *Four Quartets* and the French translations of Eliot's poem ensure the resistance and the survival of his testimony, like a light to which others can have immediate or retrospective access.

The two French translators of Eliot's *Four Quartets* are Pierre Leyris[52] and the poet Claude Vigée.[53] What is striking about the translations themselves is that both translators picked up on the work very quickly. Indeed Claude Vigée started working on the translation when he arrived in the United States after leaving France where he had participated in the Resistance, and he finished it in the spring of 1944. Like other artists of the time, who used their own aesthetic modes of resistance as they resisted the spread of Nazism — Ernst Lubitsch for instance in his humorous denunciation of the Nazi regime in *To Be or Not to Be* released in 1942 —, T.S. Eliot in his writing of *Four Quartets* and Claude Vigée in his translation of the poem can be considered as providing cultural responses to the then ongoing conflict in Europe. Pierre Leyris's translation was published later, in 1950, but presumably he had been working on it for some time. In an interview given to Anne Mounic at the Sorbonne in 2006, Claude Vigée, a poet in his own right, explained why his translation only came out in 1992[54]: indeed Pierre Leyris was Eliot's official translator and the publisher *Le Seuil* was granted all the rights to the work and its translation.

Both translations participate in the resistance and the dissemination of the source text since they ensure its survival in another language, French, by making it accessible to a wide French readership but clearly the source text is resistant *per se* — it is opaque, sometimes abstruse and the language used fairly abstract. Moreover, on several occasions in the poem, Eliot mentions the difficulty of working with his material — words that prove intractable or deficient. Both translators therefore faced the task of grappling with a source text that is cryptic and which undermines its own validity by sometimes openly questioning the writer's ability with language. Added to that, Claude Vigée's poetic sensibility is somewhat different from that of Eliot's abstract musings and voice. Conversely, the intractable nature of Eliot's text, which resists interpretation and translation, is a sure sign of its greatness. The translators' work is thus all the more challenging and intense; the end product all the more likely to be as powerful as the original. Yet do these two translations match the original and provide a target text that is a powerful equivalent bearing the stamp of the original and possessing the same vigor, the same resistant spark?

Eliot's *Four Quartets* can be considered as an enigma — it is enigmatic and requires an effort on the part of the reader who must enter into a close relationship with the text in order to make sense of it but the poem also bears on the Christian Mystery, Christ's sacrifice. *Four Quartets* rests on a living yet accessible secret. The spirit moves perhaps a little more in Leyris's translation than Vigée's because the two translators have opted for two different approaches. Pierre Leyris circles the poem, comes close to and preserves its core-secret whereas Claude Vigée's translation is rooted in the offshoots of the translator's activity — the *exegesis*, the commentary ... the unfolding of meaning.

Leyris crafts his translation in such a way as to maintain the lexis and syntax of the original. In Eliot's work the same words are often repeated twice at a close interval and Leyris proves very faithful to the source text in this respect since he does exactly the same thing in his French translation. On the other, Vigée chooses not to. Vigée practically always uses a variation, a synonym going against the grain of the original text. Then the syntactical precision apparent in Leyris's translation and the painstaking choice of words enable him to retain the polysemy and rich ambiguity of the original. Indeed it is this very precision which allows him to dig deep into the potency of the original text and keep his own text open and alive, like the original. More often than not, Leyris will translate the English words by their exact French etymological equivalent: "raid"[55] which he translates by "raid"[56] whereas Vigée opts for "incursion,"[57] "desiccation"[58] translated by "dessication"[59] (Leyris) and by "dessèchement,"[60] meaning "drying up" (Vigée), or again "calamitous annunciation"[61] which carries over into Leyris's translation as "calamiteuse annonciation"[62] and has an old-fashioned, biblical ring to it, largely due to the place of the adjective before the noun. Vigée transposes the adjective "calamitous" into a noun "désastre" ("disaster') and sticks to a more modern translation of the noun "annunciation": "l'annonce du désastre."[63] Leyris also opts for French words which echo and sometimes intensify the meaning of the original: for instance he translates the word "way"[64] by "voie"[65] which is a particularly interesting choice since it echoes the Latin *via negativa*, a concept underlying the text. Claude Vigée opts for a more target-orientated word "chemin"[66] which has other connotations, referring to a geographical or spiritual journey. Leyris also translates a transparent word "bone"[67] not by its straightforward French equivalent "os" but by "ossement"[68] which is arresting since it gives more depth to the line and is very much in keeping with the biblical tones of the following lines, in which Eliot translates verses from the *Ecclesiastes*. Leyris's words are exact, aligned with the original; his translation stands straight.

Not only does Leyris pay careful attention to words but he also uses recurrent morphemes that are relevant to the meaning of the text — for instance the prefix *in*[69] which he keeps in the French adjectives and nouns instead of modulating the sentences. This stylistic sleight of hand sometimes forces him to rely on antiquated words. Sometimes an artful strategy allows him to keep a collocation which, technically, should be considered as non-idiomatic in French. In "East Coker" for instance the path is personified since it "insists" on a "direction"[70] whereas in French such a metaphorical use of the verb "insist" with an inanimate subject is not possible. Leyris however manages to use the same verb in French — he waters down the personification by using an infinitive, not a tense.[71]

On a syntactical level, Leyris is very faithful to the original structure even if this means pushing back the boundaries of the French language: in "The Dry Salvages," he lifts the preposition "into"[72] and inserts the exact French prepositional equivalent in a structure that is unusual, awkward even, but which works.[73] Vigée clarifies the meaning and opts for an extended translation and a run-on line: "Leur visage se détend, à la peine fait place le / soulagement"[74] and his translation bears phonetic traces of the original — the assonance in the English text[75] is echoed in "détend" and "soulagement."

Leyris also finds solutions which allow him to reproduce the typological and rhythmical changes on the page. At times, instead of using canonical sentences like Vigée, he resorts to nominal phrases and a series of B of A clauses so that the French translation is as pared-down as the English text. French being a syllabic language as opposed to English which has a stress-timed rhythm, Leyris cannot hope to reproduce the very same English rhythmic pattern, but he subtly indicates the changes in the cadence and in the layout.[76] At times he is able to mirror the syntactically-based stylistic effect of the original. In the fourth section of "The Dry Salvages" for instance in which the bell can be heard,[77] the saxon genitive is clearly in an unusual position, at the very end of the line, so that there is a pause, a silence even, before the enjambment and the reference to the continuous ringing. By a twist of language, by positioning the French genitive at the very beginning of the line, Leyris creates the same powerful aesthetic effect.[78] The enjambment also appears in Claude Vigée's translation and therefore also the sense of surprised expectancy: "La cloche marine qui sonne / Son angélus perpétuel."[79] The placing of the verb "sonne" at the end of the line seems to open the line, and the pause present in the English can also be heard in Vigée's translation. Not only does Vigée keep the enjambment but he also succeeds in highlighting, beautifully, the complicated relationship between the two nouns: does the angelus belong to the sea? Does the rhythmic melodious sound stem from the surf? Are the angelus and the water one and the same thing?

Sometimes Leyris amends the text and adapts it in order to strike the right balance between the constraints of the French language and the style of the English poem. In the lines taken from the fifth section of "East Coker" however, the play on the adverb and adjective "still,"[80] cannot carry over into the French; Leyris translates the meaning but not the rich ambiguity of the line.[81] However the dynamic repetition of the personal pronoun "nous" ("us") is like a trace which very succinctly signals the presence of a repetition in the source text, as if the translation were able to store and keep alive a flicker of the meaning present in the original. Vigée translates the repetition, but also manages to capture the tension between stillness and movement through his choice of words.[82]

Leyris welcomes the poem into the French language in which he is clearly extremely at ease as his wide-ranging vocabulary,[83] inventive, canny choice of words[84] all suggest. Some of the words are so old-fashioned, precise and technical that his own text becomes resistant to the reader's probing. And at times, when he over-translates a term, his interpretation is so exact that he gets at the core meaning of the source text: for instance the slight modulation of the adjective "wrong"[85] which he does not understand in the moral sense of the word. He chooses "fourvoyée,"[86] meaning "mistaken," which sheds a light on Eliot's use of the word "hope"[87]: hope would be misleading. The two components of translation — that is text analysis and praxis come together effortlessly.

Finally, *Four Quartets* resists interpretation and translation since the two French translators sometimes differ in the interpretation not so much of the overall themes but of some of the lines; the translation of the word "time,"[88] and more surprisingly of words referring, very factually, to fauna or flora.

Both translators generate their own text; in different ways, they are involved in language. Because of his canny knack for language, his experience and craftsmanship, Leyris is able to grapple with the core meaning of words and the structure of *Four Quartets*, and therefore revive the power of the original text in French. Like the English poet[89] he enriches language and his translation illustrates Benjamin's theory of a "pure" language.[90] Because it is intricately rooted in *Four Quartets*, because it mirrors and complements the original text, Leyris's translation comes across as an offshoot of the original and seems to flow from it. It is as if this deep interconnectedness turned

Leyris's work into another facet of the same work. For one who is able to understand both languages, the original work and the translation seem to come from the same source as if the French translation were not really written in another tongue but the two works participated in one another at a deep level, at a level situated beyond language — a level to which language only pointed. In other words, to a certain extent, Leyris's translation abolishes such notions as differentiation and foreignness, the plurality of language and Babel. Almost, but not quite. Just like the hiatus between man and God which can, at times, be bridged, just like the complex oscillations between the meaning present in the original work and what the reader reads into it, there is a hiatus between the original work and how it carries over into the translation ... Leyris's translation mirrors Eliot's work. The same yearning, impetus, desire flow through their writings — the source text and its "parent-text," the translation.

To a certain extent, Claude Vigée appropriates the source text and draws it into the structures of his poetic tongue. His translation testifies to his spirit of resistance — the fact he picked up on the text so early suggests his desire to disseminate an experience which touched him — even though the publication and circulation of his work was thwarted for a long time; but his translation can also be considered as a very personal self-creative[91] act, helping him find his own poetic way.

For Eliot and his writer-translators, resistance is active hope.[92]

Notes

1. T.S. Eliot, *Four Quartets* (London: Faber and Faber, 1959), "Little Gidding," 43 (78 and following).
2. "Little Gidding," 42 (56–59).
3. Seamus Heaney, *The Government of the Tongue* (London: Faber and Faber, 1988), xvi.
4. Philippe Lacoue-Labarthe, *Lacan avec les philosophes* (Paris: Albin Michel, 1991), 34. See also "The Dry Salvages," 34 (94).
5. Georges Bataille, *Le coupable* (Paris: Gallimard, 1944, 1961), 23. Translation mine.
6. Heaney, 64.
7. Cf "Burnt Norton," 16 (119–121).
8. T.S. Eliot, *On Poets and Poetry* (London: Faber and Faber, 1957), 21.
9. Quoted in George Steiner, *After Babel* (Oxford: Oxford University Press, 1975), 194. Eugène Ionesco, *Journal en miettes* (Paris: Folio, 1967), 89.
10. "Little Gidding," 44 (126–127). See Mallarmé's poem "Le Tombeau d'Edgar Poe."
11. "East Coker," 26–27 (188–189).
12. Heaney, 43.
13. Boris Cyrulnik, *Un merveilleux malheur* (Paris: Odile Jacob, 1999), 8.

14. Cyrulnik, 19. Translation mine
15. Cyrulnik, 20. Translation mine.
16. Cyrulnik, 38–39.
17. Didi-Huberman,19, 36.
18. Didi-Huberman, 62.
19. Cf "Burnt Norton," 13–14 (20–46).
20. Didi-Huberman, 17. Translation mine.
21. Cf "Little Gidding," 41 (13–16)
22. Cf "East Coker," 25 (127–132).
23. Cf "Burnt Norton," 17 (129–134).
24. Didi-Huberman,110. Translation mine.
25. Cf "Burnt Norton," 14 (35–39)
26. "Burnt Norton," 15 (85–90).
27. "The Dry Salvages," 34.
28. "Little Gidding," 45.
29. "East Coker," 21–22 (1–46)
30. *Ecclesiastes, Holy Bible, King James version* (Nashville : Thomas Nelson Publishers, 1972), III 1–3.
31. *The Boke named the Gouernour*, 153.
32. See the use of anaphora, inverted parallel structures, repetitions.
33. "The Dry Salvages," 35 (128–132).
34. Cf "East Coker," 24 (119–121, 124–127).
35. Cf "East Coker," 25 (150–151).
36. "The Dry Salvages," 37 (215–216).
37. "East Coker," 27 (194).
38. "The Dry Salvages," 38 (224–225).
39. "Burnt Norton," 13 (8), "Burnt Norton," 13 (16/18). See Helen Gardner.
40. "Burnt Norton," 15 (62–64).
41. "Burnt Norton," 14 (47). See Helen Gardner, *The Art of T.S. Eliot* (London: Faber and Faber, 1968) 160.
42. "East Coker," 25 (136–146).
43. See "Little Gidding," 46.
44. "Little Gidding," 43 (86 ff).
45. Translation mine. "Le défaut des langues." Stéphane Mallarmé. *Crise de vers*.
46. "Little Gidding," 47 (216–217).
47. Umberto Eco, *Dire presque la même chose* (Paris: Grasset, 2007), 343.
48. Didi-Huberman,117.
49. Albert Camus, *La peste* (Paris : Gallimard, 1947).
50. Jorge Semprun, *L'écriture ou la vie* (Paris: Gallimard, 1994).
51. Steiner, *After Babel*, 30.
52. T.S. Eliot, *La terre vaine et autres poèmes,* Transl.: Pierre Leyris (Paris: Editions du Seuil, 1976).
53. T.S. Eliot, *Quatre quators*, Transl. Claude Vigée (London:The Menard Press, 1992).
54. Claude Vigée revised his translation in 1990–91.Claude Vigée, "Comment traduire les Quatre Quatuors de T.S. Eliot?" in *Palimpsestes 20 : De la traduction comme commentaire au commentaire de traduction*, Ed. Maryvonne Boisseau (Paris : Presses Universitaires de la Sorbonne), 206.
55. "East Coker," 26 (179).

56. Leyris, 189.
57. Vigée, 25 (179)
58. "Burnt Norton," 16 (119).
59. Leyris, 169.
60. Vigée, 14 (119)
61. "The Dry Salvages," 32 (54).
62. Leyris, 197.
63. Vigée, 30 (56)
64. "East Coker," 25 (143).
65. Leyris, 187.
66. Vigée, 23 (145)
67. "East Coker," 21 (8).
68. Leyris, 175.
69. Leyris, 199 "inchangés" (see "Dry Salvages," 33), 197 "inattachée" (see "Dry Salvages," 33).
70. "East Coker," 21 (18).
71. Leyris, 177.
72. "The Dry Salvages," 35.
73. Leyris, 203.
74. Vigée, 34 (134–135)
75. "The Dry Salvages," 35.
76. See Leyris, 172, 179.
77. "The Dry Salvages," 37 (182–183).
78. Leyris, 207.
79. Vigée, 36 (186–187)
80. "East Coker," 27 (204).
81. Leyris,191.
82. Vigée, 27 (205–206).
83. Leyris: "broui" 215, "finisterre" 195, "ronçaie" 181, "arroi" 179, "nordé" 199.
84. Leyris: "postvoir" 219, "le sans-fin" 217.
85. "East Coker," 24 (125)
86. Leyris, 185.
87. "East Coker," 24 (125)
88. See Henri Bergson, *Durée et simultanéité* (Paris: Quadrige 1968).
89. T.S. Eliot, *On Poets and Poetry*, 20.
90. Walter Benjamin, "La tâche du traducteur" in *Œuvres I*, Transl. M. de Gandillac, Rainer Rochlitz, P. Rusch (Paris : Gallimard, 2000) 250–51.
91. Claude Vigée, "Comment traduire les Quatre Quatuors de T.S. Eliot?," 208.
92. "The Dry Salvages," 38 (228–229).

Works Cited

Bataille, Georges (1944,1961), *Le coupable*. Paris: Gallimard.
Benjamin Walter (2000), *Œuvres I*. Transl. M. de Gandillac, Rainer Rochlitz, P. Rusch. Paris: Gallimard.
Bergson, Henri (1968), *Durée et simultanéité*. Paris: Quadrige.
Camus, Albert (1947), *La peste*. Paris : Gallimard.

Cyrulnik, Boris (1999), *Un merveilleux malheur*. Paris: Odile Jacob.
Didi-Huberman, Georges (2009), *Survivance des lucioles*. Paris: Les Editions de Minuit.
Eco, Umberto (2007), *Dire presque la même chose*. Paris: Grasset.
Eliot, T.S. (1959), *Four Quartets*. London: Faber and Faber.
_____. (1957), *On Poets and Poetry*. London: Faber and Faber.
Gardner, Helen (1968), *The Art of T.S. Eliot*. London: Faber and Faber.
Heaney, Seamus (1988), *The Government of the Tongue*. London: Faber and Faber.
Holy Bible King James Version (1972). Nashville : Thomas Nelson Publishers.
Ionesco, Eugène (1967), *Journal en miettes*. Paris: Folio.
Lacoue-Labarthe, Philippe (1991), *Lacan avec les philosophes*. Paris: Albin Michel.
Leyris, Pierre (transl.) (1976), *La terre Vaine et autres poèmes*. Paris: Editions du Seuil.
_____. (transl.) (1950 for the French translation, 2006), "La Terre vaine" in *Quatre Quatuors de T.S. Eliot*. Paris: Editions du Seuil, coll. *Points Poésie*.
Semprun, Jorge (1994), *L'écriture ou la vie*. Paris: Gallimard.
Steiner, Georges (1975), *After Babel*. Oxford: Oxford University Press.
Vigée, Claude (2007), "Comment traduire les Quatre Quatuors de T.S. Eliot?" in *Palimpestes 20 : De la traduction comme commentaire au commentaire de traduction*. Ed. Maryvonne Boisseau. Paris : Presses Universitaires de la Sorbonne, 201–230.
_____. (transl.) (1992), *Quatre quators*. London: The Menard Press, in association with King's College, London.

PART III: NORTHERN RESISTANCE

8. Basil Bunting
Resistance, History and Myth
Charlotte Estrade

Resistance, in the basic sense of fighting against an enemy or an authority, was a constant feature of Basil Bunting's life.[1] Indeed, he was a conscientious objector during World War One, enrolled in the Royal Air Force during the Second World War, and always had social preoccupations. This social consciousness was passed on to Basil early in life by his father who was a doctor for the local miners in a small town in Northumberland. His political resistance also finds its equivalent in his poetics: Bunting fought against mainstream British English readings of poetry and put forward his native Northumbrian culture in his poems, prose and lectures. Bunting's thought also resists precise categorization in the political or religious spheres. Indeed Bunting's poetry is not quite war poetry although World War One and Two are commented on; nor is it just the poetic autobiography of a poet who traveled and also had political responsibilities; and Bunting's resisting spirit, as it is formulated in his poetry or critical prose, does not form a consistent whole. Yet all these characteristics are present in his poetry.

Bunting's poems present individuals whose resistance is the driving force of history and who problematize man's relation to time. Historical or mythical individuals combine as in a mosaic to embody the concept of resistance and the poet's ideals or worst fears. Resistance is both subject-matter and a structural and formal principle informing Bunting's poetics. These individuals stand out and resist a monolithic interpretation. The term "individual" has to be taken in its full sense here, since historical or mythical figures often have to stand and face their destiny alone. Myth and history in Bunting's work as it evolves, together with the superposition of times and places, throw light on each other and draw on a range of modes of resistance in relation to various historical eras.

More complex still, poetic and political resistance are intertwined. First, Bunting resists political ideologies. Through his poetic reflection on society, he also resists what he sees as decadence and decrepitude. Second, Bunting's poetic resistance is a means of staying aloof from facile poetry; it also relies on the notion of condensation in the Ezra Pound tradition. Condensation in poetry implies economy of word, precision, selection of the essential features of language; it is about "compressing," "paring the language."[2] Consequently, it is a poetry which resists immediate comprehension. What is the link between these various forms of resistance? Does one type of resistance cause the other? How can the political and the aesthetic run so parallel? What is the link between Bunting's political resistance and his poetic choices? The aim here is to analyze how the political, the linguistic and the poetic are intertwined.

Bunting's resistance takes the form of a social critique — indeed, modern society is characterized by its decadence and uniformity, against which one should fight. This idea is present throughout the whole Bunting corpus, as the poem entitled "Attis: Or Something Missing," II, suggests. A network of negative words is present:

> In the morning
> clean streets welcomed light's renewal,
> patient, passive to the weight of buses
> thundering like cabinet ministers
> over a lethargic populace.
> [...]
> Battered, filthily unfortunate streets
> perish, their ghosts are wretched
> in the mockery of lamps.[3]

The most evident archetype to illustrate the degradation of modern life is the city of London, as can be seen, for example, from the description of the engine and machines in part II of *Briggflatts*:

> Secret, solitary, a spy, he gauges
> lines of a Flemish horse
> hauling beer, the angle, obtuse,
> a slut's blouse draws on her chest,
> counts beat against beat, bus conductor
> against engine against wheels against
> the pedal, Tottenham Court Road, decodes
> thunder [...][4]

The idea is also present in "The Well of Lycopolis," II, where the grass in parks has lost its color and days have lost their luminosity.

> The nights are not fresh
> between High Holborn and the Euston Road
> nor the day bright even in summer
> nor the grass of the squares green.[5]

The idea of a faded, discolored and wandering present is recurrent in Bunting's poems.

The poet wants to warn against the merging of the individual into the impersonal city. Hence his appeal to particular individuals or characters who are singled out from the crowd, resist this uniformity, and embody a spirit of resistance, whether in a negative or a positive way. These individuals are taken from various distant places or eras and provide an antithesis to the uniformity or sterility of present society. Resistance seems to be inextricably linked to the comparison with other times or places, which provide a counterpoint from which to judge one's situation.

Individuals are drawn from different places and historical periods. The reflection on history is always accompanied by resisting characters or speakers who are temporally and geographically alien to a modern reader. No wonder then, that Bunting should feel affinities with Chomei's *Ho-jo-ki*. Bunting condenses the prose work of this twelfth-century Japanese writer in his 1932 poem entitled "Chomei at Toyama." Here, the speaker refuses life in the city because of its lack of permanence: "This is the unstable world and / we in it unstable and our houses."[6] This instability is literal since the poem is a tribute to the victims of a particularly violent earthquake which shook Tokyo in 1177, but it seems fair to say that the instability is also moral and cultural, and also applies to modern times.

Such individuals also provide models or counter-examples. In the poem "Attis: Or Something Missing," for example, modern man is described and judged in the light of the mythical figure of Attis who emasculates himself in the context of the cult of Cybele. The stress is on the impotence of modern man who is thus satirized and whose lack of vitality and memory is underlined, together with the sense of something "disrupt" in present times:

> Out of puff
> noonhot in tweeds and gray felt,
> tired of appearance and
> disappearance;
> warm obese frame limp with satiety;
> slavishly circumspect at sixty;
> [...]
> disrupt Atlantis, days forgotten,
> extinct peoples, silted harbours.
> He regrets that brackish
> train of the huntress.[7]

Whereas Attis is emasculated for religious reasons, modern man is characterized by dereliction, loss of a spiritual dimension and longing for a time when he was at one with the goddess Cybele ("the huntress"), who is associated with forests, the earth and nature. It is clear from Bunting's poems that loss of contact with nature and the spiritual provokes apathy, a sense of meaninglessness and amnesia which Bunting deems unfulfilling for mankind. Nature, with all its vitality, is associated, in Bunting's poetry, with the spiritual, as will be seen below. Myth set in the present rarely evokes nostalgia for a long-lost past or Eden. Rather, myth creates a parallel with which to view modern society anew in order to create surprise, provoke thought in the reader, and give birth to a resisting spirit.

The idea of decadence can stretch to the mythical figures themselves. In "Attis," the Muse of rhetoric, "Polymnia, / keeps a café in Reno."[8] At the beginning of "The Well of Lycopolis," another mythical figure has undergone change: "Mother Venus, ageing, bedraggled, a / half-quarter of gin under her shawl" is on the verge of suicide.[9] As Victoria Forde underlines, Bunting meant to satirize this "detested generation" he thought he was part of. This explains the fact that the poem "The Well of Lycopolis" is a "castigation of society" and also explains its weaknesses.[10] In both the Attis and Polymnia examples mentioned above, myth is displaced into a modern context to show the present invalidity of the practice of these rites, and yet the rewritten myth is meant to create a feeling of responsibility and awkwardness regarding one's own situation in the present. Transposing myth into the present invites the reader to question his habits and provides, by contrast, a new way of seeing.[11] This idea of contrast, Bunting takes from Horace and others: "the process of association or contrast [...] I think I derive from Horace, Hafez, and the symphonic composers."[12]

Indeed, establishing a contrast, whether on the level of poetic language or ideas, entails setting something in opposition to something else, resisting an Other. The notion of contrast or contest can also be seen in subject-matter, through the theme of confrontation. Thus, there are numerous warriors or fighting figures in the Bunting corpus. Eric Bloodaxe, the ancient king of Orkney, Joan of Arc, Alexander the Great, Genghis Khan are present, sometimes in the same poem, and the war element is recurrent; and yet they resist conventional historical interpretation. Bunting's work is that of a poet, not an historian. Bloodaxe, for one, is meant to be tragic because he cannot face his own destiny and has failed to keep his father's kingdom of Norway, although he is of illustrious descent; he was eventually kicked out of York and Northumbria.[13] In a 1965 letter, Bunting notes that he has "taken care to make Bloodaxe as telling as [he could], abler age would have made a tragedy out of him as scarifying as anything the Greeks had."[14] Bunting is interested in the universal, human dimension of Bloodaxe. Similarly, Alexander the Great is present in Bunting's masterpiece *Briggflatts*. Yet it is the Persian version of the Alexander story, taken from Firdosi's *Shahnameh*, that Bunting rewrites in order to emphasize the solitude of the leader whose troops have given up following him. The climax lies in Alexander seeing the angel Israfel about to sound the horn to announce the end of the world. This vision of the apocalypse provides him with a new outlook on the world and brings him back to the stage when his troops decided to abandon him. It is not the conventional vision of Alexander as a ruthless and conquering leader which is presented here.

Although Bunting has picked his emblematic figures among the toughest warriors and heroes, these presences serve a paradoxical purpose since it is their weakness and failure which are being underlined. There is a paradox between Bunting's anti-military preoccupations and the recurrence of warring heroes in his poetry. Yet Bunting does not present these figures as models to follow. Warriors in Bunting's poetry are put forward for their human aspect and the epiphanic dimension of the experience they go through. It is not the conquest that is put forward: Bloodaxe's name is surrounded by terms evoking death and failure in the first and second parts of *Briggflatts*.[15] Alexander is pictured in the same situation in the third part of *Briggflatts*:

> But we desired Macedonia,
> [...]
> and deemed the peak unscaleable; but he
> reached to a crack in the rock
> with some scorn, resolute though in doubt
> [...].[16]

The discrepancy between army and leader is enacted in language: the pronoun "we" is separated and differentiated from "he" by an adversative "but." The collective pronoun "we" further underlines the loneliness of the leader, presumptuously wanting to conquer more and higher territory. The climax of this passage brings the character to a fuller consciousness of death: "When will the signal come / to summon man to his clay?"[17] The same kind of epiphany takes place for Bloodaxe: "By such rocks / men killed Bloodaxe."[18] Those are only two examples of the way warriors, war and battle feature in Bunting's poetry. Paradoxically, this fighting spirit is linked more to *hybris* and stubbornness than to an ideal of resistance one should follow.

There are other examples, which are sometimes linked to Bunting's own experience. Such is the case of his satire of World War Two in "The Well of Lycopolis" or in "The Spoils."[19] In the first of these two poems, the speaker laments the fact that "times have changed," and strong contrasts are presented between madness ("rave," "maniacs") and reason, cleanliness and filth ("sweating," "sticky," "smell"), love and hate ("atrocities"), conventional or mechanical behavior ("instructions") and natural behavior.[20] In "The Spoils," Bunting portrays Churchill as a clown and critically refers to the well-known iconographic representations of him with a cigar. Bunting is highly ironic regarding the "fun of fighting."[21] The critique of military figures therefore also applies to modern ones, not just to mythical or ancient ones.

Warfare is also the leading thread of Bunting's summary of Northumbrian history in his presidential addresses to the Northern Arts Council. Indeed, on these occasions, Bunting defined the thriving Northumbrian culture as one that was threatened by Roman domination and blended with the culture of the Angles. Bunting names surviving monuments of Northumbrian architecture — despite the Norman Conquest, Northumbrian culture is still very much alive and ought to be preserved.[22]

Myth and history in Bunting thus resist a clear-cut interpretation. They provide a template of purposiveness in the past while being rewritten to comment on the lethargy of present times. Myth and history serve as a powerful tool for criticism: although they evoke an alien temporal and sometimes geographical frame, they manage to serve as a mirror for the reader to reflect on himself and his society. Resistance, here, amounts to a struggle against the lethargy of society, and a consciousness of one's cultural roots. Resistance lies in the contrasted presentation of warrior figures and impotent modern mankind. Resistance, therefore, is meant to be produced in, and suggested to, the reader through the contrasts that myth and history provide.

The type of resistance or awareness Bunting wants to evoke is present in three precise though apparently unconnected fields which, in his critical prose and statements, become interdependent — the linguistic, the artistic and the religious. Bunting's linguistic form of resistance is about fighting the hegemony of Southern British English in poetry, although Bunting's spelling is not that of a Northumbrian dialect.[23] His artistic resistance aims at protecting artists from poverty and maintaining a policy of foregrounding the arts, and more particularly Northumbrian art: for Bunting, linguistic, artistic and political resistance are one.

The poet always stressed the Northumbrian element of his identity, although basic knowledge of the man's life instantly indicates his cosmopolitanism and openness to the world. For him, ancient Northumbrian art should be a guide for Northumbrian artists today. In his presidential address to the Northern Arts Council in November 1974, Bunting stressed the duty of the institution to "recover that Northumbrian spirit in painting and literature," not through "imitation of ancient models" but by encouraging and financing artists who produce new works which are created in the same "spirit." Bunting added that universities and schools also had a role to play in this.[24] This resistance to a hegemonic and unified culture is well illustrated by the variety of cultural references in Bunting's poetic corpus, which range from Persian, to Latin and Scandinavian, and reflect Bunting's travels.

The poet already had this idea of protecting Northumbrian art in mind in his 1969 lecture in Newcastle when taking the *Lindisfarne Codex* as "the central masterpiece of Northumbrian art, and also of all the art of the Dark Ages, except what you find in Byzantium."[25] Bunting's defense of Northumbrian culture, which some critics have taxed with provincialism in the past, is best understood in terms of the concept of resistance. Bunting proposes to take a new and long-neglected point of reference — his native Northumbria. In his notes to *Briggflatts*, the poet also makes clear that "all the school histories are written by or for Southrons"; hence the fact that "Northumbrians should know Eric Bloodaxe but seldom do."[26] Bunting implicitly links the conservation of one's heritage with the notion of resistance. Heritage to Bunting is both the historic landmarks he comments on and thinks should be taken as models, and the Northumbrian culture more generally speaking. This culture, Bunting underlines, is very often neglected, notably by the institutions responsible for funding the arts. The center-periphery problematic is particularly acute, as Stefan Hawlin has shown in an article entitled "Bunting's Northumbrian Tongue: Against the Monument of the Centre." In this article, Hawlin points out: "[Bunting's] rejection of the monument topos goes along with his implicit rejection of national centricity, his slighting of ideas of power, and his teasing of Southrons." This enables Bunting to contest or resist the implications of the notion of monument: "an emphasis on the stabilizing center, the apparent location of power and culture."[27] The term "teasing" which Hawlin uses here is perhaps too light. Bunting's subversive resistance to mainstream English culture may explain his long neglect in British literary studies, and his strong association with the American Modernism of Louis Zukofsky, Charles Olson, and Ezra Pound, to name but a few. Bunting's emphasis on Northumbrian architecture as *good* monument is meant to displace the point of reference for culture.

In this Northumbrian-orientated approach, reading a Northumbrian poem in the Queen's English is the worst thing one can do since the specificity of the poem is thus lost and since this goes against the intention of the author. Indeed, Bunting always stressed the aural importance of poetry, which should resist simplification into a prose synopsis and should not be read in silence: poetry "is to be heard," is about "sounds" and "must be read aloud."[28] The ideal poet according to Bunting is characterized by "an ear open to melodic analogies" and should write poetry "as a musician pricks his score."[29]

Yet this resistance cannot be effective without concrete means. This is why Bunting, from his late recognition in the sixties to his death in 1985, stressed the importance of a proper policy regarding the arts and culture. In the speeches he gave as president of Northern Arts, Basil Bunting, over the years, stressed several elements. Among them, he emphasized the need to have more funding for artists so as not to leave them in poverty (and Bunting speaks from experience here), the necessity of experimentation in the arts even if it is to be done at the expense of public taste, together with the importance of keeping the Northumbrian tradition alive. The problematic issue of patronage for artists is a recurrent theme in his poetry, as can be seen at the beginning of the well-known opening of the second part of *Briggflatts* concerning the "poet appointed" who is dependent on patronage.[30] Resistance, or fighting to live up to one's ideals, goes hand in hand with commitment to cultural values linked to place and home, and more broadly speaking, collective and cultural identity.

As far as personal identity is concerned, in the religious sphere, for instance, Bunting's resistance takes the form of a right to suspend one's judgment. His Quaker origin probably accounts for some of his reluctance to take strong political or religious stands. Moreover, Bunting was a contemporary of T. S. Eliot and Ezra Pound's poetic maturity. Eliot's conversion to the Anglican Church in 1927 and his latter-day conservative views, together with Pound's commitment to fascism in the thirties, partly explain Bunting's resistance to systems and clear-cut ideologies. As for religion, Bunting's "view of things is an extremely pantheistic one" and "finds no expression in any organized society."[31] Bunting's work resists categorization and he more than once stressed his distaste for labels and systems.

The more ambiguous form of resistance that Bunting cultivated is the resistance to facile poetry. Contrary to Pound or Eliot who at times cultivated the difficulty of their poetry and its wealth of learned allusions (one will remember Eliot's remark that "poets in our civilization, as it exists at present, must be *difficult*."[32]) Bunting is against the unnecessary in poetry and is all for "cutting down."[33] Indeed, condensation is one of Bunting's poetry-writing principles, as Ezra Pound points out in his *ABC of Reading*, originally published in 1934: "*DICHTEN = CONDENSARE*" is "Bunting's discovery and his prime contribution to contemporary criticism."[34]

Again, Bunting's model is the *Codex Lindisfarne* and its illuminations. When a scribe chooses to represent a cormorant for example, Bunting points out that he has spent a long time "evolving this form, which stands for the cormorant," and which Bunting takes as an illustration of his point; the chosen essential and remaining lines are the most specific, the most "needful"[35] ones for the viewer to recognize the pattern. This enables the illustrator, once the essential outline is drawn, to bring in his own creative touch. At this point only can he "afford to fill in the body of the bird, which is naturally a very sombre creature, with all sorts of colors which contradict the natural appearance."[36] This way of proceeding, once applied to poetry, goes through various stages: immediate perception or remembrance, the choice of essential features, the re-coloring into poetic form, which eventually provoke resistance for the reader whose perception, experience and understanding may vary from the poet's. A reading of J. H. Prynne's essay entitled "Resistance and Difficulty" would suggest that what has up to now been called *resistance* in this chapter is in fact what Prynne refers to as the "fabricated or willed" *difficulty* of poetry (as opposed to the "inherent" or "given" *resistance* of objects of the world).[37] Indeed, the process of creating this difficulty through the conscious arrangement of words in a poem does apply to Bunting, who wrote and rewrote his poems until he found the most economical way of putting his poems into words, thus creating the difficulty the reader experiences. Prynne underlines the fact that "Difficulty [...] is the subjective counterpart to resistance: I experience difficulty when I encounter resistance."[38] Difficulty is seen as prior to resistance and as its outward, symptomatic aspect. This analysis is particularly suited to Bunting's poetry which makes the reader experience difficulty while reading, while dealing with the resistance of some notions tackled by Bunting such as the impermanence of life in nature. Indeed, some notions could be said to be inherently difficult since man can never fully comprehend them. Death, for example, is everywhere in Bunting's poems and experienced by various species (man and animals) and sometimes in a reflexive way (such as the mason figure carving an epitaph in stone for a grave in *Briggflatts*). This plurality of experiences of death shows this notion to be resistant to full and clear comprehension. The second stanza of *Briggflatts*, I, is a case in point, uniting the figure of a lark, the mason carving the epitaph, "rot" and "grave":

> A mason times his mallet
> to a lark's twitter,
> listening while the marble rests,
> lays his rule
> at a letter's edge, [...]
> till the stone spells a name
> naming none,
> a man abolished. [...]
> In the grave's slot
> he lies. We rot.[39]

Men, animals and the process of decomposition are all envisaged on the same plane, as transitory elements of nature. Difficulty in this passage of the poem stems both from the economical and poetic formulation, and from the ontological resistance of man to the full grasp of such processes as death and writing.

In this context, the use of historical, mythical and literary figures should provide help. One expects them to be meaningful and provide a shortcut to an idea or theme grasped by all. Indeed, history, myth, and some elements of literature belong to the realm of common knowledge and general culture. Sometimes they are chosen because they find their equivalent in Bunting's own experience of life. For example, the use of the figure of Villon in the eponymous poem by Bunting, written in 1925, is first of all related to the poet's experience in prison during World War One. This is the way Bunting's "literary skeletons draw his experience to them," to quote Peter Makin.[40] However, the use of such figures actually contributes to the fact that the poem resists easy reading.

What is at stake is nothing less than the whole issue of literary allusion and tradition. The reader's resistance is all the more acute as Bunting mentions a whole series of other historical and mythical characters which do not seem to be connected and seem to point outside the poem in a centrifugal whirl of associations. The time frame, together with the theme of heroic death, provides a bridge between Villon and Joan of Arc. It is through the poet's rewriting Villon's introduction[41] to the *Ballade des dames du temps jadis* and then through his expanding successively on the theme of death and that of female beauty that Helen of Troy is brought into the poem. This process of contiguity and association is reminiscent of Pound's method in the early *Cantos* (*A Draft of 16 Cantos* was published, in its revised form, in 1925).[42] Pound was writing them at the same time as Bunting's "Villon." The influence of the early *Cantos* on Bunting was strong; it is therefore no coincidence that Bunting should later on in life have commented precisely on this part of the *Cantos*. In a 1974 lecture, Bunting explained that the figure of Helen of Troy in Pound's *Cantos* was to be understood as one possible illustration of war and beauty, along with other female presences which were "ramifications" or "facets" of the same idea, and which Bunting associated with a musical pattern.[43] Thus, the repetition of the same idea through different figures creates poetic difficulty, as the reader has to make sense of this web of associations, and recognize that they enrich each other and make the poetic echoes more complex.

This principle of contiguity, as opposed to formal logic, creates what Roy Fisher calls a "dislocative effect."[44] A. Kingsley Weatherhead sees this effect as the main feature of, and common point between, the modern poets whose works he analyzes in his book on poets of *The British Dissonance*. His argument is that the poets he considers (and Bunting is among them) do not use common literary devices which have, in the past, "supplied structure: a logical or narrative sequence, or repetition — rhythm and rhyme, stanzas, the reflection of the elements of the theme in varied forms, the repetition of an image [...], the reflection of the ideas in symbol or in the shape of the framework." These elements, which "for centuries have supported the reader," are subverted or no longer used by modern poets.[45]

This loss of bearings, which contributes to the difficulty of the reading process, is even stronger since Bunting's statements on poetry and his practice are sometimes contradictory or confusing. If the mythical and the historical in Bunting seem pretty well delineated, they nonetheless become intertwined. The character of Bloodaxe, for example, is treated as an historical character yet the main account of his life is present in the *Heimskringla*, which is a saga.[46] What is to be said of the *poetic* rewriting of a *mythicized historical* event? The poem thus resists immediate interpretation because categories are blurred and discourses mixed. Resistance stems from confrontation with the conscious and willed confusion between life and history on the one hand, and art and myth on the other hand. Or is this meant to suggest that poetry and history are, after all, equally valid discourses?

Many types of difficulty are accumulated in Bunting's poetry, and this, in turn, produces more than one type of resistance in the reader. If one takes up George Steiner's four types of difficulty as described in his essay "On Difficulty" and summed up in Ruth Padel's essay entitled "Reading a Poem," one can see that Bunting combines three out of the four.[47] Steiner's first main type of difficulty refers to the mention of something the reader does not know about, thus creating the most obvious type of difficulty one can come across in poetry. Indeed, Bunting's poetry is difficult, for one thing, because it is allusive. Despite Bunting's reluctance to have his readers check all his allusions in encyclopedias, Bunting uses an imperative addressed to the reader when he discusses Bloodaxe: "Piece his story together from the Anglo-Saxon Chronicle, the Okneyinga Saga, and Heimskringla, as you fancy."[48] Bunting's statement that "notes are a confession of failure" is to be understood in the context of his ideal of the self-sufficient poem.[49] His notes to his *Complete Poems* underline, and suggest a way of filling in, gaps in the reader's knowledge in the fields of myth and history, gaps of which Bunting was very much aware. In a 1977 interview, he acknowledged: "The world doesn't spend all its time reading books, and we all assumed that they [*sic*] do."[50] This "we all" of course includes Ezra Pound and T. S. Eliot, whose well-known practice of the literary allusion also produced texts which engage the notions of resistance and difficulty. Modernist poets' knowledge of classical texts and literary tradition is bound to create a sense of frustration in the modern reader who does not recognize (but can often sense there is) a literary allusion in the lines he is reading.

Steiner's second type of difficulty relates to the opaqueness a reader can still feel after reading a poem, to some "impropriety" (a term used by Aristotle and quoted by Padel) whereby the poem does not conform to one's idea of poetry.[51] This is less evident in Bunting and a second reading always proves Bunting right, confirming that the chosen form was the optimal one for a given poem. The rewriting of myth or history — that is, narrative — in a condensed and allusive modern poetic form is a truly challenging literary enterprise.

Steiner's third type of difficulty amounts to obscurity for stylistic and sometimes also political or private reasons, or the fear of censorship. It applies to Bunting's poetics of condensation, although the poet would probably argue against his *deliberate* obscuring of poems, arguing instead that they have nothing abstruse in content or in language. Yet place names and some Northumbrian words are not necessarily familiar to everyone. Despite Wallace Stevens' comment that "Poetry must resist intelligence almost successfully,"[52] one could argue, as William Empson did while commenting on various types of ambiguity, that "poetry always has multiple layers of meaning, which gives it an 'irreducible ambiguity.'"[53]

Coming back to Bunting's statement on poetry having to be read aloud, Bunting is tempted by a radical view of poetry as predominantly a matter of sound only. The silent reading of poetry makes the reader look for basic meaning yet prose, for Bunting, "exists to convey meaning," and does so better; he goes on to say, "no meaning such as prose conveys can be expressed as well in poetry. This is not poetry's business."[54] This statement seems to suggest that sounds are meaningful in themselves. Yet how can one prevent the reader from looking for meaning conventionally, in the words? Besides, there *is* meaning in Bunting's words. The poet seems to have been aware of this when he stated, in a 1977 interview that "with the sound words have meanings, you can't avoid that."[55] So Bunting qualified his initial stance.

Although Bunting was never a strong political or social activist, he expressed his political and ideological resistance in his poetry. This is particularly obvious in the way he rewrote the story of some warrior figures. Political resistance entails protecting one's ideals and fighting what Bunting saw as the general decrepitude of society, which affects all areas, cultural, religious, and inter-personal. This political resistance and the specific kind of resistance Bunting tries to inspire in the reader are embodied in the literary, mythological or historical figures featuring in his poems. Mythological references in particular seem to crystallize the problem of resistance: they embody a spirit of resistance. At the same time, because they are temporally or geographically alien, the reader is led to reflect on society and history. The reader is invited to exercise his or her critical faculties. This social aspect of Bunting's resistance extends to his practice of poetry, seen as a craft of condensation. Indeed, Bunting's poetry resists easy reading. The inherent "resistance" of things is mirrored by the complexities of Bunting's allusive style, and is further intensified by the essential nature of sound in poetic language.

Therefore, Bunting's resistance is multi-faceted: it is political, it stresses poetic condensation which demands active participation on the part of the reader, and it is meant to underline the complexity of things, in order to suggest the ideally critical yet humble position of man.

Notes

1. This is one of A. K. Weatherhead's first comments on Basil Bunting in *The British Dissonance: Essays on Ten Contemporary Poets* (Columbia, London: University of Missouri Press, 1983), 144.
2. P. Johnstone's words in his article "Basil Bunting: [Two Interviews]" in *Meantime* 1 (1977, 67–80), 78.
3. Basil Bunting, *Complete Poems* (Newcastle upon Tyne:Bloodaxe Books Ltd., 2000), 32.
4. Bunting, *Complete Poems*, 65.
5. Bunting, *Complete Poems*, 42.
6. Bunting, *Complete Poems*, 91.
7. Bunting, *Complete Poems*, 30.
8. Bunting, *Complete Poems*, 33.
9. Bunting, *Complete Poems*, 39.
10. Victoria Forde, *The Poetry of Basil Bunting* (Newcastle: Bloodaxe, 1991), 175.
11. P. Johnstone, "Basil Bunting: [Two Interviews]," 76. This is in keeping with Bunting's emphasis that the poet should observe and dissect things, in the way William Carlos Williams, as a doctor, would examine patients.
12. This is a passage from a 1951 letter from Basil Bunting to Louis Zukovsky, quoted in *Basil Bunting, Man and Poet*, Ed. Carroll F. Terrell (Orono, Maine: National Poetry Foundation, 1981), 268.
13. Peter Makin, *Bunting: the Shaping of his Verse* (Oxford: Clarendon Press, 1992), 174.
14. Makin, *Bunting: the Shaping of his Verse*, 169–70.
15. Bunting, *Complete Poems*, 62, 64, 69.
16. Bunting, *Complete Poems*, 72.
17. Bunting, *Complete Poems*, 73.
18. Bunting, *Complete Poems*, 62.
19. Bunting, *Complete Poems*, "The Well of Lycopolis," I, 40, "The Spoils," III, 56.
20. Bunting, *Complete Poems*, 40.
21. Bunting, *Complete Poems*, 56.
22. Basil Bunting, *Presidential Addresses: An Artist's View on Regional Arts Patronage* (Newcastle upon Tyne: Northern Arts, 1976), 2.
23. Matthew Hart, "A Dialect in the Spelling of the Capital: Basil Bunting Goes

Home," in *Nations of Nothing but Poetry: Modernism, Transnationalism, and Synthetic Vernacular Writing* (Oxford: Oxford University Press, 2010).

24. Bunting, *Presidential Addresses*, 2.

25. Basil Bunting, *Three Essays*, Ed. Richard Caddel (Durham: Basil Bunting Poetry Center, 1994), 4.

26. Bunting, *Complete Poems*, 226.

27. Stefan Hawlin, "Bunting's Northumbrian Tongue: Against the Monument of the Center" in *The Yearbook of English Studies* 25 (1995, 103–113), 108, 110.

28. Jonathan Williams, "A Statement" in *Descant on Rawthey's Madrigal* (Lexington, Ky.: Gnomon Press, 1968), n. p.

29. B. Bunting, "Preface" in *Complete Poems*, 21.

30. Bunting, *Complete Poems*, 65.

31. Paul Johnstone, "Basil Bunting: [Two Interviews]," 72.

32. T. S. Eliot, "The Metaphysical Poets," *Selected Essays* (London: Faber and Faber Ltd, 1969 [1932]), 289. The rest of Eliot's paragraph on this reads: "Our civilization comprehends great variety and complexity, and this [...] must produce various and complex results. The poet must become more and more comprehensive, more allusive, more indirect, in order to force, to dislocate if necessary, language into his meaning."

33. P. Johnston, "Basil Bunting: [Two Interviews]," 80.

34. Ezra Pound, *ABC of Reading* (New York: New Directions, 1987), 92.

35. Both quotations are from *Basil Bunting on Poetry*, Ed. Peter Makin (Baltimore and London: The Johns Hopkins University Press, 1999), 10.

36. Peter Makin, *Basil Bunting on Poetry*, 10.

37. Prynne 30.

38. Prynne 28.

39. Bunting, *Complete Poems*, 72.

40. "Introduction" in *Basil Bunting on Poetry*, Ed. Peter Makin (Baltimore and London: The Johns Hopkins University Press, 1999), xv.

41. V. Forde, *The Poetry of Basil Bunting*, 153.

42. Bunting's "Villon" was not published until 1930. Forde (*The Poetry of Basil Bunting*, 150) insists on Pound's importance in the writing of this poem.

43. P. Makin, *Basil Bunting on Poetry*, 137.

44. Roy Fisher, *Nineteen Poems and an Interview*, quoted in A. K. Weatherhead, *The British Dissonance*, 7.

45. Weatherhead, *The British Dissonance*, 7.

46. Peter Makin, *Bunting: the Shaping of his Verse*, 184–185. See also the whole of this chapter on "Warriors" in Bunting.

47. Ruth Padel, "Reading a Poem" in *Poetry Nation Review* 31/5 (2005), <http://www.ruthpadel.com/pages/reading_poem.htm>, accessed 15 Sept. 2010.

48. Bunting, *Complete Poems*, 226.

49. Bunting, *Complete Poems*, 225.

50. C. F. Terrell, *Basil Bunting, Man and Poet*, 249.

51. Cf. Padel, "Reading a Poem."

52. W. Stevens is quoted in Bart Eeckhout, "Wallace Stevens's Poetry of Resistance" in *Modernism Revisited : Transgressing Boundaries and Strategies of Renewal in American Poetry*, Eds. Viorica Patea and P. S. Derrick (Amsterdam and New York: Rodopi, 2007), 121–134.

53. W. Empson is quoted in Marjorie Perloff, *The Poetics of Indeterminacy: Rimbaud to Cage* (Evanston, Illinois: Northwestern University Press, 1999 [1981]), 34.

54. Jonathan Williams, "A Statement" in *Descant on Rawthey's Madrigal*, n.p.
55. P. Johnstone, "Basil Bunting: [Two Interviews]," 76.

Works Cited

Bunting, Basil(2000), *Complete Poems*. Ed. Richard Caddel, Newcastle upon Tyne: Bloodaxe Books Ltd.
_____ (1976), *Presidential Addresses: An Artist's View on Regional Arts Patronage*. Newcastle upon Tyne: Northern Arts.
_____ (1977), *Presidential Addresses: An Artist's View on Regional Arts Patronage*. Newcastle upon Tyne: Northern Arts.
_____ (1994), *Three Essays*. Ed. Richard Caddel, Durham: Basil Bunting Poetry Centre.
Eliot, T. S. ([1932] 1969), *Selected Essays*. London: Faber and Faber Ltd.
Forde, Victoria (1991), *The Poetry of Basil Bunting*. Newcastle: Bloodaxe.
Matthew Hart (2010), "A Dialect in the Spelling of the Capital: Basil Bunting Goes Home," in *Nations of Nothing but Poetry: Modernism, Transnationalism, and Synthetic Vernacular Writing*. Oxford: Oxford University Press, 79–105.
Hawlin, Stefan (1995), "Bunting's Northumbrian Tongue: Against the Monument of the Centre," in *The Yearbook of English Studies* 25 (special number: Non Standard Englishes and the New Media), 103–113.
Johnstone, Paul (1977), "Basil Bunting: [Two Interviews]," in *Meantime*, 1, 67–80.
Makin, Peter (ed.) (1999), *Basil Bunting on Poetry*. Baltimore and London: The Johns Hopkins University Press.
_____ (1992), *Bunting: the Shaping of his Verse*. Oxford: Clarendon Press.
Padel, Ruth (2005), "Reading a Poem," in *Poetry Nation Review* 31/5 (May), <http://www.ruthpadel.com/pages/reading_poem.htm>. Accessed 15 Sept. 2010.
Pound, Ezra (1987), *ABC of Reading*. New York: New Directions.
Prynne, J. H. (1961), "Resistance and Difficulty," in *Prospect*, 5, 26–30.
Terrell, Carroll F. (ed.) (1981), *Basil Bunting, Man and Poet*. Orono, Maine: National Poetry Foundation.
Weatherhead, A. Kingsley (1983), *The British Dissonance, Essays on Ten Contemporary Poets*. Columbia, London: University of Missouri Press.
Williams, Jonathan (1968), *Descant on Rawthey's Madrigal*. Lexington, Ky.: Gnomon Press.

9. Ted Hughes and "That Built-In Resistance"
Versions of the Calder Valley
Claire Hélie

> When writing by hand you meet the terrible resistance of what happened your first year at it when you couldn't write at all ... when you were making attempts, pretending to form letters. These ancient feelings are there, wanting to be expressed. When you sit with your pen, every year of your life is right there, wired into the communication between your brain and your writing hand. There is a natural characteristic resistance that produces a certain kind of result analogous to your actual handwriting. As you force your expression against that built-in-resistance, things become automatically more compressed, more summary and, perhaps, psychologically denser.[1]

Ted Hughes came to such conclusions after having been on the judging panel of the W.H. Smith children's writing competition for a few years. He could not but notice a difference between texts composed on typewriters, rather long texts displaying "mastery of words," texts he deemed "boring"[2] though, and hand-written texts, shorter, denser texts. According to the poet, when handwriting, not only does one feel the resistance of the tip of the pen against the texture of the page and against the command of one's brain, but, more importantly, one experiences the feelings of inadequacy and incapability one felt as a child, when one was learning to form letters. These "ancient feelings" also draw one back to the first steps of humanity, since Ted Hughes sees in handwriting "a subtext of a rudimentary picture language."[3] Resistance is the sign of a split between the brain and the body, between the childhood self and the adult self, between prehistory and contemporary history, and writing is tantamount to bridging these gaps. In other words, resistance can be seen as the cause of Ted Hughes's writing; the struggle against resistance, the struggle for expression, would be his poetic method; and overcoming the resistance to be whole again, might be considered his lyrical and ethical aim, his "poethical"[4] aim, to take up Jean-Claude Pinson's coinage, in *Habiter en poète* (1995), a book that takes up Martin Heidegger's understanding of Hölderlin's phrase to analyze its meaning and bearing on contemporary French poetry.

Indeed, Ted Hughes, in his poems, critical essays and prose pieces, dreams of finding a way to "dwell" poetically that would both question and motivate the link between living and writing. More than loco-descriptive poetry in which verse is at the service of place, his works do not give precedence to one over the other but intermingle the two, constantly searching how a sense of place has influenced his poetry[5] and how his poetry can change the place we live in.[6] This is most notably the case in three works in which the poet comes back to his native Yorkshire: the essay "The Rock,"[7] which describes the gloomy and ominous shadow cast by Scout Rock at Mytholmroyd, his hometown; the collection *Remains of Elmet*,[8] which traces the history of the region from the ancient Celtic kingdom of Elmet to the Calder Valley the poet grew up in; and *Elmet*,[9] a reworked version of the previous collection in which the poet draws particular attention to the inhabitants of the region and especially to his own family as well as including an extended preface in which he delineates the history of the place through the ages. Taken together, these three pieces tell the story of how Edward Hughes from Mytholmroyd came to be Ted Hughes, a poet who forced his expression against built-in resistances and gained worldwide recognition.[10]

The Calder Valley is situated in Yorkshire, in the North of England, which is historically famous for its seditious character, from the Northumbrian resistance to centralization in the Middle Ages, to the Wars of the Roses, the Pilgrimage of Grace or the Northern Rising during the Renaissance, to the debate on devolution at the beginning of the 21st century.[11] This drive towards sedition informed much dialect poetry and broadsheet ballads in the 19th century,[12] but also more contemporary poets such as Basil Bunting (1900–1985) and Tony Harrison (1937–). Ted Hughes has proved himself eager to turn such a poetic *topos* of resistance associated with the North into the North as a *locus* of poethical resistance. Indeed, the way up north, back to his childhood, is the way for him to try and mend the severance of man from nature and find salvation. However the fact that the poet had to come back and write about the North over and over again shows that the place and the word resist him. Analyzing the three works as milestones in his career will enable us to delineate the evolution of his poetic style.

In spite of his continued interest in his native region, Hughes was known for being protective of his private life: "The Rock" shows his resistance to autobiographical readings of his poetry; *Remains of Elmet* turns life into myth, whereas *Elmet* unashamedly uses autobiographical facts. His work on the

North therefore redefines lyricism from impersonality to impersonification. Besides, the three works depict the valley in the constant throes of agony. *Agon*— or struggle — is everywhere to be found as the natural process that drives (*agein*) history, especially in *Remains of Elmet*: the valley has been fighting against the forces of industrialization, Methodism, the Enlightenment, technological warfare.[13] Nature and culture, like two armies are therefore opposed and resistance becomes a means to achieve salvation through a search for equilibrium. In *Elmet*, the inhabitants of the valley do not so much resist as endure mechanically and try to survive. Yet the possibility of dwelling poetically in a disenchanted world raises the question of the meaning of the poetry of place itself.

"The Rock" and the Resistance to Autobiographical Readings

One of the many definitions of the word resistance reads "opposition, freq. unconscious, to allowing memories or desires which have been repressed as unacceptable or disruptive to emerge into the conscious mind."[14] Interestingly enough, Ted Hughes wrote his first poems by doing exactly the opposite, which, in a letter to his sister Olwyn Hughes dated 1962, he finally deemed counter-productive:

> I'm aghast when I see how incredibly I've confined & stunted my existence, when I compare my feeling of what I could be with what I am. What I am, is completely a consequence of certain ideas which I arrived at quite rationally & imposed like laws. Such as my decision, when I read Jung when I was 18, to inhibit all conscious thought & fantasy, so that my unconscious would compensate with an increased activity — maybe it worked but it rendered me so incapable of mental control & deliberate mental play that my whole life has been shut up in a self-imposed curfew.[15]

By the time he was 32, Hughes had understood that control over and resistance to the figments of his conscious mind was a sham that stiffened his poetic activity. In the same letter, there is a draft poem called "Heptonstall," after the name of the Yorkshire village where Sylvia Plath would be buried a few months later, a poem which Hughes calls "experimental & lyrical."[16] This poem is followed by considerations on the relocation of his wife, whom he was separated from by then, in Spain. The poet fiddles with the psychological mechanism of resistance to turn its workings into a poetic paradigm — the conscious and the unconscious minds, poetic writing, the question of the lyrical voice, the North, Sylvia Plath and death are intermingled and constitute a lens through which his work can be understood.

It then comes less as a surprise that, only seven months after Plath committed suicide, the first piece he published, "The Rock," is a short text in prose in which he describes the effect his native region had on him. The fact that he does not mention his wife at all should not read as a refusal to deal publicly with the traumatic event. There is no doubt that critics and readers eager to learn scandalous revelations about the tragic death of the poetess must have been disappointed: Hughes's first official statement is a demonstration that putting ostensibly to the fore his private life could not be further from his mind. Yet the piece teasingly relies on autobiography since it describes the poet's native region, its inhabitants, its atmosphere and the different adventures that nourished Hughes as a budding poet. Scout Rock becomes a site of resistance to the traumatic event of mourning, taking up all the space Plath, the cause of the trauma, cannot take yet.

"The Rock" is deeply influenced by William Wordsworth's poems of revisiting such as "Tintern Abbey" or "Yarrow Revisited," as well as by the Romantic poet's claim that "the child is father of the man."[17] In this prelude to Hughes's poetic collections on the North, in this prose version of the growth of his poetic mind, parts of the Yorkshire landscape are imbued with emotions, so that pathetic fallacy is one structuring pattern. For instance, the depression of the valley is not only geomorphologic but also spiritual, since the inhabitants are all depressed. The way out of this depression is the way up Scout Rock to the moorland where, in the pure Romantic fashion, the physical elevation is also spiritual (it brings a feeling of elation) and aesthetic (it gives a sense of the sublime).

The overtly Romantic inspiration of this piece is actually corrected by Hughes' use of the Modernist notion of "objective correlative"—"a set of objects, a situation, a chain of events which shall be the formula of that particular emotion; such that when the external facts, which must terminate in sensory experience, are given, the emotion is immediately evoked," as Eliot defined it.[18] Indeed, by the end of the text, the rock has become the objective correlative to melancholy, and the simple mention of its name or of the matter it is made of evokes that particular emotion. The weight of the stone evokes the *gravitas* of the North.

Sylvia Plath is present *in absentia*. First, she had written "Ocean-1212-W"[19]—a revisiting of the place where her grandparents lived and where she used to spend her holidays as a child—only a few months before Ted Hughes wrote "The Rock." Hughes had had her text published in *The Listener* just one month before he published his own text in the same magazine, which can therefore be read as his own northern version of Plath's text. This is one more example of the collaboration of the two poets, even beyond the grave. Plath had also written quite a few mineral poems after her visits to Hughes's parents' house in Yorkshire,[20] poems in which rock — the element that rules over the valley — takes center stage. Finally, the poet's strategy of radical avoidance fails and her image, far from being erased, resurfaces, most notably when the poet alludes to suicides in the region: "The oppression cast by that rock was a force in the minds of everyone there. I have heard that valley is notable for its suicides, which I can believe, and I could also believe that rock is partly to blame for them."[21] Plath committed suicide in London but she is buried in Heptonstall at the heart of the Calder Valley. In Hughes's text, her ghostly presence is therefore everywhere to be felt.

So, instead of dealing head on with his wife's suicide, Hughes draws a map of his own psyche and poetics. Paradoxically this resistance to the traumatic event led him, maybe not to a period of writer's block, but at least to a decade in which theoretical writing and children's poetry took precedence over poetry for adults. Breaking down the resistance and allowing the trauma to inform the poem meant embarking on a quest for Sylvia. This is the quest he started on in *Remains of Elmet*. The collection is indeed one that believes in the therapeutic function of poetic writing and is considered by many critics as a turning point in his poetic career.

Yet, even in this collection, the poet resists the autobiographical temptation of the almighty "I" and writes what he calls "impersonal mood pieces" instead, that is to say, rather short poems focusing on the atmosphere — climatic and spiritual — of the region.[22] The sense of impersonality is created by the scarcity of first and second personal pronouns (there are less than fifteen occurrences of "I," "you" and "we") and by the use of impersonal structures. Instead of an "I" describing the place or narrating a story, a de-centered eye, maybe a third eye or the eye of nature itself, offers snapshots of the place, and the impression of impersonality is enhanced by Fay Godwin's photographs.

Throughout the collection, Plath's presence becomes more and more conspicuous. She first appears under the many guises of the Great Goddess — from the unleashed winds that howl and threaten destruction in "Where the Mothers,"[23] to the motherly and fecund natural elements in "Curlews in April."[24] The natural landscape of the region is thus imbued with her metamorphic presence. However, she is less a physical presence than an auditory one — she is to be found in the many sounds of nature, in the wind, in the cries of new-born animals, in the songs of birds. She is progressively fleshed out, first as Catherine Earnshaw at Heathcliff's window in "You Claw the Door,"[25] then as a version of the author of *Wuthering Heights* suffering from pneumonia on the moorland in "Emily Brontë,"[26] and then as her own self, "Sylvia," flanked with her *Doppelgänger*, "Esther," in "Heptonstall Cemetery."[27] She is therefore present, but dying and finally dead.

The last poem, "The Angel" reads as a sort of poem *à clé*, in which the "square of satin"[28] the angel is wearing refers, according to Ann Skea,[29] to the way Plath had been dressed in her casket. This square of satin is to be seen in a dream and is enigmatic — the poet admits he could not make any sense of "that strange head-dress"; at the end, he cannot lift the veil but he can touch it, thus taking a symbolical step towards accepting the horror of what happened, putting it behind, or more precisely, "under [his] feet" i.e. in the earth and in his verse, where everything can be regenerated.[30] *Remains of Elmet* thus mythologizes Sylvia Plath's death to place it at the heart of Hughes's poetics.

Fifteen years later, in *Elmet*, Hughes seems to have overcome his trauma — he mentions the poetess right from the start as a dead person and does not transform her into a myth of regeneration, for instance in "Two Photographs at Top Withens."[31] The image of Plath endures — she has her former shape, her former self, that of a poetess and a necromancer, a voice, a poetic voice, a voice of the past. Yet the reader will have to wait another four years, till 1998 and the publication of *Birthday Letters*, to see the poet taking stock of his first marriage.

Hughes's resistance to the inscription of Plath as his wife in his poetry, his resistance to the handling of autobiographical data, has led him to work on a redefinition of lyricism, from T.S. Eliot's objective correlative to what Jonathan Bate has called a "song of the earth,"[32] an attempt at finding a cure in the many sounds of nature, to come back to Wordsworth's "spontaneous overflow of powerful feelings [that] takes its origins from emotion recollected in tranquility"[33] — only with a note of despair for the death of the valley.

The Agony of the Valley in Remains of Elmet

In a war context, resistance is defined as an "organized covert opposition to an occupying or ruling power,"[34] be it military, cultural or linguistic. Resistance is not passive, it is a strategy in its etymological sense, that is to say what drives the army. Ted Hughes has many memories of World War Two and of German invasions, which he mentions in such pieces as the note to "A Masque for Three Voices."[35] More importantly, his poems work the symbolical debt he inherited from his father who survived a traumatic experience during the Gallipoli disaster. In "The Rock," he writes that the "the whole region is in mourning for the first world war" and looks like "a pre-first-world-war snapshot of itself, grey and faded, yet painfully bleak and immovable,"[36] and that he and the inhabitants live under the rock as "under the presence of a war, or an occupying army."[37] Trying to get rid of the psychological burden of war and not allow it to be a defining human and cultural experience while recognizing that nature itself is driven by all kinds of wars is one of the paradoxes the poet deals with.

The two poetic collections on the Calder Valley take up the idea of a land at war and give it personal and historical depth. In the very short preface to *Remains of Elmet*, Ted Hughes describes Elmet, the name the valley was given up to the 6th century, as "the last British Celtic kingdom to fall to the Angles."[38] What might be striking is that the founding moment for the identity of the region according to him is not the fusion between the Britons and the Angles but the state of war that preceded it. The invasion of the land by the Vikings is the starting point of other wars to come, most notably World War One, which "bled the valley to death."[39] Yet, in spite of the constant attacks, the North and its inhabitants resist and are regenerated.

In other words, Hughes rewrites history in a slightly different light than that shed by official history books in the sense that he focuses on autochthonous traditions that have been colonized and marginalized. The geographical and historical center of Elmet is displaced from Leeds to Heptonstall so that the medieval kingdom is aligned with the poet's personal space. The history of the valley is filtered through his consciousness, which allows him to shed a light on subjects that have been left unsaid: he gives expression to alternating communal voices (those of the inhabitants but also that of the valley itself) and lists places, martyrs, legends and heroes. The poems themselves contain few toponyms or ethnonyms but refer to local traditions. Furthermore, in the locations of the photographs that "moved [the poet] to write" his poems, Fay Godwin mentions little known places like Abel Cross or Churn-Milk Joan to give two examples. His poetry can be considered as poetry of resistance, dealing with margins, and suggesting an alternative to official history — it is Celtic, not English, just as Yeats's and Heaney's are.

By tracing the history of the region up to the Calder Valley he grew up in the aftermath of the Second World War, Hughes claims a prestigious epitome of political resistance as a poetic paradigm for many other kinds of resistance — to land conquests, the Enlightenment, Methodism, to industrialization and de-industrialization, mass tourism and everything that imposes grids through which the land has to be read. Yet since he did not want to write a historical narrative but his own personal myth of the region, these historical events are not mentioned chronologically throughout the collection but in terms of penetration, dissemination, expansion, as a disease inscribed in the body of the valley, taking many different forms and spreading into every pore of the Calder Valley.

The collection argues that nature and men are in a constant state of war, each trying to resist the attacks of the other. The poet's insistence on the natural cycles of life and death are due to his rejection of Puritanical repression and to his interest in environmental research, which started rather early in his career and became more and more prominent in his poetry. As early as 1970, at the onset of the environmental movement, he had already connected nature, Western culture and Christianity in his poetic version of history:

> The fundamental guiding ideas of our western civilization are against conservation. They derive from reformed Christianity and from Old Testament Puritanism. They are based on the assumption that the earth is a heap of raw materials given to man by God for his exclusive profit and use. The story of mind exiled from nature is the story of western man. It is a story of spiritual romanticism and heroic technological progress. It is a story of decline.[40]

Since nature is not benevolent and men are not noble savages, they are constantly opposed, polarized, at war. The cyclical patterns of victory and defeat inevitably lead to the consumption of the energies of each of the two parties, as the law of entropy has it. On the one hand, men try to control nature through pillaging, colonization, the enslavement of the land — all in the name of progress. They inevitably fail and yet they persist, as if stubbornness were a common trait of theirs. On the other hand, nature does not seem to care about these attacks and is characterized by its survival instinct.[41] The poem suggests that nature resists through transference of energy: men's futile attempts at controlling nature end in corruption and become fertilizers for the soil so that nature is restored to itself. "The poetry of the earth is never dead" as Keats writes in "On the Grasshopper and the Cricket." Nature's resistance to man's destructive bent has led many critics such as Terry Gifford to read the poems as belonging to the genre of eco-poetry.

Therefore, against Cartesianism, Hughes suggests that man should not act as if he owned nature. Some of the poems, such as "Hardcastle Crags," "The Trance of Light" or "Walls" to name but a few,[42] even read as nature itself protesting against the damages caused by the age of Enlightenment, industrialization, Methodism, and intellectualism. This gives way to a messianic reading of the collection, in which redemption can be found if man respects nature, lays down his guard and accepts the mysteries of nature, if he becomes conscious that he is part of the world. Resistance therefore takes on a new meaning as "the opposition offered by one body to the pressure or movement of another."[43] To strike a balance between contradictory forces is one of the lessons of Taoism which deeply inspired Hughes, as Leonard M. Scigaj has shown.[44] The collection desperately tries to enact such harmony between place and people.

Yet balance is hard to find between these contradictory forces, especially since men have trouble remembering and taking stock of the past. History and the past are depicted ambivalently in *Remains of Elmet* since, as was said above, Hughes rewrites history in a way that potentially brings about regeneration, but memory is also under suspicion and the inhabitants suffer from amnesia. Origins keep on receding. For instance in the poem "The Ancient Briton Lay Under his Rock,"[45] children have to dig deeper and deeper to find the grave of their British ancestor, without ever finding it. Yet the collection is rather hopeful because regeneration is considered possible, as Ann Skea has shown.[46] Resistance is not linear but cyclical: it lies in the ability to give in and be reborn. Hence the apparent repetitiveness of some of the poems within and across the collections, which, instead of being a flaw, is really an attempt at finding a form capable of resisting and standing the test of time while at the same time imitating the process of memory loss and recovery.

On the contrary, the second version of *Elmet* is far more pessimistic — balance simply cannot be found because it is impossible to remember, or to speak of history (which is epitomized by the recurring figure of the muted father, unable to tell the horrors he witnessed during the war), or not to become mad because of knowledge, like the lunatic in "Climbing into Heptonstall."[47] *Men* cannot learn his lessons from his past experiences. The story Elmet tells is no longer one of redemption and regeneration but one that wavers between endurance and survival.

Endurance and Survival in Elmet

The OED also defines resistance as "the fact of enduring (pain, hardship, annoyance) (...) duration or continued existence in time. Also, power of lasting, capacity of continued existence."[48] In "The Rock," the inhabitants resist the oppression cast by the shadow of Scout Rock which leaves them no more than half-alive. Endurance to the rock seems to have been passed on from one generation to the next, up to the point that it has become an atavistic character as Hughes states in his introduction to the reading of *Remains of Elmet* for the BBC:

> I used Elmet, then, to signify not just a vaguely featured Celtic and criminal and non-conformist inheritance but a naturally evolved local organism, like a giant protozoa, which is made up of all the earlier deposits and histories animated in a single glance, an attitude, an inflection of speech. If you imagine all those things distilled into a lens with filters and distortions peculiar to the ingredients, then the characteristics of this lens, would be, in a sense, *Remains*

of Elmet. This showed up, commonly at the time, in a bedrock, laconic perversity of character.⁴⁹

In *Elmet*, many of the inhabitants described in the two collections — in "Billy Holt," "Dick Straightup," or "Crown Point Pensioners"⁵⁰ — show such endurance of character, which is linked to the characteristics of the valley itself. More than that, parallels are established between the region and them. One of the dangers linked to the over-determination of place and people is to fall into what Patricia Boyle Haberstroh calls "racial history,"⁵¹ especially when one considers Hughes's depiction of the "shivery"⁵² Pakistanis in Yorkshire and their counterparts, the rhododendrons, unsightly, like "a brass band in India."⁵³ In that context, resistance, understood as the passing of characteristics from one generation to the next sounds like a defense mechanism against otherness that may have dangerous nationalistic undertones.

Yet rampant xenophobia is counteracted in *Remains of Elmet* by the use of foreign traditions, most notably Taoism, to describe the flux of energies that circulate in the valley, and also because the landscape is sometimes Americanized (for instance through the word "badlands," the images of the wilderness and the presence of the moorland which is closer to the American plain than to English enclosures): the valley is really a melting pot of cultures. Such syncretism destabilizes a homogenous description of the region and enables the poem to go beyond localism, provincialism, and regionalism.

In *Elmet*, xenophobia is also kept at bay through humor: the portraits are more numerous and so are the northern characteristics described — taciturnity, physical resistance to unfavorable climate, resistance to death. All this is exemplified in the poem "Football at Slack"⁵⁴ in which the football players, regardless of the bracing weather, the pouring rain and the raging wind, keep on playing football. The sublime description of the unleashed elements turns the football players' pugnacity into a mock-epic. This satiric trend is followed in several other poems, for instance in "Sacrifice"⁵⁵ where the uncle's repeated failures at making money turns him into a puppet of destiny that uses the mechanisms Bergson described in *Le Rire*. Consequently, more often than not, the humor is grim. There is a dark side to the fact that the inhabitants are like machines, in the sense that they are dehumanized. *Elmet* shows that regeneration is no longer possible, that redemption will not and cannot happen.

Besides, Ted Hughes added poems he had already published in previous collections, such as "The Horses," from his first collection, *The Hawk in the Rain*, a poem in which the poet compares the horses to megaliths.⁵⁶ These poems have in common rock and the geographical features of the poet's childhood landscape. Seamus Heaney in "Englands of the Mind," writes: "That rock is the equivalent in his poetic landscape of dialect in his poetic speech. The rock persists, survives, sustains, endures and informs his imagination, just as it is the bedrock of the language upon which Hughes found his version of survival and endurance."⁵⁷ Resistance is deeply ingrained in the language itself through the use of dialect, and in the poetic rhythm through alliterative patterns that are reminiscent of Middle English poetry and especially of the Gawain poet, a poet considered by Ted Hughes, and later Simon Armitage, as an ancestral local poet.

Hughes's narrative of the Calder Valley reads like "a great driving force meeting solid resistance."⁵⁸ He rewrote the same collection so many times that the different versions of *Remains of Elmet* and the poems themselves seem to resist completion. The poetic forms resist categorization — they are certainly not fixed, but are not free either. The lines themselves resist memory and memorization. A feeling will linger but the exact words are soon forgotten, as if poetry itself were resisting total grasp. In that sense, Hughes's poetry is a good example of self-resistance, leading the reader to "read for the resistance, not in spite of it."⁵⁹ One could therefore say that the project is overcoming resistance to be whole again is a failure since fragmentation of everywhere to be found. Yet it would be more genuine to Ted Hughes's project to claim that fragmentation — the resistance to wholeness — is the very nature of man's "dwelling" and has to find an expression in poetry. Only this way can man, the world he lives in and the word be connected.

Ted Hughes's collections on the Calder Valley epitomize the many definitions of the word resistance. "The Rock," *Remains of Elmet* and *Elmet* all resist rationalism, Cartesianism, the Enlightenment, and historic optimism — in other words, they all resist the injunctions of modernity. In that sense, Ted Hughes can be said to be an "anti-modern" to use Antoine Compagnon's phrase in his essay, *Les Anti-Modernes*. However, Hughes's resistance is not reactionary, but a way for him to think of the way we inhabit the earth. His life-long poetic treatment of the region he grew up in is not akin to melancholy or nostalgia, but it enacts, in a poethical manner, a poetic dwelling.

Notes

1. Drue Heinz, "Ted Hughes : The Art of Poetry LXXI" in *Paris Review* 37 :134 (Spring 1995, 54–94), 65.
2. Heinz, "Ted Hughes : The Art of Poetry LXXI," 65.
3. Heinz, "Ted Hughes : The Art of Poetry LXXI," 65.
4. Jean-Claude Pinson, *Habiter en poète : Essai sur la poésie contemporaine* (Seyssel : Champ Vallon, 1995).

5. The recent discovery of some of his letters to his sister Olwyn Hughes has shown how critical he was of the negative influence the U.S. had on his creativity for instance.

6. Terry Gifford has shown how the poet's two collections on the Calder Valley have led to a renewed interest in the region as a touristic place. Terry Gifford, "'Dead Farms, Dead Leaves': Culture as Nature in *Remains of Elmet* and *Elmet*" in *Ted Hughes: Alternative Horizons*, Ed. Joanny Moulin (London: Taylor and Francis, 2005), 23–31.

7. Ted Hughes, "The Rock," *The Listener* 19 September 1963 (421–423).

8. Ted Hughes, *Remains of Elmet* (London: Faber and Faber, 1979).

9. Ted Hughes, *Elmet* (London: Faber and Faber, 1994).

10. There is actually yet another version of this collection still under the title of *Remains of Elmet* published in *Three Books* in 1993, but since it was to be read as part of a triptych including *Cave Birds* and *River*, we shall not analyse it here.

11. Helen Jewell, *The North-South Divide: The Origins of Northern Consciousness in England* (Manchester: Manchester University Press, 1994).

12. Martha Vicinus, *The Industrial Muse: A Study of Nineteenth-Century British Working-Class Literature* (London: Croom Helm; New York: Barnes and Noble, 1974).

13. Cf. Patricia Boyle Haberstroh, "Historical Landscape in Ted Hughes's *Remains of Elmet*" in *CLIO* 14 (1985, 137–154).

14. *Oxford English Dictionary* (Oxford: Oxford University Press, 1989), vol. XIII, 717.

15. Christopher Reid (ed.), *Letters of Ted Hughes* (London: Faber and Faber, 2007), 204.

16. Reid, *Letters of Ted Hughes*, 205.

17. William Wordsworth, "My heart leaps up when I behold," *Poetical Works* (Oxford: Oxford University Press, 1936), 62.

18. T.S. Eliot, "Hamlet and His Problems," *The Sacred Wood: Essays on Poetry and Criticism* (London; New York: Routledge, 1989), 101–102.

19. Sylvia Plath, "Ocean 1212-W.," *The Listener* 29 August 1963, 312.

20. "November Graveyard," "The Snowman on the Moor," "Hardcastle Crags," "Two Views of Withens," "The Great Carbuncle," "Wuthering Heights" to name but a few.

21. Ted Hughes, "The Rock," 421.

22. Christopher Reid, *Letters of Ted Hughes*, 133.

23. Ted Hughes, *Remains of Elmet*, 10.

24. Ted Hughes, *Remains of Elmet*, 28.

25. Ted Hughes, *Remains of Elmet*, 95.

26. Ted Hughes, *Remains of Elmet*, 96.

27. Ted Hughes, *Remains of Elmet*, 122.

28. Ted Hughes, *Remains of Elmet*, 124.

29. Ann Skea, *Ted Hughes: The Poetic Quest* (University of New England: University of New England Press, 1994), 254.

30. Ted Hughes, *Remains of Elmet*, 124.

31. Ted Hughes, *Remains of Elmet*, 19.

32. Jonathan Bate, *The Song of the Earth* (Cambridge: Harvard University Press, 2000).

33. William Wordsworth, "Preface to the Second Edition of the *Lyrical Ballads* (1802)," *Poetical Works*, 740.

34. *Oxford English Dictionary*, vol. XIII, 717.

35. Ted Hughes, *The Collected Poems of Ted Hughes* (London : Faber and Faber, 2003), 1219–1222.

36. Ted Hughes, "The Rock," 422.
37. Ted Hughes, "The Rock," 421.
38. Ted Hughes, *Remains of Elmet*, 8.
39. Ted Hughes, *Remains of Elmet*, 34.
40. Ted Hughes, "Review of Max Nicholson's *The Environmental Revolution*," *Winter Pollen: Occasional Prose* (London: Faber and Faber, 1995), 129.
41. Ted Hughes, *Remains of Elmet*, 14.
42. Ted Hughes, *Remains of Elmet*, 13, 20, 33.
43. *Oxford English Dictionary*, vol. XIII, 717.
44. L.M. Scigaj, "The Ophiolatry of Ted Hughes" in *Twentieth-Century Literature* 31: 4 (1985, 380–398).
45. Ted Hughes, *Remains of Elmet*, 84.
46. Ann Skea, "Regeneration in *Remains of Elmet*" in *The Challenge of Ted Hughes*, Ed. Keith Sagar (London: St Martin's Press, 1994).
47. Ted Hughes, *Elmet* (London: Faber and Faber, 1994), 117–118.
48. *Oxford English Dictionary*, vol. V, 236.
49. Ted Hughes, *Poems and Short Stories*. "The Spoken Word" series, British Library: BBC, 2008.
50. Ted Hughes, *Elmet*, 51, 78, 89.
51. Patricia Boyle Haberstroh, "Historical Landscape in Ted Hughes's *Remains of Elmet*" in *CLIO* 14 (1985, 137–154), 137.
52. Ted Hughes, *Remains of Elmet*, 107.
53. Ted Hughes, *Remains of Elmet*, 87.
54. Ted Hughes, *Elmet*, 16.
55. Ted Hughes, *Elmet*, 124.
56. Ted Hughes, *Elmet*, 100.
57. Seamus Heaney, "Englands of the Mind," *Finders Keepers: Selected Prose 1971–2001* (London: Faber, 2002), 85.
58. Ted Hughes, "Ted Hughes and *Gaudete*" in *Ted Hughes: The Unaccommodated Universe*, Ed. Ekbert Faas (Santa Barbara: Black S. Press, 1980), 214.
59. James Longenbach, *The Resistance to Poetry* (Chicago: Chicago University Press, 2004), XII.

Works Cited

Compagnon, Antoine (2005), *Les Anti-Modernes: de Joseph de Maistre à Roland Barthes*. Paris: Gallimard.

Eliot, T.S. (1989), "Hamlet and His Problems," in *The Sacred Wood: Essays on Poetry and Criticism*. London; New York: Routledge.

Faas, Ekbert (1980), *Ted Hughes: The Unaccommodated Universe*. Santa Barbara: Black S. Press.

Haberstroh, Patricia Boyle (1985), "Historical Landscape in Ted Hughes's *Remains of Elmet*" in *CLIO*, 14, 137–154.

Heaney, Seamus (2002), *Finders Keepers: Selected Prose 1971–2001*. London: Faber and Faber.

Heinz, Drue (1995), "Ted Hughes: The Art of Poetry LXXI," in *Paris Review*, 37 :134 (Spring), 54–94.

Hughes, Ted (2003), *The Collected Poems of Ted Hughes*. London: Faber and Faber.
_____ (1994), *Elmet*. London: Faber and Faber.
_____ (2008), *Poems and Short Stories* in "The Spoken Word" series (British Library: BBC).
_____ (1979), *Remains of Elmet*. London: Faber and Faber.
_____ (1963), "The Rock," *The Listener* (19 September), 421–423.
_____ (1995), *Winter Pollen: Occasional Prose*. London: Faber and Faber.
Jewell, Helen (1994), *The North-South Divide: The Origins of Northern Consciousness in England*. Manchester: Manchester University Press.
Longenbach, James (2004), *The Resistance to Poetry*. Chicago : Chicago University Press.
Moulin, Joanny (ed.) (2005), *Ted Hughes: Alternative Horizons*. London: Taylor and Francis.
Pinson, Jean-Claude (1995), *Habiter en poète : Essai sur la poésie contemporaine*. Seyssel : Champ Vallon.
Plath, Sylvia (2002), *The Collected Poems*. London: Faber.
_____ (1963), "Ocean 1212-W.," *The Listener* (29 August), 312–313.
Reid, Christopher (ed.) (2007), *Letters of Ted Hughes*. London: Faber and Faber.
Sagar, Keith (ed.) (1994), *The Challenge of Ted Hughes*. London: St Martin's Press.
Scigaj, L.M. (1985), "The Ophiolatry of Ted Hughes," in *Twentieth-Century Literature*, 31: 4, 380–398.
Skea, Ann (1994), *Ted Hughes: The Poetic Quest*. University of New England: University of New England Press.
Vicinus, Martha (1974), *The Industrial Muse: A Study of Nineteenth-Century British Working-Class Literature*. London: Croom Helm; New York: Barnes and Noble.
Wordsworth, William (1936), *Poetical Works*. Oxford: Oxford University Press.

PART IV: THE CELTIC STRAIN

10. "The Embattled Stance"
Late Yeats
Elizabeth Muller

Yeats's poetry might aptly be termed an art of resistance, owing partly to his Platonic conception of the poet's role.[1] In effect, poets are demiurges with a mission, that of recreating the world. They ignore so-called "reality," dismissed as "the struggle of the fly in marmalade,"[2] and go about their own business, which is to write about another reality no one has ever seen, for a public which does not exist, like Yeats's fisherman, his ideal audience: "A man who doesn't exist, / a man who is but a dream."[3] Following the rules of this archetypal art, artists are supposed to struggle against the kind of reality which does not accord with the ideal. Thus Yeats also undertook to change the world and, consequently, embarked upon numerous crusades which are, on the whole, considered legitimate, at least as regards the early and middle stages of his career: Yeats in his fight to revive "Irish self-confidence"[4] and his stand against the British Empire is a welcomed familiar figure. Yeats's middle career when he acquired his zest for rhetoric and vented his spleen against the Dublin middle classes and the Catholic clergy is also deemed acceptable. Yet his later public stand has been appraised very differently, and what concerns me here is the disreputable Yeats of the *Last Poems* with his famous (or infamous) resistance to progress, science and democracy. Indeed, critics have often objected to Yeats's late poetry, not on the ground that it is dross but, on the contrary, too-well written, especially when voicing unpopular opinion. As Terence Brown pointedly remarks about "Under Ben Bulben," the poem "could be tolerated easily enough ... were it not so mesmeric a performance."[5] This raises interesting questions about the very nature of literary criticism as shall be argued; but, in order to make out a case for Yeats, I shall examine four of his late poems, all composed during the last year of his life: "Hound Voice," "Under Ben Bulben," "Cuchulain Comforted" and "The Black Tower." The last two were written on the poet's death-bed since he died on January 29th, 1939, and produced "Cuchulain Comforted" on the 13th and

"The Black Tower" on the 21st. All four poems have been appraised differently by critics although they embody the same kind of "embattled stance": each poem is part of a coherent whole while displaying different technical skills. However if scholars and critics have responded warmly to "The Black Tower," and "Cuchulain Comforted," they have often balked at "Hound Voice" and "Under Ben Bulben."

By the late nineteen-thirties, Yeats had long been considered a prominent Modernist, as T. S Eliot was to confirm in an essay dedicated to him: "what Yeats did in the middle and later years is a great and permanent example ... a kind of moral as well as intellectual excellence."[6] Yet in spite of his acceptance into the Modernist clan, Yeats's first form of resistance was his refusal to write free verse and to the very end, he defiantly resorted to the traditional forms of the past: "The Black Tower" is a ballad written in sixains with an incremental refrain; "Under Ben Bulben" exemplifies the ongoing energy of tetrameters, what Helen Vendler has identified as the Yeatsian expository stance[7]; "Hound Voice" is written in rhyme royal, the shorter version of the prestigious ottava rima; and finally "Cuchulain Comforted" is composed in terza rima, the verse form Dante chose for *The Divine Comedy* and the only example of its kind in Yeats's work.

Perhaps the most popular of the four poems is "The Black Tower" which (aside from its prestige as Yeats's very last poem) represents the apotheosis of Yeats's later rebellion. From the outset, the poem makes a cryptic statement in favor of some mysterious fortress which is besieged:

> Say that the men of the old black tower,
> Though they but feed as the goatherd feeds,
> Their money spent, their wine gone sour,
> Lack nothing that a soldier needs,
> That all are oath-bound men:
> Those banners come not in.
>
> There in the tomb stand the dead upright,
> But winds come up from the shore:
> They shake when the winds roar,
> Old bones upon the mountain shake.[8]

The usual interpretation views the "oath-bound men" as resisting the banners of modernity: instead of complying with the times, the soldiers seem bent on waiting for the return of a hypothetical king whose great horn fails to be heard in spite of the treacherous cook's asseverations to the contrary:

> The tower's old cook that must climb and clamber
> Catching small birds in the dew of the morn
> When we hale men lie stretched in slumber

> Swears that he hears the king's great horn.
> But he's a lying hound:
> Stand we on guard oath-bound!⁹

These allusions to a lost king have an Arthurian ring and seem reminiscent of the powerless Fisher King in *The Waste Land* by T. S. Eliot. Furthermore, the missing or sleeping king (who also recalls the sleeping Emperor in the earlier "Byzantium") is a common figure in comparative mythology and stands for some kind of *deus otiosus* or idle god, in other words a god who has turned away from the affairs of men and has let lesser deities rule in his stead.¹⁰ His absence informs "The Black Tower" with the same nostalgia we find in other works of the same period:

> I sing what was lost and dread what was won,
> I walk in a battle fought over again,
> My king a lost king, and lost soldiers my men.¹¹

On a more positive note, the tower is a famous Rosicrucian symbol for the soul's resilience and capacity to withstand the turmoil raging in the outside world: "Our, the true believers,' dwelling place is a dark, grey and sinister castle, bewitched, surrounded by a very thick cloud, so that no one may come near it."¹² As Kathleen Raine remarks: "The symbol of the Tower belongs to Yeats's later work; the tree of life gives place to the edifice of wisdom, whose 'winding ancient stair' becomes the 'steep ascent' of gnosis."¹³ In Greek mythology, the *deus otiosus* is Cronos, also associated with a tower situated near the Greek paradise as attested by Pindar: the souls of the just are said to "travel the road of Zeus to the tower of Kronos, where ocean breezes blow around the Isle of the Blessed."¹⁴ Yeats, who was well-versed in Greek mythology, knew of this association and in "The Black Tower," he offers us an earthly replica: since the tower stands in the realm of everyday reality, all that the oath-bound men can do is resist the banners, not defeat them. This does not detract from the warriors' heroism: quite the contrary, for, as Yeats asserts elsewhere, "The one heroic sanction is that of the last battle of the Norse gods, of a gay struggle without hope."¹⁵ Thus, the poem provides the esoteric dimension courted by many Yeatsian critics and the banners that "come not in" are easily identified as Yeats's own personal refusal to surrender. Furthermore, the poem's allusive multi-layered symbolism has probably ensured its success as it seems to preclude didacticism. Unlike the earlier volume entitled *The Tower* centered around Thoor Ballyllee as the emblematic reification of the poet's life and work, "The Black Tower" regains some of the magical evasiveness of Yeats's early poetry. As such it affords a wider scope for varied interpretations: the decried banners for instance could designate all kinds of enemies, including the poet's own approaching death.

Yet the attentive reader is bound to own that the oath-bound men stand in monolithic fashion, like their dead buried upright, and that they display a fine contempt for "the base born,"[16] the goatherd in the first stanza or the cook in the last one who still has to serve "in the dew of the morn" while "we hale men lie stretched in slumber." This eulogizes what Albright calls "the happy rigidity of hierarchy"[17] and the war-like, epic mood of the poem clearly fore-grounds a fight for an ancient order, which, as Yeats reminds us elsewhere, "cannot long persist without the rule of educated and able men."[18] This "rule of educated and able men" is also what Yeats advocates in *On the Boiler* and that which prompts him to call democracy into question. Such a stand drove Yeats to write more didactic and rhetorical poetry such as "Under Ben Bulben" which was harshly criticized.

The change of title from the original "Creed" or "His Convictions" to "Under Ben Bulben,"[19] is significant as, in his work, Yeats constantly hankers back to a famous crevice on the side of Ben Bulben which is one of the entrances to the other world and a location which he seems to associate with the oracle at Delphi. Thus, in the first station, the poem duly sets the scene, haunted by a fairy host:

> Swear by those horsemen, by those women,
> Complexion and form prove superhuman,
> That pale, long-visaged company
> That airs an immortality
> Completeness of their passions won;
> Now they ride the wintry dawn
> Where Ben Bulben sets the scene.
>
> Here's the gist of what they mean.[20]

This clearly points to the main motif of the poem and its leading thread: the interpenetration of the two worlds, mundane and spiritual, as the supernatural horde instructs the future artists of Ireland. Under a certain crevice, beneath the mountain of Ben Bulben, any transmutation is possible, and the chosen title, by reinforcing this magical propensity, mitigates the didactic message. Furthermore, with this first station, Yeats is avowedly targeting the realms of myth and aesthetics, not propounding theories on science and politics.

In the second station, Yeats (via the spirits) states his main declaration of faith in the immortality of the soul by re-affirming his undaunted belief in reincarnation, which (in his opinion) is part of the natural heritage of Ireland:

> Many times man lives and dies
> Between his two eternities,
> That of race and that of soul,

> And ancient Ireland knew it all.
> Whether man dies in his bed
> Or the rifle knocks him dead
> A brief parting from those dear
> Is the worst man has to fear.[21]

The immortality of the soul is indeed the pre-requisite for Yeats's kind of art but it is only one side of the coin since, as regards life on earth, the continuity of family or race provides us with another sort of eternity. What Yeats understands by "race" is of course, as Albright notes, civilization, and more particularly, Ireland, the ship he wishes to steer on the right course: the poem "commands poets to assist in the rebirth of an admirable civilization."[22] Here, as elsewhere in Yeats's work, the reader is reminded of the poet's oft-reiterated view of Ireland as a bastion of Paganism which centuries of Catholicism could never bring to heel. Yeats was never to waver in this: at the beginning of his career, he held that "Ireland under a new cycle would return to paganism and sacrifice a mullet to Artemis"[23]; and in "The Statues," another of Yeats's *Last Poems*, the line "We Irish, born into that ancient sect" points to the secret affinities between Ireland and the Pythagoreans whose belief in reincarnation was notorious.[24] This amply justifies the phrase "And ancient Ireland knew it all" although this allusion to one of Yeats's favorite theories is sometimes overlooked.[25]

The next station of "Under Ben Bulben" is concerned with war, a problematic term, since "war" is often (wrongly) interpreted in the literal sense. In fact, war was an important philosophical concept Yeats had derived from Heraclitus. War in its philosophical acceptation means the principle of life or individuation, and one also has to draw on Empedocles to grasp this notion fully. Empedocles talks of Love as the divine round-shaped *Sphairos* which is all-encompassing. However, if one wants to exist, one has to dissociate oneself from this absolute sphere and gain some form of identity. According to Yeats, this movement of separation from eternity is what Heraclitus calls "war," hence the famous fragment: "War is father of all and king of all."[26] After Yeats became acquainted with the pre–Socratic philosophers, he consistently used the term "war" as synonymous with the forging of an identity, either personal or collective.[27] In this third station Yeats, still the interpreter of the host, addresses the future artists of Ireland as individuals who need to define themselves before accomplishing their task:

> Know that when all words are said
> And a man is fighting mad,
> Something drops from eyes long blind,
> He completes his partial mind,

> For an instant stands at ease,
> Laughs aloud, his heart at peace,
> Even the wisest man grows tense
> With some sort of violence
> Before he can accomplish fate,
> Know his work or choose his mate.[28]

It is clear from these lines that the concept of war needs to be interiorized and that the remaking of the artist precedes his recreating the world. In fact, the stanza simply reformulates Yeats's famous maxim: "We make out of the quarrel with others, rhetoric, but of the quarrel with ourselves, poetry."[29] Interpreting this third station as a battle call for a general extermination of the "base born" mentioned in stanza V does not make much sense, given the last lines of the stanza or the general framework of the poem.

Unsurprisingly, station IV can *now* equate poets with sculptors, the supreme compliment for, in Yeats's later production, sculpture is increasingly equated with a demiurgic kind of poetry:

> Poet and sculptor, do the work,
> Nor let the modish painter shirk
> What his great forefathers did,
> Bring the soul of man to God,
> Make him fill the cradles right.
> Measurement began our might:
> Forms a stark Egyptian thought,
> Forms that gentler Phidias wrought....[30]

We note the importance of measurement and form, with form repeated twice in the second stanza. As mentioned above, the location of the poem, the fairy spot under Ben Bulben where two worlds meet, is the ideal space of magic art, the sort that was practiced in ancient Greece or Egypt. Because of the comparison between Ireland and other prestigious civilizations long gone, Ireland, unlike the rest of Europe, is still this timeless place where hagiography is possible, and the same theme is tackled in "The Statues." As Brown points out, "Yeats's later poetry inhabits a kind of world geography in which ancient Ireland—with its mystic sites, Celtic crosses and mounds—is made to seem the spiritual kin of India, Japan, China, Alexandrine Egypt."[31] Thus, at the end of the first stanza, we note that only a particular kind of artist can "bring the soul of man to God" and "make him fill the cradles right," in other words this improvement of mankind or civilization depends solely on the relation between the artist and God, a pagan God of supernatural forces since the "he" is not capitalized. This movement of ascent to and descent from the supernatural makes the incarnation complete, so that this filling of the cradles can only be grasped as a *figure* for a perfect aesthetic creation in which soul and matter are fused into one, the image somehow suggesting the fabrication of a statue cast in bronze.

In station V, the last before Yeats's famous epitaph, the poet is now ready to drive his Platonic point home:

> Irish poets learn your trade,
> Sing whatever is well-made,
> Scorn the sort now growing up
> All out of shape from toe to top,
> Their unremembering hearts and heads
> Base-born products of base beds....[32]

Since, as we know, ordinary reality has to be molded into shape, it is impossible to understand "out of shape" in any other way but as synonymous with the Platonic *amorphos*, a notion which informs Yeats's entire oeuvre. The theme of evil as shapelessness or unshapeliness relates to a fundamentally Yeatsian tenet and is found very early in his poetry:

> The wrong of unshapely things is a wrong too great to be told
> I hunger to build them anew and sit on a green knoll apart,
> With the earth and the sky and the water, re-made, like a casket of gold[33]

In addition, the phrase "unremembering hearts and heads" designates the reincarnation theory expounded upon in Plato's *Phaedrus*: only the soul who forbears drinking from the waters of Lethe (oblivion) in Hades will be able to remember the Plain of Truth in his/her next life and consequently be reincarnated as "a seeker after wisdom or beauty, a follower of the Muses, and a lover."[34] The "sort" the true artists are meant to scorn, "the base-born hearts and heads" are first and foremost bad artists but, in any case, the statement directly points to souls who suffer from amnesia and have no use for what Yeats called elsewhere "traditional sanctity and loveliness,"[35] while the "base beds" provide a striking contrast with the idyllic "cradles" of the preceding station. Thus it is clear that the stigma attached to "unremembering" or "base born" is moral as well as aesthetic. Yeats's play *Purgatory*, first performed in 1938, highlights his idea of moral responsibility: in this ambiguous play, a noble house is destroyed through the fault of the aristocratic young heiress who falls in love with the loutish groom and marries him. In this plot, one can indeed recognize a defense of hierarchical society, a common stance in authors who advocate resistance to "the degeneration of literature, newspapers, amusements."[36] However, the social prejudice against misalliance in *Purgatory* should not make us forget that the first step towards the ruin of the house is taken by the young girl who feels drawn to the very man bound to destroy her entire heritage. Thus, Yeats's pro-aristocratic bias, which has been so much decried, is never crude, for aristocracy is not an absolute panacea,[37] nor is good "stock" sufficient to ensure the desirable rule of "able and well-educated men." In fact, the moral flaw can be found even among the inheritors of the proper kind of tradition and, in "Meditations in Time of Civil War," Yeats surprisingly faces the possibility of "degeneracy" in his own descendants who may very well prove unworthy of Thoor Ballyllee:

> And what if my descendants lose the flower
> Through natural declension of the soul,
> Through too much business with the passing hour,
> Through too much play, or marriage with a fool?
> May this laborious stairs and this stark tower
> Become a roofless ruin that the owl
> May build in the cracked masonry and cry
> Her desolation to the desolate sky.[38]

Surely, if Yeats's own descendants may conceivably turn out to "lose the flower," their responsibility will be a moral one, similar to the blame which is laid at the young girl's door in *Purgatory*. Indeed, when required to give an explanation for his play, Yeats intimated as much: "In my play, a spirit suffers because of its share, when alive, in the destruction of an honored house; that destruction is taking place all over Ireland today. Sometimes it is the result of poverty, but more often because a new individualistic generation has lost interest in the ancient sanctities."[39]

The "base-born" in Yeats's "Under Ben Bulben," therefore, are hardly to be equated with any social class but they can be identified as Yeats's enemies throughout his career: politicians, journalists, bad artists, demagogues. This denunciation of commonness starts in Yeats's mid-career as in "The Fisherman," where the poet bemoans the state of mercantile Dublin in lines which are reminiscent of *Hamlet*:

> The craven man in his seat
> The insolent unreproved....
> The witty man and his joke
> Aimed at the commonest ear
> The clever man who cries
> The catch-cries of the clown,
> The beating down of the wise
> And great art beaten down.[40]

Yet the wealthy Philistines of Dublin and, more generally, the rule of money is a constant preoccupation in poems where "base" simply means "rich":

> I lived among great houses,
> Riches drove out rank,
> Base drove out the better blood,
> And mind and body shrank.
> No Oscar ruled the table....[41]

In this, Yeats follows the Modernists' lead and their fear of *Usura* taking over the world,[42] but the warning against a sort of standardized sub-culture which transforms individuals into an amorphous mob begins even earlier. One thinks of George Gissing and the quarter-educated, also denounced by Oscar Wilde, hence, possibly, the conspicuous absence of Oscar, the poet and wit, at the table of the newly rich.

Finally, as might be expected, the new poets of Ireland in "Under Ben Bulben" are exhorted to find their inspiration in the past:

> Cast your mind on other days
> That we in coming days may be
> Still the indomitable Irishry.[43]

The "indomitable Irishry" has caused much heated debate but Yeats, being Anglo-Irish himself as well as often criticized for not being "really Irish," could never think of "the indomitable Irishry"[44] as a "race" in our present understanding of the term but rather in the more general sense of the Greek *genos* which can mean anything from a family or a clan to a group of people or a culture. What Yeats means by "Irishry" can be much clarified by his oft-reiterated belief in Ireland's superiority over England: England had been destroyed by the leveling wind and had "shaped itself in the printing press,"[45] a fate Ireland should avoid at all cost. In Yeats's mind, Ireland still retained a traditional art with a vivid oral tradition exemplified by itinerant poets such as Raftery, the Irish Homer. This poetry of the wandering beggar, fiddler or countryman was what Yeats hoped to perpetuate in his country: "In Ireland today the old world that sang and listened is, it may be for the last time in Europe, face to face with the world that reads and writes."[46]

As a partial conclusion regarding "Under Ben Bulben," the poem certainly deserves better than the misrepresentation to which it is frequently subjected by hasty readers who often isolate one or two lines to quote the phrase out of context and give it an ugly twist. This results in a nasty caricature which a serious study of Yeats's whole opus simply cannot countenance. While reviewing any poem of Yeats's late period (and this is particularly true of "Under Ben Bulben"), it is of paramount importance not to mistake "the part for the whole" and to take into account the larger picture of the poet's philosophy.[47]

"Hound Voice" has also been severely criticized by Terence Brown as "a fluently nasty celebration of social elitism, of terror transcended in bloodlust," a judgment which, again, seems widely off the mark, for the text refers to a hunt of an immaterial kind.[48] It is true that, in Yeats's poetry, horses frequently appear in connection with aristocratic characters such as Major Gregory and above all Con Markiewicz, conspicuous for her clear voice and superb horsewomanship.[49] Her presence is suggested in the first and second stanza:

> Because we love bare hills and stunted trees
> And were the last to choose the settled ground,
> Its boredom of the desk or of the spade, because
> So many years companioned by a hound,
> Our voices carry; and though slumber bound,
> Some few half wake and half renew their choice,
> Give tongue, proclaim their hidden name — "hound voice."
>
> The women that I picked spoke sweet and low
> And yet gave tongue. "Hound voices" were they all.[50]

Con Markiewicz was a revolutionary whose radical politics antagonized Yeats but she came from an aristocratic family of the Ascendancy and, as such, was one of the members of the Anglo-Irish community whom Yeats admired because "They gave though free to refuse."[51] However, the poem tackles another reality than the realm of politics — the ghostly company is described in Yeats's best "Host of the Sidhe" manner.[52] The mysterious hunters are all "slumber bound/Some few half-awake," which sounds reminiscent of the men in "The Dark Tower" and, in addition, they seem associated with the hound as a totemic animal. This hound immediately suggests Cerberus, the dog which guards the gate to the other world, and the word "hound," repeated at different places and in different contexts, conveys a sense of the ineffable, thus raising the poem to a form of incantatory ritual. The choice of the hound fits with Irish mythology as well since it is the totemic animal of the Irish hero, Cuchulain, Yeats's chosen alter ego, whose Gaelic name means either Hound of Culan or Beautiful Hound. The wild ride itself evokes the lord of shades, Hades and his infernal hunt, a common theme in European folklore which Yeats adapted severally in his poetry.[53] Consequently, this grim company is composed of the hordes of the dead riding with ancient gods, as in the first station of "Under Ben Bulben." Finally, the poem is obviously some kind of answer or echo to Pound's "The Return" which Yeats believed was about the return of Pagan gods — hence the mythological allusions and the fantastic fairy ride. This, like "The Black Tower" is a multi-layered poem imbued with mysterious symbolism, although not always recognized as such. Furthermore, the last stanza with its accumulation of strong stresses and slant rhymes betokens the pathos of uncertainty:

> Some day we shall get up before the dawn
> And find our ancient hounds before the door,
> And wide awake know that the hunt is on;
> Stumbling upon the blood-dark track once more,
> Then stumbling to the kill beside the shore;
> Then cleaning out and bandaging of wounds,
> And chants of victory amid the encircling hounds.[54]

Indeed, the kind of victory which is at stake is far from decisive: it might concern the victory of past heroic times returning once more upon the gyre of history, or the victory of beings long dead in some mythical other world which persists alongside our drab reality. However, because of Pound's poem which stresses a painful, slow process of reawakening and in view of Yeats's philosophy in later years, this hunt can be interpreted as a war against the self; thus the same theme is addressed as in the third station of "Under Ben Bulben." The effort and violence implied by expressions such as "bloodtrack," "stumbling to the kill," "bandaging of wound" seem to point to the mysterious war which artists and heroes have to wage before finding their destiny: like Dante, Yeats's perfect artist in "Ego Dominus Tuus," the members of the hunt have set their "chisel to the hardest stone," namely themselves.[55] The "blood-track" is stained with their blood just as the "bandaged wounds" are their wounds and the poem reverberates with the echo of self-inflicted pain.

One final point, a pivotal one, is that Yeats's artists wage a heroic war to reach their mask or contrary self in order to achieve unity of being. This war against the self is another form of resistance in Yeats's poetry, and it is sometimes the sole theme of one poem, as is the case, I believe, in "Hound Voice"; at other times, Yeats composes two totally conflicting poems answering one another like reflecting mirrors. In the last two poems Yeats ever wrote, the effect is uncanny: nothing is further removed from the staunch men of "The Black Tower" than the apparent pliancy we find in "Cuchulain Comforted."

"Cuchulain Comforted" takes place in the after-life, which justifies the use of Dante's favored terza rima. Yet the description fits Homer's *Odyssey* much more closely for, as in the Greek Hades, the shades "seem not to know they are dead and continue after death in the activities and thoughts of the last moments on earth."[56] Thus Cuchulain is still haunted by his violent demise and, like Achilles in the last book of Homer's *Odyssey*, has difficulty reconciling himself to his new shadowy existence.

> A man that had six mortal wounds, a man
> Violent and famous, strode among the dead;
> Eyes stared out of the branches and were gone.
>
> Then certain Shrouds that muttered head to head
> Came and were gone. He leant upon a tree
> As though to meditate on wounds and blood.[57]

As in the Homeric after-life, the lesser shades are transformed into birds or bats flitting about in the trees: "Eyes stared out of the branches and were gone."[58] In Yeats's poem, those lesser dead turn into singing voices wrapped in shrouds and they manage to convince Cuchulain to sing and weave, a rather unexpected occupation for the arch-hero of Ireland:

> "We thread the needles' eyes, and all we do
> All must together do." That done, the man
> Took up the nearest and began to sew.[59]

To add to the incongruity, the shrouds are "convicted cowards all" and, consequently, represent the hero's anti-selves.

> "Now must we sing and sing the best we can,
> But first you must be told our character:
> Convicted cowards all, by kindred slain
> Or driven from home and left to die in fear."
> They sang, but had nor human tunes nor words,
> Though all was done in common as before[60];

In Yeatsian or neo–Platonic lore, this is a stage of purification after death known as the Shiftings in which, Yeats explains, "the victim must ... live the act of cruelty, not as victim but as tyrant; whereas the tyrant must ... become the victim."[61] The result of such an exchange will be purgation so that a new life may begin — the shrouds of the poem symbolizing the bodies of the next incarnation. The cowards, therefore, compensate and redeem their past cowardice through Cuchulain's own valor, whereas the Irish hero, a man of violence, agrees to embrace the opposite of what he is. The result is perfect harmony, hence the last line of the poem: "They had changed their throats and had the throats of birds." Of course, the weaving of linen as well as the singing are famous classical metaphors for the art of poetry, and the poem deserves much better than this summary; but the very idea of the Shiftings is that of tolerance, an acceptance of whatever is most alien to one's nature which counter-balances the rigidity we find in the other more war-like poems of the same period. Yet embracing one's opposite cannot be achieved without inner struggle, and this fight for unity within the self constitutes the ultimate form of resistance in Yeats's poetry.

To conclude, when confronted with Yeats's later work, critics often seem to beg the question like Terence Brown on "The Statues" and "A Bronze Head": both poems are said to "endow elitist poetry with a terrible sublimity. A rhetoric and imagery of the sublime allow a politics of elitist prejudice to *seem* a form of heroic spirituality."[62] Yet if the poems express an ideal of "heroic spirituality" by means of "a rhetoric and imagery of the sublime," reading "elitist prejudice" into them smacks of arbitrariness. As Jonathan Allison points out, this sort of criticism "raises an interesting question about the aesthetics of the late poetry, whereby that which is most attractively seductive ("mesmeric") is perceived to be the most objectionable and dangerous," the basic assumption being that "Yeats is at his most dangerous when he is most enchanting and persuasive."[63] So poetic skill, it seems, is not what is in question, but the impropriety of voicing objectionable ideas. This retaliates on Yeats's didacticism with a vengeance, to say nothing of the dubiousness of judging poetry on ethical or political grounds.[64] Another alternative is amusingly rebutted by Yvor Winters: "We have been told many times that we do not have to take the ideas of W. B. Yeats seriously in order to appreciate his poetry; but if this is true, Yeats is the first poet of whom it has ever been true."[65] My own contention is that we can neither reject good poetry on the grounds that it is "nasty" nor claim a poem merely derives its force from its "mesmeric" style — form and matter are not to be dissociated, especially in the case of Yeats whose poetry was informed by philosophy all his life. That this philosophy was sometimes "esoteric" and often drew upon the more obscure texts of Antiquity does not signify: one just has to make the effort even though, as Kathleen Raine remarks, Yeats's poetry often reaches beyond the pale of "such things as critics discuss."[66]

In fine and despite all detractors, Yeats's last poems, poems of resistance as they are, can be perceived as poems about freedom to which, indeed, the poet's entire philosophy bears witness, revolving as it does around the opposition between losing oneself in the exterior world, or freeing oneself from it[67]: this emancipation Yeats calls "war," a Thermopylae of the mind which entails merciless work upon the self and a complete disregard for public opinion. In *On the Boiler*, what Yeats deplores about democracy is not that it ensures liberty but that it produces an illusion of liberty which in fact aims at making everyone alike: "Try to be popular and you think another man's thought."[68] In spite of Yeats's interest in eugenics, his aim was never to duplicate any form of ideal hero *ad infinitum* but, on the contrary, to contribute to the making of what he called free "upstanding men."[69] This entailed resisting those who tried to substitute "for the old humanity with its unique irreplaceable individuals something that can be chopped and measured like a piece of cheese."[70] Yeats's uncompromising plea for freedom has been duly recognized by critics such as Edna Longley, who contends that his "individual voice opposes propaganda and conformity."[71] Similarly, Seamus Heaney holds that Yeats is essentially a non-conformist and that a great poet should have the right to be judged on his own terms: "I assume that this peremptoriness, this apparent arrogance is exemplary in an artist, that it is proper and even necessary for him to insist on his own language, his own vision, his own term of reference."[72] However, I shall let the infamous Yeats conclude for himself. In *On the Boiler*, Yeats opposes mere "mass instinct" to the Sophoclean ethos, and quotes from the chorus in *Oedipus the King*:

> ... I would be praised as a man,
> That in my words and deeds I have kept those laws in mind
> Olympian Zeus, and that high, clear Empyrean,
> Fashioned, and not some man or people of mankind.[73]

Notes

1. The title of this essay, "The Embattled Stance," is borrowed from a phrase in Roy Foster's biography of Yeats: *Yeats, A Life: II The Arch-Poet* (Oxford: Oxford University Press, 2003), xxiii.

2. "Ego Dominus Tuus," W. B. Yeats, *The Poems*, Ed. Daniel Albright (London, Everyman, rev. 1994), 211.

3. "The Fisherman," *The Poems*, 198.

4. Foster, 426.

5. Terence Brown, *The Life of W. B. Yeats* (Dublin: Gill & Macmillan, 1999), 369.

6. "Yeats" in *Selected Prose of T. S. Eliot*, Ed. Frank Kermode (London: Faber & Faber, 1975), 252.

7. Helen Vendler, *Our Secret Discipline* (Cambridge: Belknap Press of Harvard University Press, 2007), 206–208.

8. "The Black Tower," *The Poems*, 378–79.

9. "The Black Tower," *The Poems*, 379.

10. I believe this notion of a *deus otiosus* or sleeping god also informs Eliot's *The Waste Land*.

11. "What Was Lost," *The Poems*, 359.

12. From *Secret Symbols of the Rosicrucians*, given by F. A. C. Wilson, *W. B. Yeats and Tradition* (New York: Macmillan, 1958), 227.

13. Kathleen Raine, *Yeats, the Initiate* (Savage, Maryland: Barnes and Noble Books, 1990), 243. The idea of the tower as representing the fortress of the soul can be found as early as Plato: "they [disruptive desires] seize the citadel of the young man's soul,

finding it empty and unoccupied by studies and honorable pursuits and true discourses ... those braggart discourses close the gates of the royal fortress within him." *Republic,* 560, b, 560, d, *The Collected Dialogues of Plato,* Eds. Edith Hamilton and Huntington Cairns, transl. by Paul Shorey (New York: Pantheon Books, 1961; rev. 1963). The old watch tower beaten by the storms to symbolize the higher soul can also be found in Plotinus (*Enneads,* 4. 8. 2) as Brian Arkins points out in *Builders of My Soul: Greek and Roman Themes in Yeats* (Savage, Maryland: Barnes and Noble Books, 1990), 67.

14. *Pindar I,* Transl. William H. Race (Harvard: Loeb Classical Library, 1997) 71.

15. *W. B. Yeats and Sturge Moore, Their Correspondence 1901–1937,* Ed. U. Bridge (London: Routledge & Kegan Paul, 1953), 154.

16. "Under Ben Bulben," *The Poems,* 375.

17. *The Poems,* 787.

18. *The Variorum Edition of the Poems of W. B. Yeats,* Eds. P. Allt and R. K. Alspach (London: Macmillan, 1957), 543.

19. *The Poems,* 809.

20. "Under Ben Bulben," *The Poems,* 373.

21. "Under Ben Bulben," *The Poems,* 373.

22. *The Poems,* 808.

23. Wilson, *W. B. Yeats and Tradition,* 165. The prophecy according to which the Irish will in time "sacrifice a mullet to Artemis" comes from "Rosa Alchemica." Yeats's early short fiction constantly toys with the idea of an imminent revival of paganism in Ireland. It is the main theme in "Rosa Alchemica," "The Tables of the Law" and "The Adoration of the Magi."

24. *The Poems,* 384.

25. Brown, 369, is a case in point: to him the stanza displays "a charge of savage energy and a cold dogmatic power ('Ancient Ireland knew it all') that makes it especially appalling as a very dubious aesthetic experience."

26. Fragment LXXXIII in Charles Kahn's edition (LIII in Diels'), *The Art and Thought of Heraclitus* (Cambridge: Cambridge University Press, 1981), 67.

27. As Yeats asserts, he started reading the pre–Socratic philosophers as well as other Greek philosophers in the early 1920's after the first proof sheets of *A Vision* came; see *A Vision* (London: Macmillan, 1981; first edn. 1937), 19–20.

28. "Under Ben Bulben," *The Poems,* 374.

29. W. B. Yeats, *Mythologies* (London: Macmillan, 1959), 331.

30. "Under Ben Bulben," *The Poems,* 374.

31. Brown, 353.

32. "Under Ben Bulben," *The Poems,* 375.

33. "The Lover tells of the Rose in his Heart," *The Poems,* 73.

34. *Phaedrus,* 248, d, *The Collected Dialogues of Plato,* Transl. by R. Hackforth,

35. "Coole and Ballylee, 1931," *The Poems,* 294.

36. W. B. Yeats, *Explorations* (London: Macmillan, 1962), 423.

37. If anything, the (for Yeats) disastrous example of the Gore-Booth sisters was definite proof to the contrary: both dedicated their lives to radical politics and dragged out "lonely years conspiring with the ignorant," "In Memory of Eva Gore-Booth and Con Marckiewicz," *The Poems,* 283.

38. Part IV, entitled "My Descendants," *The Poems,* 249.

39. A. Norman Jeffares, *A Commentary on the Plays of W. B. Yeats* (London: Macmillan, 1975), 275.

40. *The Poems,* 197.

41. "A Statesman's Holiday," *The Poems*, 371.
42. See Ezra Pound's Canto XLV (1937), *Selected Poems* (London: Faber & Faber, 1975), 147.
43. *The Poems*, 375.
44. "Under Ben Bulben," *The Poems*, 375.
45. *Explorations*, 206.
46. *Explorations*, 206.
47. This is Augustine Martin's view, given by Jonathan Allison, "The Reception of Yeats in Ireland since 1950" in *The Reception of W. B. Yeats in Europe*, Ed. Klaus Peter Jochum, (London, Continuum, 2006), 243.
48. Brown, 368.
49. In "Easter, 1916" her voice was "sweet ... when she rode to harriers," and in "On a Political Prisoner," she is again hunting under Ben Bulben: "When long ago I saw her ride/Under Ben Bulben to the meet.... She seemed to have grown clean and sweet" in *The Poems*, 228 and 232 respectively.
50. *The Poems*, 388.
51. "The Tower" III, *The Poems*, 244.
52. Countess Markiewicz died in 1927.
53. As Robert Graves points out, in Irish, Welsh, Highland and English folklore, the king of the underworld is a huntsman on a horse accompanied by the Hounds of Hell. *The White Goddess*, (London: Faber and Faber, 1988; first edn. 1961), 50.
54. *The Poems*, 388–89.
55. *The Poems*, 210.
56. Raine, 262.
57. *The Poems*, 379–80.
58. *The Poems*, 380.
59. *The Poems*, 380.
60. *The Poems*, 380.
61. *A Vision*, 238.
62. Brown, 369 (italics mine).
63. Allison, 248.
64. Allison, 244, quotes Denis Donaghue on the subject: according to Donoghue "it is improper to level a political judgment on poetry."
65. Yvor Winters, *The Poetry of William Butler Yeats* (Denver: Alan Swallow, 1960), 1. (Now on Questia Online Library.)
66. Yeats was extremely knowledgeable about the Hellenistic period of Antiquity which is not as thoroughly studied as the Classical one. For instance, apart from Plotinus, he was familiar with Plutarch's essays, Porphyry, Proclus and Iamblichus among others.
67. As Steven Helmling observes, Yeats's "motive [in writing *A Vision*] was surely to enlarge freedom," *The Esoteric Comedies of Carlyle, Newman and Yeats* (Cambridge: Cambridge University Press, 1988), 210.
68. *Explorations*, 410.
69. "The Tower," *The Poems*, 244.
70. *Explorations*, 436
71. Allison, 245.
72. Seamus Heaney, *Preoccupations, Selected Prose 1968–1978* (London: Faber & Faber, 1980), 101.
73. *Explorations*, 443.

Works Cited

Allison, Jonathan (2006), "The Reception of Yeats in Ireland since 1950," in *The Reception of W. B. Yeats in Europe*. Ed. Klaus Peter Jochum. London: Continuum.
Arkins, Brian (1990), *Builders of My Soul: Greek and Roman Themes in Yeats*. Savage, Maryland: Barnes and Noble Books.
Brown, Terence (1999), *The Life of W. B. Yeats*. Dublin: Gill & Macmillan.
Eliot, T. S. (1975), *Selected Prose*. Ed. Frank Kermode. London: Faber & Faber.
Foster, Roy (2003), *W. B. Yeats, A Life, II. The Arch-Poet*. Oxford: Oxford University Press.
Graves, Robert (1988; first edn. 1961), *The White Goddess*. London: Faber and Faber.
Hamilton, Edith, and Cairns, Huntington (1961; rev. edn. 1963), *The Collected Dialogues of Plato*. New York: Pantheon Books.
Heaney, Seamus 1980), *Preoccupations, Selected Prose 1968–1978*. London: Faber& Faber.
Helmling, Steven (1988), *The Esoteric Comedies of Carlyle, Newman and Yeats*. Cambridge:
Cambridge University Press.
Jeffares, Norman, and Knowland, A. S (1975), *A Commentary on the Collected Plays of W. B. Yeats*. London: Macmillan.
Kahn, Charles H. (ed. and transl.) (1981), *The Art & Thought of Heraclitus*. Cambridge: Cambridge University Press.
Pound, Ezra (1975), *Selected Poems 1908–1969*. London: Faber and Faber.
Race, William H. (1997), *Pindar I*. Harvard: Loeb Classical Library.
Raine, Kathleen (1990), *Yeats the Initiate*. Savage, Maryland: Savage and Noble Books.
Vendler, Helen (2007), *Our Secret Discipline*. Cambridge: Belknap Press of Harvard University Press.
Wilson, F. A. C (1958), *W. B. Yeats and Tradition*. New York: Macmillan.
Winters Yvor (1960), *The Poetry of William Butler Yeats*, Denver: Alan Swallow.
Yeats, W. B., and Sturge Moore, T. (1953), *Their Correspondence 1901–1937*. Ed. U. Bridge. London: Routledge & Kegan Paul.
Yeats, W. B.Yeats, W. B. (1981; first edn. 1937), *A Vision*. London: Macmillan.
_____ (1962), *Explorations*. London: Macmillan.
_____ (1959), *Mythologies*. London: Macmillan.
_____ (1994), *The Poems*. Ed. Daniel Albright. London: Everyman.
_____ (1957), *The Variorum Edition of the Poems*. Eds. P. Allt and R. K. Alspach. London: Macmillan.

11. W. B. Yeats and Resistance

Catherine Phillips

W. B. Yeats once famously wrote, *We make out of the quarrel with others, rhetoric, but of the quarrel with ourselves, poetry.*[1] This would seem to suggest that resistance, both to the views of others and within himself, was at the heart of Yeats's intellectual endeavor. And yet, of course, it is not as straightforward as the statement suggests. Not only do the terms sometimes exchange partners so that Yeats quarrels with himself in prose and aggravates others poetically but "quarrel" suggests two opposing positions and Yeats was seldom so simple. I have divided up my investigation of this aspect of his work into three parts: an initial phase in which he sought a "voice"; a mature phase in which resistance molded the form of poems and the organization of volumes of his poetry, and old age, in which some of the struggle had to be in the opposite direction to his earlier efforts.

In December 1921, when Yeats was writing his *Memoirs*, he wrote to Olivia Shakespear, with whom he had had his first liaison, "I send Four Years which is the first third of the complete memoirs. As they go on they will grow less personal, or at least less adequate as personal representation, for the most vehement part of youth must be left out, the only part that one well remembers and lives over again in memory when one is in old age, the paramount part."[2] It was most probably the first version of his very frank Memoirs that Yeats sent. This was not published until 1972. In it Mrs. Shakespear was disguised as Diana Vernon and the course of their affair described openly; the final version published in Yeats's lifetime as his *Autobiography* omitted any mention of her. His poems on the events of the same period are more revealing, though without mentioning names, which Yeats perhaps thought sufficiently discreet. The Memoirs show that "The Lover mourns for the Loss of Love" depicts Mrs. Shakespear's grief when the poet turned away from her on the reappearance after her sojourn in Paris of Maud Gonne, for whom he felt perhaps the deepest love in his life.[3] The statement about the memories of old age is, however, also a generalized claim that Yeats, who was not yet sixty, was in actuality yet to experience.

The autobiographical prose account gives a rather different impression from the poetry and early drama of the poet as a young man. In particular the poems gathered in *The Rose* (1893) often concern unrequited love. They fit neither the "quarrel" with others, nor that with the speaker, who is only too single-minded. The early plays, *The Countess Cathleen* (1899) and *The Shadowy Waters* (1900) fit the same lovesick mode. However, that more was going on is clearer in the prose. As one of the group of young people influenced by the Irish patriot, John O'Leary, Yeats was strategically developing a "voice" that would both speak in an unmistakably Irish way, and would appeal to and educate the Irish people about their own cultural heritage. This meant not only being involved in such practical schemes as the establishing of public libraries, and editing of a series of books to "de-Anglicize" Ireland[4] but also carrying out the literary task of compiling books of Irish legends. He wrote for and edited journals such as *Samhain* and *Beltaine*, in which he espoused polemical views of the value of Irish traditions and set out the nationalist aims of the Irish Literary Theater.[5] Such valuing of national culture was widespread in Europe in the second half of the nineteenth century and in Ireland, as elsewhere, it had political implications. Trumpeting the quality of Irish legends was to resist the derogatory conclusions about them of the official English Education commission, which would report in 1900 that "there was no imagination or idealism in the whole range of Irish Literature."[6] In 1890, reviewing Douglas Hyde's *Beside the Fire*, Yeats was able to claim that there had been published in the previous three years as much Irish mythology as in the preceding fifty.[7] "Our legends," he recorded,

> are always associated with places, and not merely every mountain and valley, but every strange stone and little coppice has its legend, preserved in written or unwritten tradition. Our Irish romantic movement has arisen out of this tradition, and should always, even when it makes new legends about traditional people and things, be haunted by places. It should make Ireland, as Ireland and all other lands were in ancient times, a holy land to her own people.[8]

In his *Autobiography* he writes of his longing to hold a sod of earth from Sligo while he was living in London, a connection with the land he ascribed to "some old race instinct."[9] At this time many of the tales and the main cycles of Irish mythology, the Ulster cycle and the Fenian cycle, were available in Gaelic. Yeats, who was not a strong linguist, had no Gaelic, but Lady Gregory, who befriended him in the 1890s, had learnt it and translated enough to fill several volumes that were published and contributed material for Yeats's poems, plays and prose for the rest of his life.[10] The volumes had complimentary prefaces written by Yeats.

The organization in editions of Yeats's poems tends to emphasize one or other side of his development, so that either the love poems or the Irish ones dominate: Macmillan tucked the long mythological poems at the back of *Collected Poems* and began with the collection called *Crossways* (1889) and its first poem, "The Song of the Happy Shepherd" of 1885. This begins "The woods of Arcady are dead," binding Yeats into an English poetic tradition. More recently, since Macmillan's copyright ran out, Daniel Albright's *W. B. Yeats: The Poems* (1990), in which he generally tried to follow Yeats's proposed final sequence,[11] opens with the long poem, "The Wanderings of Oisin" (1889), in which Oisin is by his second verse paragraph situating the tale he will tell. The heroes were near

> ... the cairn-heaped grassy hill
> Where passionate Maeve is stony-still;
> And found on the dove-grey edge of the sea
> A pearl-pale, high-born lady, who rode
> On a horse with bridle of findrinny; [white bronze][12]

This locates the story near the mountain of Knocknarea where the perhaps historical, perhaps mythological Queen Maeve is said to have been buried in one of the largest cairns in Ireland. Thus Yeats anchors his mythical, imaginary world to physical reality. The location of the relevant beach was probably intended by Yeats as Sligo Bay but today Rossbeigh Beach some two hundred miles to the south is touted by guesthouses as the spot of the meeting, adding romance to the allure for tourists of its natural beauty. The ballad form and romantic story may disguise the subtleties with which Yeats is playing with the genre. The poem's rhymes allude to ballad form with rhymed couplets and wrenched rhymes ("high-born *la dý*," for example) but the pattern is a complex one and is played off against the rhythm; for example, in the passage cited above, a listener would assume that "lady" was placed at the end of a line leaving the section with aa,bbb rhymes and a long last line. Yeats unsettles that expectation, making a more sophisticated rhythm by forcing a pause after "rode." That technical alertness to the form is also evident in the handling of the story, which on one level is simply romance but, on another, plays out allegorically the tensions in the psychology of a young man.

The story is that Oisin, who is one of the mythological Irish heroes called the Fianna, is chosen by Niamh, daughter of the god of the sea, as her lover and rides away with her into the land of the "other folk." He ultimately decides to return to Ireland leaving Niamh behind and the mythological worlds of the lands of dancing and perpetual youth, of heroic conflict and feasting, and of forgetfulness which he has shared with her, in order to try to regain the riskier companionship of his former heroic comrades, though he does give each world a good try — a hundred years apiece. However, when he returns to Ireland, it is to find that the Fianna have died out and the land is under Catholic domination. It is the bleak, harsh lore of the Church as preached to him by St Patrick that Oisin rejects most vehemently. The poem thus sketches out the conflict between a sensual mythology and a repressive Church that Swinburne had elaborated in such poems as "Laus Veneris."[13] Yeats establishes an internal conflict in his protagonist between sensual longing for female intimacy on one hand and on the other the attraction of a male world of celebrated heroism and companionship that he continued to depict as enviable decades later, for example in "Meditations in Time of Civil War" (sections II and V, 1922).

By contrast with the allegorical exploration of the male psyche in "The Wanderings of Oisin," *Crossways* has the poem, "The Stolen Child," which sketches more simply a conflict between a fairy world of eternal but bland life and human existence. Here the pain of the latter is outweighed by an attractive, cosy homeliness of rural existence:

> Away with us he's going,
> The solemn-eyed:
> He'll hear no more the lowing
> Of the calves on the warm hillside
> Or the kettle on the hob
> Sing peace into his breast,
> Or see the brown mice bob
> Round and round the oatmeal-chest.
> *For he comes, the human child,*
> *To the waters and the wild*
> *With a faery, hand in hand,*
> *From a world more full of weeping than he can understand.* (1886)

Again, the apparent simplicity of the poem belies a technical sleight of hand as the mysteriousness of the fairies and the passiveness of the child under their sway is conveyed through the syntactic inversions that repeatedly (though not always) remove him from the dominant topic position at the beginning of a sentence.

By 1914 Yeats was seeking to establish a very different relationship between the poet and his poems from that of T. S. Eliot a few years later who, in "Tradition and the Individual Talent," compared the writer to a catalyst. Eliot was rather less impersonal in his *Four Quartets* of the late 1930s and 1940s but he never related the writer and work as closely as Yeats, who described his approach most clearly shortly before his death. The poet, he said, "is never the bundle of accident and incoherence that sits down to breakfast; he has been reborn as an idea, something intended, complete. A novelist might describe his accidence, his incoherence, he [that is, the poet] must not; he is more type than man, more passion than type."[14] As Joe Ronsley puts it,

> Yeats's purpose in his *Autobiography* was not to recount his life candidly for the psychological interest or entertainment of the curious, or to provide simple psychological or biographical readings of his poems, but to arrange his life into patterns of experience informed by philosophy and moving toward a preconceived goal. It is quite apparent that some parts of his life that would have contributed to this design were eliminated because they were too intimate, but others resisted inclusion by their irrelevance.[15]

Yeats found that writing the memoirs assisted him in constructing his own identity privately and from these he selected a public compilation of ideas and emotions that would give significance to the published poetry.

The earliest part of this construction was "Reveries over Childhood and Youth" in which he set out a family tree and circle of friends who would locate his social position (1916). Yeats had become interested in his middle-class Protestant ancestors around 1909 and used material provided by his sister Lily, who shared his interest. His family gave him conflicting sets of values, the anti-intellectual, mercantile but superstitious Pollexfens on his mother's side in opposition to the fiercely social, anti-materialist and intellectual ideals of his father. The type of status available to an Irish man at this time had a number of constraints. Yeats wanted to suggest that he was from a family with influence, and therefore there had to be some attention paid to the established residences and material wealth of his ancestors and yet in ways that distinguished these ancestors from English counterparts whose society had at its center the king or queen — not the most popular figurehead in Ireland. They had, therefore, to be people who were locally important but distinguished as individuals by their personality and eccentricity: of his relatives the Middletons he said, "they let their houses decay and the glass fall from the windows of their greenhouses, but one among them at any rate had the second sight." Judgmental comments he passed about them, such as the following, are suggestive of what he was trying to construct for himself: "They were liked but had not the pride and reserve, the sense of decorum and order, the instinctive playing before themselves that belongs to those who strike the popular imagination."[16] His maternal grandfather, William Pollexfen, owner of a number of ships, had "the reputation of never ordering a man to do anything he would not do himself," and was "so looked up to and admired that when he returned from taking the waters at Bath his men would light bonfires along the railway line for miles."[17] Yeats lists various ancestors who took part in nationalist Irish politics, concluding, "I am delighted with all that joins my life to those who had power in Ireland or with those anywhere that were good servants and poor bargainers."[18] Wanting to play a role in the history of Ireland, he increasingly strove to make himself a voice for Ireland: "My house" from "Meditations in Time of Civil War" (1922) poetically grafts the speaker to the "man-at-arms" who "Gathered a score of horse and spent his days/In this tumultuous spot." Yeats,—and the elision of poet and speaker is invited,— chose the tower as his house, he tells us, "that after me/ My bodily heirs may find,/To exalt a lonely mind,/ Befitting emblems of adversity." ("Meditations in Time of Civil War," II). The construction of arduous ideals was to stem the decline into laxity, into a lack of achievement that he knew from his own youth to be such a temptation and from which his father's brusque exhortations had deflected him; W.B. had not had much success at school and much of what he had learnt had been drummed into him by his father. The only things he had absorbed easily had been natural history and the paternal readings of literature.[19] John Butler Yeats, who had given up his position as a solicitor to follow the more precarious existence of a painter, had subsequently dissuaded W.B. from getting a regular job that would have given him the security of a salary, pushing him instead towards constant freelance achievements.[20]

By 1910 Yeats was working on achieving a more international reputation and adopted a range of reference that suggested a greater grasp of the classics than he seems to have had of these staples of upper class education. Thus Maud Gonne becomes Helen in "No Second Troy," etc. As his self-belief strengthened Yeats began to write more poems that have political implications. In the final version of *The Green Helmet and Other Poems* (1910) one of the first of his occasional poems is "On hearing that the Students of our New University have joined the Agitation against Immoral Literature." In it Yeats takes his stand as the voice of advanced thought, of more sophisticated social views and seeks to link himself with urbane European attitudes. Much of what follows in the volume is similarly outspoken criticism of Irish conventionality. Yeats's main resistance to his age was to its diluting of individuality. Years later, in "Among School Children" (1927), he was more gently to question the standardizing type of education provided by the Church; those nuns from whom "The children learn to cipher and to sing,/ To study reading-books and histories,/ To cut and sew, be neat in everything"(ll.3–5). In his middle phase (which I consider to run roughly from 1910 to 1930) he calls the wealthy Irish landowners to account in poems such as "Ancestral Houses" in which he queries whether too much luxury dissipates the strength of character leaders require:

> O what if leveled lawns and graveled ways
> Where slippered Contemplation finds his ease
> And Childhood a delight for every sense,
> But take our greatness with our violence?....
>
> What if those things the greatest of mankind
> Consider most to magnify, or to bless,
> But take our greatness with our bitterness?

"Ancestral Houses" is the first part of the "Meditations," a type of "poem of poems" that Yeats developed during his middle period where he is able to add to the complexity of his argument by linking a series of "sub-poems" that deal with its different facets. In "Meditations in Time of Civil War" he makes his most concentrated examination of the theme he had approached repeatedly of the relative value of active, perhaps military, life and solitary, individual artistic endeavor. How, in a world of increasing ease, does one foster the qualities of personality necessary for achievement? Too much engagement with violence and hardship simply blunts the sensibility, hardens the heart (section VI) while too protected a life can lead to dissipation or an inability to cope with ordinary existence. The topic is given personal relevance in his decision in the final (seventh) poem that, no matter what the attractions of the active life, he must validate what he has achieved by continuing to live as a writer. But the theme is also apposite in his consideration (sections I, II, and IV) of how to guide his children, both of whom were born shortly before the poem was written. The interrelation of life and artistic production (section III — "My Table") occupies the central portion. These poems differ from the many he wrote through characters' voices, such as "The Ballad of Moll Magee" or "The Lamentation of the Old Pensioner," where he sometimes simply versified stories he had heard or, at other times, expressed one side of an argument in which he was interested. The dramatized positions impose a distance between the poet and his speaker, leaving the organization of the volume to establish a sense of different aspects of a theme rather than the more directed quarrel of pairs of opposing views. This is true, for instance, of *The Wind Among the Reeds* with contrasting poems about women's lives. In the "The Song of the Old Mother" the speaker compares her hard domestic toil which is her lot because she is old and no longer beautiful with the idleness of the young and beautiful. This is immediately followed by "The Heart of the Woman," where the speaker is a young woman who consciously abandons the comfort of her home provided by her mother to follow her lover into the wilds.

Yeats not only dramatized others' voices, he was quite capable of striking a pose, constructing a platform or stage from which he held forth. This was apparent in the titles of early poems such as "He bids his Beloved be at Peace,"

"He reproves the Curlew," "He remembers Forgotten Beauty", "He gives his Beloved certain Rhymes" (all from *The Wind Among the Reeds* (1899)) but it is also true in poems such as "September 1913" when he addresses those who "add the halfpence to the pence" with little to gain from rebellion and everything to lose, and lambasts them for their caution, an idea revised publicly in "Easter 1916," in which sacrifice for "home rule" has led to "a terrible beauty." In the latter poem the use of the chorus line allows the poet to step back from involvement — the repeated sentiment providing a lens through which a reader can consider each of the incidents to which the stanzas are devoted. It is perhaps significant that as a Senator in the newly independent Irish Assembly he chose to talk on domestic issues such as the design of coins, or the place of art and education, rather than the issues of greater moment such as foreign affairs more fitting for more active men. His most controversial stance was on divorce.

From 1915 in *A Vision* he systematized opposition into both personality types characterized by a palette of qualities requiring effort to achieve a balance of opposite traits and a metaphysical and political system in which eras are seen as having dominant tendencies provoking the onset of an age with opposite qualities. Like the *Autobiography* it was to provide background information that might otherwise have distorted the dramatic voices in his poems with prosy lectures. *A Vision* never found its place as viable analysis of politics or character but only as explanation of Yeats's efforts to develop his own personality and as a key to the more obscure lines in his poems, such as, perhaps, the reference to "Juno's peacock screamed" at the end of "My Table" ("Meditations in Time of Civil War," III) where it seems to suggest the incursion of Western ideas of artistry growing out of individual experience into Japanese traditions where methods were passed unaltered from father to son.

With encroaching age Yeats's voice grew more vigorous, energized sometimes by indignation as in the poems about Roger Casement, a British consul who obtained arms from Germany for the Irish and was hanged by the British for treason. Yeats considered Casement "not a very able man but he was gallant and unselfish and had surely his right to leave ... an unsullied name,"[21] a protest against the use of what at the time were thought to be forged diaries suggesting that Casement was homosexual. Yeats sought continued relation to his times, writing, for example, "Lapis Lazuli," about fears of the impending war, catching the flavor of contemporary conversation, as T. S. Eliot had done in "The Waste Land" some ten years earlier: "For everybody knows or else should know /That if nothing drastic is done"— and then the tone changes with the register, capturing another voice: "Aeroplane and Zeppelin will come out,/ Pitch like King Billy bomb-balls in/ Until the town lie beaten flat," a reference perhaps uniting Kaiser Wilhelm II and King William III in his conquest of Ireland in 1690.

Yeats also started to think about how he might be remembered. One aspect of "The Circus Animals' Desertion" is contrition at having cared less for his friends than for what he could make of them as material for his poems. As in his youthful *Autobiography*, he enhanced his status by projecting elevated pictures of his friends. "The Municipal Gallery Revisited" (1937) is a striking case in point:

> Mancini's portrait of Augusta Gregory,
> "Greatest since Rembrandt," according to John Synge;
> A great ebullient portrait certainly;
> But where is the brush that could show anything
> Of all that pride and that humility?
> And I am in despair that time may bring
> Approved patterns of women or of men
> But not that selfsame excellence again.

In this poem the quarrel with the self is not smoothed into artistic artifact so that the reader follows the lines of the argument with ease. Instead, we are left to follow as best we can the jumps in thought from one position to another. The effect is of seeing into Yeats's mind as he walks through the galleries. There is no longer the regret and partial guilt of "Meditations in Time of Civil War" where he turns away after conversing with the soldier and feels envy for the man's social utility. The ambiguity is in the balance between a sense of irreparable personal loss of his dead friend with its associated mourning for his own decline, and a more public nostalgia for the disintegration of the national movement of which they had both been part. In the course of the latter he asserts again the belief of his early writings that "all that we did, all that we said or sang/ Must come from contact with the soil, from that/ contact everything Antaeus-like grew strong" (st.vi). There is considerable pride in his claim that "We three alone in modern times had brought/ Everything down to that sole test again,/ Dream of the noble and the beggarman" (st.vi). The "three" were Synge, Lady Gregory and Yeats himself.

Among his poems in the final phase are those that work as photographs in an album. Such is his description of Lady Gregory as she withstood threats of violence during the troubles.

> Augusta Gregory seated at her great ormolu table,
> Her eightieth winter approaching; Yesterday he threatened my life.
> I told him that nightly from six to seven I sat at this table,
> The blinds drawn up ("Beautiful Lofty Things." 1938)

The poem exemplifies that change in emphasis as physical beauty, so admired in the early poems, is more and more balanced by admiration for courage, for the strength of personality that he praised in his ancestors. Yeats's struggle against physical weakness and impotency was carried out in the real world and in the world of his poetry where he adopted the rough strength of colloquial language and wrote poems for characters whose wants were simply and graphically expressed such as in the poems attributed to Crazy Jane. She is a dramatized speaker, based on an old woman who lived in Gort "with an amazing power of audacious speech"[22] who challenges the life-denying dictates of the anonymous "Bishop" with whom she converses, asserting the vitality of sexual relations ("Crazy Jane talks with the Bishop," *The Winding Stair and other Poems* [1933]).

Yeats rearranged his final volume of poems for the Coole edition, a collection in over thirty volumes of all his works that was not published at the time because of the outbreak of the Second World War. The rearrangement splits the final volume into two volumes and is most clearly different in the placing of what was the final poem, "Under Ben Bulben," so that it now opens rather than closing *Last Poems*. This exhorts thus:

> Irish poets, learn your trade,
> Sing whatever is well made,...
> Cast your mind on other days
> That we in coming days may be
> Still the indomitable Irishry.

... and establishes Yeats's place:

> Under bare Ben Bulben's head
> In Drumcliff churchyard Yeats is laid,
> An ancestor was rector there
> Long years ago; a church stands near,
> By the road an ancient cross.
> No marble, no conventional phrase,
> On limestone quarried near the spot
> By his command these words are cut:
>> *Cast a cold eye*
>> *On life, on death.*
>> *Horseman, pass by!*
> September 4, 1838.

Statements of this sort adhere to the picture of lonely tragic heroism that Yeats had presented in plays such as the second version of *The Hour Glass* and in the weaving of event around place. In the re-ordered Coole edition, which is followed by Daniel Albright, Yeats makes his farewell with "Politics":

> How can I, that girl standing there,
> My attention fix
> On Roman or on Russian
> Or on Spanish politics,
> Yet here's a traveled man that knows
> What he talks about,
> And there's a politician
> That has both read and thought,
> And maybe what they say is true
> Of war and war's alarms,
> But O that I were young again
> And held her in my arms.
> (23 May 1938)

Having accosted the reader with his rhetorical question, the poem alludes to the apparently rational assessments of the traveled man and politician and the growing fears of yet another war — subjects with which Yeats had engaged energetically during his writing life — only to end by becoming confessional, intimate. It asserts the validity of the statement to Olivia Shakespear that it is love that remains most important to us. It thus forms the closing bracket round Yeats's work with its complex patterns of resistance that *Crossways* had opened over forty years earlier.

Notes

1. W. B. Yeats, *Per Amica Silentia Lunae* (London: Macmillan, 1918), 25, printed in "Anima Hominis," *Mythologies* (New York: Collier, 1959, 1969), 331.

2. Joseph Ronsley, *Yeats's Autobiography: life as symbolic pattern* (Cambridge, Massachusetts: Harvard University Press, 1968), 25.

3. W. B. Yeats, *Memoirs: Autobiography — First Draft; Journal*, transcribed and edited by Denis Donoghue (London: Macmillan, 1972, 89): After dining with Maud Gonne, Yeats records that his "trouble increased" and notes that when Diana Vernon [his name for Olivia Shakespear in this draft] next visited him, "My friend found my mood did not answer hers and burst into tears. 'There is someone else in your heart,' she said. It was the breaking between us for many years." See too R. F. Foster, *W. B. Yeats: a Life. Vol. I: The Apprentice Mage* (Oxford: Oxford University Press, 1998), 173.

4. *Collected Letters* vol.I, p.xvi.

5. *Beltaine: the Organ of the Irish Literary Theatre* had three issues: May 1899, February 1900 and April 1900. *Samhain* ran for longer from October 1901-November 1908. Each journal was reprinted in one volume with an Introductory Note by B. C. Bloomfield (London: Frank Cass and Co., 1907). Beltaine is the name of an ancient Irish Spring festival and "Samhain," according to WBY, is "the old name for the beginning of winter" (*Samhain*, 10); both were times when the Irish Literary Theater put on their season of plays.

6. Eleanor Knott and Gerard Murphy, *Early Irish Literature* (London: Routledge and Kegan Paul, 1966, 1967), 150-4.

7. W. B. Yeats, *Uncollected Prose*, collected and ed. John P. Frayne (London: Macmillan, 1970), 188.

8. John Eglinton, *W. B. Yeats, A.E., William Larminie: Literary Ideals in Ireland* (New York: Lemma Publishing Co., 1973), 11.

9. The *Autobiography of William Butler Yeats*, (New York: Collier Books, 1916, 1965), 19.

10. Augusta Gregory, *Gods and Fighting Men*. The story of the Tuatha de Danaan and of the Fianna of Ireland, arranged and put into English by Lady Greory with a preface by W. B. Yeats (Gerrards Cross: Colin Smythe, 1904, repr. 1970). *Cuchulain of Muirthemne*: the story of the men of the red branch of Ulster, arranged and put into English by Lady Gregory. With a preface by W.B. Yeats. London, 1902. *Visions and beliefs in the west of Ireland*, collected and arranged by Lady Gregory: with two essays and notes by W. B. Yeats (New York and London: G. P. Putman's Sons, 1920).

11. *W. B. Yeats: The Poems*, Ed. Daniel Albright, (London: Dent, 1990). The Coole edition, named after Lady Gregory's home, was fully prepared, with proofs checked by Yeats in the 1930s but it was not printed because of the outbreak of war, Yeats's death and the shortage of paper during and just after the war. It is the proofs for this edition, housed in the National Library of Ireland, that Daniel Albright is following.

12. Quotations from the poems are taken from the *Collected Poems of W. B. Yeats*, 2nd edn. (London: MacMillan, 1950, 1976).

13. The unflattering picture of Catholicism in "The Wanderings of Oisin" was not without its consequences, stimulating a watchfulness in the Catholic clergy that no doubt contributed to the negative reaction Yeats received a few years later in the "Souls for Gold" controversy, in which his play, *The Countess Cathleen*, was condemned for suggesting that one might sell one's soul for gold. While Marlowe's Faust had sold out to the Devil to extend his earthly enjoyment, Yeats's Countess Cathleen sells hers for grain to distribute to the starving poor. However, certain anti-Catholics used the play as an opportunity to stimulate anti-clerical demonstrations and Yeats had to ask for police protection. (*Autobiography*, 276–80).

14. W. B. Yeats, "A General Introduction for My Work" in *Essays and Introductions* (New York: Collier, 1961), 509.

15. Ronsley, *Yeats's Autobiography*, 28.

16. *Autobiography*, 9.

17. *Autobiography*, 3.

18. *Autobiography*, 12.

19. *Autobiography*, 19, 29–31, 42–3.

20. WBY to Katharine Tynan, 12 February [1888] in *The Collected Letters of W. B. Yeats*, Vol. I 1865–1895, Ed. John Kelly, Associate Ed. Eric Domville (Oxford: Clarendon Press, 1986), 48, 50. See too R. F. Foster, *W. B. Yeats: a Life. Vol. I: The Apprentice Mage* (Oxford: Oxford University Press, 1998), 65.

21. Albright, 788, quoting *Letters on Poetry from W. B. Yeats to Dorothy Wellesley* (London: Oxford University Press, 1964), 867.

22. *Poems*, Ed. Albright, p.730, quoting *The Letters of W. B. Yeats*, Ed. Alan Wade (London: Rupert Hart Davis, 1954), 785–6.

Works Cited

Eglinton, John (1973), *W. B. Yeats, A.E., William Larminie: Literary Ideals in Ireland*. New York: Lemma Publishing Co.

Foster, R. F. (1998), *W. B. Yeats: a Life. Vol. I: The Apprentice Mage.* Oxford: Oxford University Press.

Gregory, Augusta (1904, repr. 1970), *Gods and Fighting Men: The Story of the Tuatha de Danaan and of the Fianna of Ireland.* Arranged and put into English by Lady Gregory with a preface by W. B. Yeats. Gerrards Cross: Colin Smythe.

Gregory, Augusta (1902), *Cuchulain of Muirthemne: The Story of the Men of the Red Branch of Ulster.* Arranged and put into English by Lady Gregory. With a preface by W.B. Yeats. London: John Murray.

Gregory, Augusta (1920), *Visions and Beliefs in the West of Ireland.* Collected and arranged by Lady Gregory: with two essays and notes by W. B. Yeats. New York and London: G. P. Putman's Sons.

Knott, Eleanor and Murphy, Gerard (1966, 1967), *Early Irish Literature.* London: Routledge and Kegan Paul.

Ronsley, Joseph (1968), *Yeats's Autobiography: Life as Symbolic Pattern.* Cambridge, Massachusetts: Harvard University Press.

Yeats, W. B.(1916, 1965), *The Autobiography of William Butler Yeats.* New York: Collier Books.

_____ (Ed.) (1907), *Beltaine: The Organ of the Irish Literary Theatre* reprinted in one volume with an Introductory Note by B. C. Bloomfield. London: Frank Cass and Co.

_____(1950, 1976), *Collected Poems of W. B. Yeats.* 2nd edn. London: MacMillan.

_____(1986), *The Collected Letters of W. B. Yeats.* Vol. I 1865–1895. Ed. John Kelly, Associate Ed. Eric Domville (Oxford: Clarendon Press).

_____(1961), "A General Introduction for My Work" in *Essays and Introductions.* New York: Collier.

_____(1972), *Memoirs: Autobiography—First Draft; Journal.* Transcribed and ed. Denis Donoghue. London: Macmillan.

_____ (1959, 1969), *Mythologies.* New York: Collier.

_____ (1918), *Per Amica Silentia Lunae.* London: Macmillan.

_____(1990), *The Poems.* Ed. Daniel Albright. London: Dent.

_____(1970), *Uncollected Prose.* Collected and ed. John P. Frayne. London: Macmillan.

_____(ed.) (1907), *Samhain* reprinted in one volume with an Introductory Note by B. C. Bloomfield. London: Frank Cass and Co.

12. Responding, Rewording and/or Resisting
Edwin Morgan
Shona M. Allan

Edwin Morgan (1920–2010) was undoubtedly, and indeed still is, Scotland's pre-eminent and best-loved poet of the late 20th and early 21st century. He was recently referred to as "the most wide-ranging, expansive and inclusive poet Scotland has ever had."[1] Despite the fact that he ultimately had a bad back, became rather hard of hearing and suffered from prostate cancer for the last eleven of his ninety years on this planet, he continued to write; his last collection *Dreams and Other Nightmares: New and Uncollected Poems 1954–2009* was published to coincide with his 90th birthday at the end of April 2010, as was *Eddie @90*, a book of birthday greetings in the form of prose and poetry from many fellow poets and friends, including then Glasgow Poet Laureate Liz Lochhead,[2] Britain's Poet Laureate Carol Ann Duffy, Morgan's biographer, James McGonigal,[3] poets Jackie Kay and Seamus Heaney, and writers Ian Rankin, Ali Smith and Alasdair Gray. Morgan's popularity and success have not gone unnoticed elsewhere either. Winner of a plethora of prizes not only for his poetry — most recently the Scottish Arts Council award for book of the year 2008 for his 2007 collection *A Book of Lives*, which was also shortlisted for the T.S. Eliot prize — Scotland's Makar seemed, up until relatively recently, quite simply to be indefatigable: in essence, he resisted succumbing to illness, and his response to his cancer diagnosis in 1999, when doctors gave him anything between six months and six years, was apparently quite simply, "I think I'll take the six years."[4]

Translation, for which Morgan also won several prizes (including the Weidenfeld translation prize in 2001 for his translation of Racine's *Phèdre*), forms a significant part of his output.[5] This is more than evident from his hefty 500-page tome *Collected Translations*, published in 1996, a collection which includes some but not all of Morgan's translations: adding his other translations of *Beowulf, Phèdre, Cyrano de Bergerac*, or the Dutch morality play *The Apple Tree*, for example, would easily have produced a volume of at least double the length. It is perhaps no surprise then that, because of his prolific output, Morgan is generally fêted as Scotland's foremost translator of poetry.[6] As a young man searching for his own poetic voice, the translation of poetry from Anglo-Saxon into modern English proved inspirational. Utterly antagonistic, from a political point of view, to the rather right-wing political stance linked with the likes of Ezra Pound and T.S. Eliot, Morgan soon turned to the Russian avant-garde poets, particularly Mayakovsky,[7] for poetic stimulation, attracted by a much more innovative and forward-looking style, intrigued about how these Russian avant-garde writers dealt with the revolutionary situations they happened to find themselves in aesthetically, linguistically and politically.[8]

Indeed, although Morgan did not resist using more traditional poetic forms such as the sonnet (as is perceptible from his sequence "Glasgow sonnets" in *From Glasgow to Saturn*, and the collection *Sonnets from Scotland*), it is clear that his inspiration was almost blinkered to focus more or less exclusively on the present and into the future in both time and space. Not only did Morgan write poems about outer space, such as "The First Men on Mercury," "Spacepoem 1: from Laika to Gagarin" or "Spacepoem 3: Off Course," in the 1960s, he actually put his name down on a list of those people wanting to be among the first space travelers. While he never managed to fulfill that space dream literally — the closest he got was traveling faster than the speed of sound on Concorde — it is certainly true that these worldly boundaries have long been surpassed by his poetry. In tune with the title of his 1973 collection, he certainly did creatively travel from Glasgow to Saturn. Although physically and emotionally rooted in Glasgow where he was born, brought up and lived all his life, Morgan and his imagination can be said to have taken that imaginative journey to Saturn. On the way, this trip made a number of metaphorical stopovers in various countries to take on board inspiration and translation from French, German, Russian, Hungarian, Italian, Latin, Old English and Spanish,[9] and, for a little variety, Morgan also collaborated with musicians from both contemporary music and jazz.[10] It is surely a measure of Morgan's eclecticism that his funeral in the University of Glasgow's grand Bute Hall on 26 August 2010 was attended by hundreds of people from all walks of life, ranging from the worlds of academia, music and the arts to the world of politics.[11]

Morgan's gargantuan appetite for so many new and different things can be rather daunting in general, and in particular within the context of poetry and resistance, as it can seem as if he resisted almost nothing and welcomed almost everything. Yet, since by far the greatest number of the poems which

Morgan translated are from either Russian or Hungarian, these selections may reveal something about what Morgan and his poetry may or may not be resisting. As Peter McCarey highlights, even though Morgan was not literally faced with having to choose between poets, considering his choices in this way does help to throw some light on these choices; why did he select "Montale not Pasolini, Mayakovsky not Mandelstam, Aigi not Brodsky, Brecht not Rilke?"[12] In some cases, the choices came about by chance, dictated by whatever Morgan happened upon, influenced by his own "affinity with the other poet," or simply because someone requested a translation of him.[13]

Of the eleven Hungarian poets who feature in the *Collected Translations*, the most prominent in terms of number of poems translated are Attila József (1905–1937) and Sándor Weöres (1913–1989).[14] In light of the fact that, when Morgan first happened upon the former, it was in Italian translation and Morgan had no knowledge of the Hungarian language, it is a measure of the "immediate and powerful impact" the Italian translation exercised that Morgan then "got hold of a Hungarian dictionary and grammar, and began making English versions through the medium of the Italian."[15] What exactly was it then that Morgan found so appealing, so irresistible, in a poetry, language and culture which may at first appear to be so far removed from that of Morgan's native Glasgow at that time? Was this strong response provoked by a political, aesthetic and/or linguistic fascination, or does this choice reveal a conscious, or unconscious, resistance to his native poetry, language and culture?

Over the years, Morgan was often asked about his choice of poets for translation, about his reasons for translating in the first place, and about how he actually went about the process of translating. If a general interest in language itself and the possibilities of language can, to some extent, be said to have fuelled Morgan's interest in the practice of translation,[16] Morgan also admitted that he had a rather more "missionary aim" and wanted to broaden his own and his fellow countrymen and women's horizons: he "[did] want to bring this range of other European writers into the Scottish awareness' and make Scots and the wider English-speaking world 'aware of what's going on elsewhere.'"[17] This desire to disseminate something of foreign cultures into his own, to facilitate intercultural transfer, to let an English-speaking audience feel some of the irresistibility of the poetry he had come across and to feel some of the excitement he too had experienced, is also evident in this comment more than ten years later:

> It seems clear that the translation of poetry [...] tends to begin when the translator comes across some foreign poetry which interests him, and he wants to convey, to bring across, to translate that interest and excitement for people using his own language.[18]

As far as Hungarian poetry is concerned, it is clear that there were a number of factors, apart from Morgan's initial fascination, which facilitated his initial translation of and subsequent long-term engagement with Hungarian poetry. The fact that the Italian translation that Morgan had come upon was a bilingual Hungarian-Italian edition assisted insofar as the original was there in front of him just waiting to be explored by a mind as open to new and foreign stimulation as Morgan's. As Morgan underlines in the preface to the *Collected Translations*, a significant role was played by the fact that his translations became known in Hungary and, when Morgan went to Budapest in 1966, he "was encouraged by writers and editors who thought [he] had captured the 'feel' of József to make further translations of Hungarian poetry, which [he] did, and indeed with increasing fervor over the years."[19] The Hungarians were not just happy that some of their poetry was being made accessible to the English-speaking world: what is consistently evident in collections of Hungarian poetry in English and guides to Hungarian literature in English is the unfailing praise for the quality of Morgan's translations,[20] a quality which is surely reflected in the fact that Morgan received several awards for these translations, including the Hungarian Order of Merit in 1997.[21] It would seem then as if, at least in the eyes of some (or perhaps even many) Hungarians, Morgan's translations are, at least, to some extent successful; it seems as if the Hungarian originals have not resisted rewording in a foreign language and culture, in spite of the existence of what must sometimes have appeared insurmountable linguistic and/or cultural obstacles.

The idea of what constitutes a successful and/or accurate translation is, of course, notoriously slippery, not to mention controversial. Morgan was well aware of the different considerations, requirements, dangers and constraints when translating different genres and reveals an understanding of the primacy of voice no matter whether the genre be poetry or drama: when being interviewed about his translation of the Dutch play, *The Apple Tree*, he strongly emphasized the fact that "it is no use — ever — having a translation which might be pedantically accurate or scholarly if it cannot be spoken on stage."[22] In this way, Morgan may easily be compared with many other poets who have tried their hands at translation. Simon Armitage, for example, whose translation of the Middle English poem *Sir Gawain and the Green Knight* was published in 2006, also emphasized this primacy of voice, claiming that the task of translating the poem was "not an exercise in linguistic forensics or medieval history; the intention [was] always to produce a living, inclusive and readable piece of work in its own right. In other words, the ambition [was] poetry."[23] Morgan was evidently not daunted by the traditional idea that something would inevitably be lost in the translation process, that something would have resisted translation, and could even have concurred with recent views on translation, which suggest that "there might be a process of gain."[24]

Despite the amount of work involved in translating from Hungarian, a language with which he, initially, was completely unfamiliar, the translation process was for Morgan undoubtedly a productive and stimulating activity. As time went on, however, his meticulous perusal of the original Hungarian texts and translation allowed him to pick up "a good deal of the language."[25] Yet, even with excellent knowledge of a foreign language and its culture, translation of that country's poetry is no mean feat, so it is all the more remarkable that the techniques which Morgan (with a less than perfect knowledge of the Hungarian language) employed to "get to know the original poem or play as deeply as possible," "to soak [him]self in it, to let it float into [his] mind at different times until [he] [got] a feeling for what the work [was] like at various levels other than that of the literal meaning"[26] were at all successful. This process was complemented by the help which Morgan needed and relied on — and that many Hungarian poets and academics were more than happy to provide — in order to complete these translations. This rather unwieldy and undoubtedly long process did bear the fruit of making at least some Hungarian poetry accessible to a wider audience whatever its limitations might be. Morgan was, however, also fully alert to these limitations and to the fact that this way of translating József and Weöres was by no means a one-size-fits-all solution: "Without my feeling of eager identification with these poets, particularly József and Weöres, the method would not have worked."[27]

Why then did Morgan identify so eagerly with József and Weöres in particular? Was his motivation for exploring Hungarian poetry a desire to familiarize himself with that foreign culture, or was it a conscious or unconscious desire to resist his own, which he believed to some extent to be stagnating? Tom Hubbard makes the pertinent suggestion that Morgan's intentions are rather to "absorb Hungary but not to break with Scotland,"[28] making this engagement with Hungarian poetry less of a resistance to his native culture and rather more of an openness to otherness. In interviews, Morgan stressed the affinities he perceived between Scotland and Hungary, two small countries he saw as being somewhat at the mercy of their geographically and culturally bigger and more dominant neighbors, England and Russia. Morgan suggested that in writing a distinctively Scottish or Hungarian poetry, poets reveal a desire to resist the influences of a dominant other culture, whether they be political, aesthetic and/or linguistic.[29] Hubbard also claims that Scottish and Hungarian cultures are linked because they are both "a mystery to the rest of Europe" and considered "exotic."[30] While, as a Scot who has never been to Hungary, I could subscribe to the view of Hungary as "mysterious" and "exotic," I have never thought of my country as especially "exotic" nor heard of it frequently referred to as such. From a language point of view, palpable affinities are less easy to find between either Hungarian and English, or Hungarian and Scots. The Hungarian language belongs to the Finno-Ugric group of Uralic languages, and, as such, is undeniably "exotic" and "a mystery to [much of] the rest of Europe"; hence it has little in common with either English or Scots (no matter whether Scots is considered an English or Germanic dialect or language). Nonetheless, the notion of both nations' poets attempting to deal with political, aesthetic and/or linguistic pressure from outside and still keep something distinctive from their own culture would seem to reveal a plausible affinity between Scotland and Hungary.

As a poet who was always sensitive to his own urban environment, it is no surprise that what especially appealed to Morgan about József was the urban nature of his poetry. The cities of Glasgow and Budapest play a central role in both poets' work. For all Morgan may have computers writing Christmas cards, apples singing, a cancer cell and a normal cell having a conversation, and men visiting Mercury, his native city is utterly intrinsic to the success of urban poems such as "Glasgow Green," "In the Snack Bar," "At Central Station," "Death in Duke Street" or "Stobhill." On the one hand, both Glasgow and Budapest are cities with beauty and tradition, but, on the other, the sense of a Jekyll-and-Hyde nature would appear to be omnipresent. While the underbelly of Budapest may not be as familiar (at least not to many Western or Northern Europeans), the image of Glasgow as "no mean city," as a crime-ridden and dangerous place, rather than the "dear green place" of legend, endures to some extent even today, in spite of Glasgow being European City of Culture 1990, City of Architecture 1999, the venue for the 2014 Commonwealth Games, and the focus of the 1980s Mr. Happy campaign with the slogan "Glasgow's miles better." Considering the fact that a Glasgow kiss is actually a head-butt, and a Glasgow smile a slashing of the mouth and then a kick in the groin to make the smile even broader, the city of Glasgow could still well be that *City of Dreadful Night*, depicted in such vivid detail by James Thomson B.V. in 1874. Hubbard highlights the influence which Thomson also had on Morgan, as Morgan did not shy away from depicting his city in all its facets: the underbelly is simply not resisted, and the rose-tinted glasses are nowhere to be seen.[31]

József, "the great working-class poet of the city,"[32] does not resist presenting these less than attractive facets of his city, its underclass and gloomy and depressing cityscapes either, and Morgan acknowledged that these poems probably had some bearing on his own poetry about Glasgow.[33] Hubbard goes on to offer a persuasive and detailed comparison of the similarities between some of the urban images used by Morgan in his sequence of "Glasgow Sonnets" and by József (in Morgan's translation) in "A View of Things," concentrating on how human life has degenerated to the level of the bestial, where humans need the survival skills of animals.[34] In the "Glasgow Sonnets," the stark contrast between the regularity of the sonnet form and the irregularity of the lives of these deprived people living in a dismal decaying environment simply paints the reality of these people's lives all the more vividly. These images show a clear affinity not only with József but also with a more general acceptance of a realistic rather than an idealistic vision. In both poets, this is clearly a resistance to beautifying reality in order to sell a fake picture-postcard version of either Glasgow or Budapest, and a willingness to give a voice to those who would otherwise have no voice.

In Sándor Weöres, Morgan found another kindred spirit. *Sándor Weöres: Selected Poems,* a selection of 24 poems, was published in 1970, and in the afterword to the 1988 edition, *Eternal Moment,* Morgan elaborates on the importance of empathy between poet and translator and a certain dedication to the task. Again, however, he does not fail to accentuate the importance of the translator being willing and able to "project himself confidently and happily into the mind of the target poet [so] that his work gains the lift and fluency we all want to see."[35] Morgan then underlines the fact that because Weöres's poetry "is often difficult; it is characterized by unusual variety of form, content, and 'voice,'"[36] it presents an even greater mountain for any potential translator to climb. In his introduction to *Modern Hungarian Poetry,* Miklós Vajda stresses the uniqueness of Weöres in Hungarian poetry, the fact that he resists categorization and the fact that he was able to "spin mankind's entire culture like a striped ball on the tip of a finger."[37] Vajda believes Weöres's poetry to be so universal that, had Weöres not had the misfortune to be writing in Hungarian, his fame elsewhere would have been guaranteed.[38] The breadth and depth of Weöres's poetic voices is quite simply staggering, displaying

> a magic virtuosity manipulating the poetic self, shifting the poem's focus back and forth in time and space, up and down the scale of human emotion, while narrowing and widening his poetic lens at will to include microcosm and macrocosm or both. Anyone on anything can be made abstract or concrete, sublime or intimate, infantile or prophetic, sarcastic or hymnlike, infinitely simple or infinitely complex.[39]

Here is a breadth and depth of poetic voice which is strikingly similar to that found in Morgan too.

In Morgan's afterword to the Weöres anthology, Morgan then proceeds to explain in some detail the affinities between himself and Weöres:

> By a lucky chance, I found that my own approach to poetry coincided at several points with that of Weöres: I have always enjoyed the use of many different voices and personas, I like variety of verse technique from the most free and exploratory to the most strict and metrical, and I relish giving immediacy to distant or mythical events in place and time. Although in other respects there are important differences between us, I felt that I had a certain *entrée* into Weöres's poetry.[40]

This way in, or *"entrée* into Weöres's poetry," and this feeling for the many voices of Weöres's poetry, which give Morgan a sense of legitimacy in his task as translator tie in very much with similar comments made by other contemporary poet translators: both Seamus Heaney and Simon Armitage, for example, experienced something comparable when approaching their translations of *Beowulf* (Heaney) and *Sir Gawain and the Green Knight* (Armitage).[41] These poetic affinities undoubtedly inspired Morgan in both his translations and his own poetry and encouraged him to further his own poetic experimentation, and the fact that Morgan and Weöres apparently had a "warm personal and professional relationship" surely also had an effect.[42] In his original 1970 introduction (where the description which Morgan offers of Weöres could equally well be applied to the Scots Makar himself), Morgan had drawn attention to the explorative and experimental nature of Weöres's poetry by quoting the poet himself on what poetry is and what it can do:

> [...] I think one should explore everything. Including those things which will never be accepted, not even in the distant future. We can never know, at the start of an experiment, where it will lead ... It may take decades or centuries to prove whether it was a useful experiment or a useless one. It may never be proved at all.[43]

If poetry can or should explore everything, then surely it must resist nothing. This constant desire to explore everything and give anything and everything a voice, from an apple, to the Loch Ness monster, a cancer cell, or the mummy of Ramses II, is also unmistakable in many Morgan poems. In fact, in 2007, the poet Sean O'Brien suggested that "there appears to be nothing Morgan is not interested in, nothing he considers too small to deserve or too big to lend itself to his attention, no form he will not explore."[44]

Kindred spirits in many ways all three. It seems clear now that the appeal of József and Weöres in particular, and Eastern European poets in general, was rather less political and rather more aesthetic or linguistic. The pull was towards new and innovative experiments with form and content and towards inspiration to forge new paths to finding a voice for one and all. If this was a resistance to a lack of, in Morgan's eyes, inspirational contemporary poetry either north or south of the border in the UK, then it could only have been an unconscious resistance. No particular malice aforethought or really tangible political agenda to resist what could be perceived as English (or, in the case of Hungary, Russian) domination. Any resistance on Morgan's part was surely overwhelmed by the irresistible appeal of the exotic and exciting poetic voices being projected by József and Weöres. Of course, everything in this Hungarian poetry was not new, and many things could be considered to some extent universal. It may then not be too far-fetched to suggest that József and Weöres's poetry both inspired and forced Morgan to see certain familiar things in an unfamiliar way. By using this technique of defamiliarization in his own poetry, Morgan was then able to heighten awareness and perhaps even to lessen resistance to seeing the familiar in an unfamiliar and perhaps enlightening way. While there are certain subversive ideas in József and Weöres (and indeed in several of the poets and poems which Morgan chose to translate), Morgan seemed to be far more attracted by poetry and poets with rather more strings to their bows. Morgan frequently claimed that he was "not a political animal"[45] or a great supporter of the Scottish Nationalist Party, but he was a supporter of the Scottish Parliament which was re-established in 1999 after almost 300 years, and did write a poem for its opening.[46] This commitment to Eastern European poetry in general, and Hungarian poetry in particular, was far more a conscious acceptance of new ideas and a desire to bring some of the apparently wonderful but unfortunately linguistically inaccessible poetry produced in Hungary to the English-speaking world. If Morgan's translations go some way to overcoming the stubborn resistance of native English speakers to reading translations, to engaging with the literatures of other countries, to widening the audience for the poets he chose to translate, then this is unequivocally to be applauded.

Morgan's decision to translate both József and Weöres into standard English rather than Scots is also worthy of comment within the context of resistance. Morgan did sometimes use Scots in his own poetry, and indeed in his translation of Mayakovsky as *Wi the Haill Voice*,[47] though he acknowledged that, because of his education and family background, his native tongue was English.[48] He used Scots in several translations though (including Racine's *Phèdre*), and the choice of language would appear to have less to do with any political agenda and far more to do with whatever feel Morgan got from the original. When talking about translating French and Dutch plays into what he called "straight English," Morgan admitted that the plays "work[ed] all right, but they lack[ed] that spice which you get from something slightly different."[49] That something different would, of course, be Scots, which would seem to offer, in some cases, a rather livelier and not an especially more politically aware voice than Standard English for a Scottish poet and translator.

Of course, the choice of Scots could make a political point about resisting the cultural and linguistic dominance of English, but, in the case of József and Weöres, it would appear as if the choice of English supports Morgan's great desire to make these poets available to the widest possible English-speaking audience.[50]

In fact, bringing poetry to the people was always one of Morgan's main aims. When still able, Morgan was an enthusiastic performer of his own poetry and, because of the fact that there is often a playfulness in much of his poetry, and some of it simply delights in the sounds themselves, he was often more than capable of grabbing and keeping the attention of a class of primary-school children. The sound poem "The Loch Ness Monster's Song" was sure to keep even the most restless of schoolchildren spellbound. During the Big City Read in 2008 (when free copies of 50 selected Morgan poems were distributed through libraries), one little boy remarked to Liz Lochhead that he did not believe that all that could be inside one man's head.[51] It is to be hoped that this event may just have done something to pierce that balloon of stubborn resistance to poetry in the next generation and to encourage audiences of all ages to open up their minds to verse which can even be fun.[52] If the "role of art in the modern world is [indeed] to challenge and provoke, to resist stagnation and to question complacency" as Moffat and Riach suggest, then Morgan fits the bill perfectly.[53]

When asked just after his 90th birthday last year about what he thought about being professor of English literature at his *alma mater*, the University of Glasgow, and having had the opportunity to pass on his vast literary knowledge and unending enthusiasm to students, Morgan responded thus:

> A poet regards himself or herself as a kind of link in a very long chain, although you can't lay down the law about poetry. A lot of poetry, like any other art, slides past the rational part of the mind. There is something mysterious about poetry in the end, something that resists being explained too much.[54]

As far as József and Weöres are concerned, Morgan responded, reworded and even resisted. He did not give up his translation attempts; he went from Glasgow to Budapest (both literally and figuratively), as the desire to let others experience what he found in these poets was evidently greater than the difficult task of translating from a language with which he was only relatively vaguely familiar. Right up to the very end of his life, Edwin Morgan was a man who still felt the draw of unexplored poetic terrain, a man who "still had lines of poetry in his head" and would not (or could not) resist them.[55]

Notes

1. *Eddie@90*, Eds. Robyn Marsack and Hamish Whyte (Edinburgh: Scottish Poetry Library and Mariscat Press, 2010), 1.
2. Liz Lochhead was appointed Morgan's successor as Scots Makar in January 2011.
3. McGonigal's biography was published in September 2010 only a few weeks after Morgan's death (James McGonigal, *Beyond the Last Dragon: A Life of Edwin Morgan* [Dingwall: Sandstone Press, 2010]).
4. Martyn McLaughlin, "He touched hearts: Farewell to Makar Edwin Morgan," *The Scotsman* 27 August 2010, *http://thescotsman.scotsman.com/news/He-Touched-hearts— farewell.6498061.jp?*.
5. Morgan also received the American Soros Award for Translation in 1985, the Hungarian PEN Memorial medal in 1972 and was awarded the Order of Merit by Hungary in 1997. (Douglas Gifford, "Obituary: Edwin Morgan OBE, poet," *The Scotsman* 20 August 2010, *http://news.scotsman.com/obituaries/Obituary-Edwin-Morgan-OBE-poet.6485326.jp?*).
6. See, for example, Matt McGuire and Colin Nicholson, "Edwin Morgan" in *The Edinburgh Companion to Contemporary Scottish Poetry*, Eds. Matt McGuire and Colin Nicholson (Edinburgh: Edinburgh University Press, 2009), 99.
7. Matt McGuire and Colin Nicholson, "Edwin Morgan," 98.
8. Interview with Robin Hamilton (Glasgow, 5 August 1971), printed in full in *Edwin Morgan: Nothing Not Giving Messages: Reflections on his Work and Life*, Ed. Hamish Whyte (Edinburgh: Polygon, 1990), 38.
9. Robert Crawford, *Scotland's Books: The Penguin History of Scottish Literature* (London: Penguin, 2007), 608.
10. The sequence of poems "Planet Wave," "commissioned by the Cheltenham International Jazz Festival and set to music by Tommy Smith, was first performed in Cheltenham Town Hall on 4 April 1997" (Edwin Morgan, *New Selected Poems* (Manchester: Carcanet, 2000), 168). Along with other authors such as Louise Welsh and A. L. Kennedy, Morgan collaborated with Roddy Woomble and the group Idlewild and their CD *Ballads of the Book* came out in 2007.
11. See Martyn McLaughlin, "He touched hearts...." The eulogy was given by Dr George Reid, former presiding officer of the Scottish Parliament; First Minister Alex Salmond was in attendance, as was former First Minister Lord McConnell of Glenscorrodale, who was the one to bestow the title of Scots Makar on Morgan in 2004. Tributes were paid to Morgan by many, including many poets and jazz saxophonist Tommy Smith, with whom Morgan had collaborated on "Planet Wave."
12. Peter McCarey, "Edwin Morgan the Translator" in *About Edwin Morgan*, Eds. Robert Crawford and Hamish Whyte (Edinburgh: Edinburgh University Press, 1990), 96.
13. Marco Fazzini, "Edwin Morgan: Two Interviews" in *Studies in Scottish Literature* 29 (1996, 45–57), 54.
14. The other Hungarian poets who appear in the *Collected Translations* are Endre Ady, Ágnes Gergely, Lászlo Kálnoky, Lajos Kassák, Ottó Orbán, Miklós Radnóti, Dezsö Tandori, Mihály Váci and István Vas.
15. Edwin Morgan, *Collected Translations* (Manchester: Carcanet, 1996), xxi. James McGonigal tells a slightly different story of how Morgan first discovered József, stressing

the involvement of Hugh MacDiarmid who initially wanted Morgan's assistance translating some of József's poems, and ultimately passed the whole task on to Morgan (James McGonigal, 113).

16. *Edwin Morgan: Nothing Not Giving Messages...*, 22.

17. Interview with Marshall Walker (Glasgow, 25 August 1975), reprinted in *Edwin Morgan: Nothing Not Giving Messages: Reflections on his Work and Life*, 82.

18. Edwin Morgan, "The Third Tiger: The Translator as Creative Communicator" in *Channels of Communication*, Eds. P. Hobsbaum, P. Lyons and J. McGhee (Glasgow: University of Glasgow Department of English Literature, 1992), 43.

19. Edwin Morgan, *Collected Translations*, xxi.

20. See, for example, *Modern Hungarian Poetry*, Ed. and intro. Miklós Vajda, foreword by William Jay Smith (New York: Columbia University Press, 1977), xxxii–xxxiii, where Vajda refers to Morgan as that "indefatigable and brilliant Scottish poet [...], for whom nothing seems untranslatable." In 2001, the *Babel Guide to Hungarian Literature* praised Morgan's translations of Weöres in particular: "a small section of Weöres's output has been very capably presented by Edwin Morgan, one of the most important translators of the second half of the century, in the *Penguin Modern European Poets Series*, along with another important poet Ferenc Juhász" (Ray Keenay, Vivienne Menkes-Ivry and Zsuzsana Varga et al, *Babel Guide to Hungarian Literature* (Oxford: Boulevard, 2001), 107). Praise does come from a native English speaker perspective too: Christopher Whyte, for example, notes the quality of Morgan's translations, stating that they were "of such merit that they would eventually form a collected volume to set beside his original work" (Christopher Whyte, *Modern Scottish Poetry* (Edinburgh: Edinburgh University Press, 2004), 136).

21. Douglas Gifford, "Obituary: Edwin Morgan OBE, poet." See also Tom Hubbard, "Doing Something Uncustomary: Edwin Morgan and Attila József" in *International Journal of Scottish Literature* 1 (Autumn 2006, 1–9), 6.

22. Joseph Farrell, "Edwin Morgan: Language at Play. In Conversation with Joseph Farrell" in *Stages of Translation*, Ed. and intro. David Johnston (Scarborough: Absolute Classics, 1996), 221.

23. Simon Armitage, "The Knight's Tale," *The Guardian* 16 December 2006, *http://www.guardian.co.uk/books/2006/dec/16/poetry.simonarmitage*.

24. *Post-colonial Translation: Theory and Practice*, Eds. Susan Bassnett and Harish Trivedi (London: Routledge, 1999), 4.

25. Edwin Morgan, *Collected Translations*, xxi.

26. Joseph Farrell, "Edwin Morgan: Language at Play. In Conversation with Joseph Farrell," 226–227.

27. Edwin Morgan, *Collected Translations*, xxi.

28. Tom Hubbard, "Doing Something Uncustomary...," 1–2.

29. *Edwin Morgan: Nothing Not Giving Messages...*, 38–39.

30. Tom Hubbard, "Doing Something Uncustomary...," 2.

31. Tom Hubbard, "Doing Something Uncustomary...," 2. Hubbard also mentions the fact that much of Morgan's introduction to *The City of Dreadful Night* could well have been said about József and the author himself.

32. Ray Keenay, Vivienne Menkes-Ivry and Zsuzsana Varga et al., *Babel Guide to Hungarian Literature*, 108.

33. Tom Hubbard, "Doing Something Uncustomary...," 2.

34. Tom Hubbard, "Doing Something Uncustomary...," 2–4.

35. Edwin Morgan, "Afterword: The Challenge of Weöres" in *Sándor Weöres: Eternal*

Moment. Selected Poems, Ed. and intro. Miklós Vajda (London: Anvil Press Poetry, 1988), 147.
   36. Edwin Morgan, "Afterword: The Challenge of Weöres," 147.
   37. Miklós Vajda, *Modern Hungarian Poetry*, xxvii.
   38. Miklós Vajda, *Modern Hungarian Poetry*, xxvii.
   39. Miklós Vajda, *Modern Hungarian Poetry*, xxvii–xxviii.
   40. Edwin Morgan, "Afterword: The Challenge of Weöres," 147.
   41. Simon Armitage, "The Knight's Tale," and Seamus Heaney, "Seamus Heaney on *Beowulf* and his Verse Translation," http://www.wwnorton.com/college/english/nael/beowulf/introbeowulf.htm.
   42. Tom Hubbard, "Doing Something Uncustomary...," 1.
   43. Quoted in Edwin Morgan, *Selected Poems: Sándor Weöres and Ferenc Juhász*, Transl. and intro. Edwin Morgan (Harmondsworth: Penguin, 1970), 9.
   44. Quoted in Alison Flood, "Edwin Morgan, Scotland's national poet, dies aged 90," *The Guardian* 19 August 2010, http://guardian.co.uk/books/2010/aug/19/edwin-morgan-scotland-national-poet.
   45. Interview with John Schofield, reprinted in *Edwin Morgan: Nothing Not Giving...*, 49.
   46. Edwin Morgan, "For the Opening of the Scottish Parliament, 9 October 2004" in *A Book of Lives* (Manchester: Carcanet, 2007), 9–10. On the day itself, the poem was recited by Liz Lochhead, as Morgan was too frail to make the trip to Edinburgh.
   47. Edwin Morgan, *Wi the Haill Voice: 25 poems by Vladimir Mayakovsky*, Transl. Edwin Morgan (South Hinksey: Carcanet, 1972).
   48. Interview with John Schofield, 49.
   49. Joseph Farrell, "Edwin Morgan: Language at Play. In Conversation with Joseph Farrell," 226.
   50. Had Morgan chosen to respond to and reword József and Weöres in Scots rather than English, then the potential audience would have been much smaller. Although, according to the Scottish Government's recent survey, a large percentage of adult Scots claim to have some knowledge of the Scots language, the survey also showed that most use the language only in spoken form and do not read or write it.
   http://www.scotland.gov.uk/Publications/2010/01/06105123/4. Some Scots poets would of course have also had the option of translating these poems into Gaelic, but, as Morgan was not a Gaelic speaker, and the Gaelic-speaking population still makes up only a very small percentage of Scotland's population, this would hardly have served Morgan's desire to bring József and Weöres to a much wider audience.
   51. This was one of the stories which Liz Lochhead herself told during the Edwin Morgan tribute evening on 9 March 2008 at Glasgow's Aye Write! book festival.
   52. See Ian Bell, "Why is our nation so poorly versed in the art of poetry?," *The Herald* 21 August 2010, 13.
   53. Alexander Moffat and Alan Riach with Linda MacDonald Lewis, *Arts of Resistance: Poets, Portraits and Landscapes of Modern Scotland* (Edinburgh: Luath Press, 2009), back cover.
   54. Lesley Duncan, "Poetry—Edwin Morgan at 90," *The Herald* 27 April 2010, http://www.heraldscotland.com/poetry-edwin-morgan-at-90-1.023542.
   55. Edd McCracken, "Edwin dreamed lines of poetry until the very end," *The Herald* 22 August 2010, http://heraldscotland.com:80/news/home-news/edwin-dreamed-lines-of-poetry-until-the-very-end-1.1049719.

Works Cited

Armitage, Simon (2006),"The Knight's Tale," *The Guardian* (16 December), London. *http://www.guardian.co.uk/books/2006/dec/16/poetry.simonarmitage.*
Ballads of the Book. (2007). Chemikal Underground. Compact disc.
Bassnett, Susan and Harish Trivedi (eds.) (1999), *Post-colonial Translation: Theory and Practice.* London: Routledge. *http://www.bbc.co.uk/news/uk-scotland-glasgow-west-12227515.*
Bell, Ian (2010), "Why is our nation so poorly versed in the art of poetry?," *The Herald* (21 August), Glasgow, 13.
Campbell, James (2010), "Edwin Morgan obituary," *The Guardian* (19 August), London. *http://www.guardian.co.uk/books/2010/aug/19/dewin-morgan-obituary.*
Crawford, Robert (2007), *Scotland's Books: The Penguin History of Scottish Literature.* London: Penguin.
_____and Hamish Whyte (eds.) (1990), *About Edwin Morgan.* Edinburgh: Edinburgh University Press.
Duncan, Lesley (2010), "Poetry — Edwin Morgan at 90," *The Herald* (27 April), Glasgow. *http://www.heraldscotland.com/poetry-edwin-morgan-at-90-1.1023542.*
_____ (2010), "Edwin Morgan: An Appreciation," *The Herald* (21 August), Glasgow, 18.
Farrell, Joseph (1996), "Edwin Morgan: Language at Play. In conversation with Joseph Farrell," in *Stages of Translation.* Ed. and intro. David Johnston. Scarborough: Absolute Classics, 219–27.
Fazzini, Marco (1996), "Edwin Morgan: Two Interviews," in *Studies in Scottish Literature,* 29, 45–57.
Flood, Alison (2010), "Edwin Morgan, Scotland's national poet, dies aged 90," *The Guardian* (19 August), London. *http://guardian.co.uk/books/2010/aug/19/edwin-morgan-scotland-national-poet.*
Gifford, Douglas (2010), "Obituary: Edwin Morgan OBE, poet," *The Scotsman* (20 August), Edinburgh. *http://news.scotsman.com/obituaries/Obituary-Edwin-Morgan-OBE-poet.6485326.jp*?
Heaney, Seamus (1999), "Seamus Heaney on *Beowulf* and his Verse Translation." *http://www.wwnorton.com/college/english/nael/beowulf/introbeowulf.htm.*
Hubbard, Tom (2006), "Doing Something Uncustomary: Edwin Morgan and Attila József," in *International Journal of Scottish Literature,* 1, 1–9.
Idlewild (2002), *The Remote Part.* Parlophone. Compact disc.
József, Attila (2001), *Sixty Poems.* Transl. Edwin Morgan. Glasgow: Mariscat.
Keenay, Ray, Vivienne Menkes-Ivry and Zsuzsana Varga et al. (2001), *Babel Guide to Hungarian Literature.* Oxford: Boulevard.
McCarey, Peter (1990), "Edwin Morgan the Translator," in *About Edwin Morgan.* Eds. Robert Crawford and Hamish Whyte. Edinburgh: Edinburgh University Press, 90–104.
McCracken, Edd (2010), "Edwin dreamed lines of poetry until the very end," *The Herald* (22 August), Glasgow. *http://www.heraldscotland.com:80/news/home-news/edwin-dreamed-lines-of-poetry-until-the-very-end-1.1049719.*
McGonigal, James (2010), *Beyond the Last Dragon: A Life of Edwin Morgan.* Dingwall: Sandstone Press.
McLaughlin, Martyn (2010), "He touched hearts: Farewell to Makar Edwin Morgan,"

The Scotsman (27 August), Edinburgh. *http://thescotsman.scotsman.com/news/He-touched-hearts—farewell.6498061.jp?*.
Marsack, Robyn and Hamish Whyte (eds.) (2010), *Eddie@90*. Edinburgh: Scottish Poetry Library and Mariscat Press.
Moffat, Alexander and Alan Riach with Linda MacDonald Lewis (2009), *Arts of Resistance: Poets, Portraits and Landscapes of Modern Scotland*. Edinburgh: Luath Press.
Morgan, Edwin (1988), "Afterword: The Challenge of Weöres," in *Sándor Weöres: Eternal Moment. Selected Poems*. Ed. and intro. Miklós Vajda. London: Anvil Press Poetry, 147.
_____ (2007), *A Book of Lives*. Manchester: Carcanet.
_____ (1990), *Collected Poems: 1949–1987*. Manchester: Carcanet.
_____ (1996), *Collected Translations*. Manchester: Carcanet.
_____ (2010), *Dreams and Other Nightmares: New and Uncollected Poems 1954–2009*. Edinburgh: Mariscat.
_____ (1973), *From Glasgow to Saturn*. Cheadle: Carcanet.
_____ (2000), *Jean Racine's Phaedra: A Tragedy*. Manchester: Carcanet.
_____ (2000), *New Selected Poems*. Manchester: Carcanet.
_____ (1970), *Selected Poems: Sándor Weöres and Ferenc Juhász*. Transl. and intro. Edwin Morgan. Harmondsworth: Penguin.
_____ (1984), *Sonnets from Scotland*. Glasgow: Mariscat.
_____ (1992), "The Third Tiger: The Translator as Creative Communicator," in *Channels of Communication*. Eds. P. Hobsbaum, P. Lyons and J. McGhee. Glasgow: University of Glasgow Department of English Literature, 43–59.
_____ (1972), *Wi the Haill Voice: 25 poems by Vladimir Mayakovsky*. Transl. Edwin Morgan. South Hinksey: Carcanet.
Pollock, David (2007), "Playing Around by the Book," *The Herald* (21 April), Glasgow, 6–7.
Scottish Government (2010), "Public Attitudes Towards the Scots Language," *http://www.scotland.gov.uk/Publications/2010/01/06105123/0*.
Thomson B.V., James (1993), *The City of Dreadful Night*. Intro. Edwin Morgan. Edinburgh: Canongate.
Vajda, Miklós (ed. and intro.) (1977), *Modern Hungarian Poetry*. Foreword by William Jay Smith. New York: Columbia University Press.
Whyte, Christopher (2004), *Modern Scottish Poetry*. Edinburgh: Edinburgh University Press.
Whyte, Hamish (ed.) (1990), *Edwin Morgan: Nothing Not Giving Messages: Reflections on his Work and Life*. Edinburgh: Polygon.

PART V: IRONY, PLAY AND PLEASURE

13. Auden's Irreducible Art

Boutheina Boughnim Laarif

Auden's lifelong commitment to formal, metrical poetry, as opposed to his predecessors Eliot and Pound who tried their hand at free verse, does not stem from a mere aesthetic choice aiming at sophistication and technical accomplishment, but is rather grounded on a whole poetics, that which Gotlieb identifies as Auden's "poetology,"[1] which envisions the poem as an "analogy" to paradise in the sense of "perfect order."[2] Such heavenly harmony — endemic, in Auden's view, to metrical verse — may be thought of as operating against a current state of ubiquitous disarray and anxiety. Among the aspects bearing on this heavenly harmony is the sublime experience of poetic rhythm which, in an age, oppressively turned towards "reducibility" and digitalization,[3] may be thought of as countering that general propensity to reducibility by conferring something which is intrinsic to the ineffable power of poetry's rhythm whose appeal and effect exceed the confines of linguistic and semantic reduction, being fundamentally a physical, bodily experience. The present article aims to identify the ways formal poetry turns into a tool of resistance to reduction by referring to three emblematic poems by Auden. The first two that may be qualified as public — that is bearing on political, social, existentialist themes — are "September 1, 1939" and "Spain, 1937"; the other, pertaining to the private biographical poems of Auden's personal experiences, is entitled "This Lunar Beauty."[4] These poems will be read in the light of two approaches to poetry's irreducibility — Derrida's, through his hedgehog figure and notion of "poematic experience" expounded in his essay "Che cos'è la Poesia"[5]; and Aviram's, through his allegorical theory of poetry clarified in "Telling Rhythm."[6]

One of the most striking metaphors alluding to the untamable, irreducible character of poetry is Derrida's catachresis of the "hedgehog"[7]; a striking metaphor which brings to the fore poetry's twofold essence as both extremely fragile and dauntingly impenetrable. Derrida draws on the description of poetry as a "hedgehog" "rolled up" in itself, counting on its "spines" to ward off the danger of being manhandled, in order to imply that, likewise, poems are language "turned in onto"⁸ itself and count on their intrinsic difficulty or impenetrability to resist discursive reduction. Poetry's defense-system, keeping to Derrida's catachrestic hedgehog, can be seen as its endemically abstruse character. In his essay, Derrida identifies poetry's vocation — the "gift" of the poem⁹ — as lying outside Western — more specifically German — idealistic tradition, notably Heideggerian, which hallows poetic discourse's ascendancy over other discourses:

> Most of all do not let the *hérisson* be led back into the circus or the menagerie of *poiesis*: nothing to be done¹⁰ (*poiein*), neither "pure poetry," "nor pure rhetoric," nor *reine sprache*, nor "setting-forth-of-truth-in-the-work..." The gift of the poem cites nothing, it has no title [...], it comes along without your expecting it, cutting short the breath, cutting all ties with discursive and especially literary poetry. In the very ashes of genealogy. Not the phoenix, not the eagle, but the *hérisson*, very lowly, low down, close to the earth. Neither sublime, nor incorporeal....¹¹

Thus, relying on Derrida's definition of the poetic "gift," we may infer that poetry's resistance lies precisely in its adherence to humility, its earthly character which is to be understood outside the Heideggerian "world" vs. "earth." Heidegger opposes the two notions of "world" and "earth," identifying the former as basically "self-disclosing openness," "the tangible," but also "the ever-non objective" reality that binds us in the very history of our being to the external world; "world" is opposed to "earth," upon which the world, i.e. the art work's material, is "grounded," is fundamentally "self-secluding" and reveals itself as such.¹² Derrida's notion of the earthly essence of the poem is, on the contrary, as suggested in the last sentence of the passage quoted above, far removed from Heidegger's ontological idealism, if one may venture the expression. Derrida stresses the earthly nature of poetry to imply its down-to-earth, palpable essence, akin to its own material — language.

This "lowly" essence of poetry is inscribed in Derrida's alternative to the "poietic" essence of poetry, which he refers to as the "poematic" experience.¹³ Such experience calls upon one vital element for poetry's condition of possibility: the heart. The latter, as identified by Derrida, is not the heart in the biological, metaphorical, philosophical or even ethical senses.¹⁴ Rather, the heart in Derrida becomes the site of two presumably contradictory notions, interiority/inwardness (of the most intimate feelings and thoughts¹⁵) and the exterior mechanism of the poetic sign.¹⁶ The "heart,"¹⁷ as construed by Derrida, is a common territory for both notions; it fuses affective inwardness with prosodic mechanism, which ascribes a universal dimension to poetic discourse governed by these rules of the "heart." In this sense Clark argues: "to learn by heart is also to learn by rote, to be dictated, ventriloquized. It is to commit to a mnemotechnique, to the automatism of signs that seems thus to supplant the apparent immediacy of what is entrusted to them [poems], possessing the psyche they touch."[18] Accordingly, the allegedly contradictory notions of "inwardness" and "automatism" are brought into joint play within the site of the heart and their antagonism is substituted for by a mutual contamination[19]: "*Heart*, in the poem, 'learn by heart' (to be learned by heart), no longer names only pure interiority [...] The memory of the 'by heart' is confided like a prayer [...] to a certain exteriority of the automaton, to the laws of the mnemotechnics, to that liturgy that mimes mechanics on the surface [...]."[20] Thus, for Derrida, the notion of "heart" is the throbbing pulse of poetry; the latter its incarnation. The poematic experience can thus be seen as the "desire"[21] to "learn by heart" that which broaches the heart: "*Literally*: you would like to retain by heart an absolute form, an event whose intangible singularity no longer separates the ideality, the ideal meaning as one says, from the body of the letter. In the desire of this absolute non-absolute, you breathe the origin of the poetic [...]."[22]

Such "absolute" form is consigned, then, to the consecration of "heart" as Derrida conceives it, an interplay between interiority and interiorization, a form of "ideality" which equally binds "body" and "letter," and hence: "[...] better binds the presenting to the presented,"[23] conducive to both "full presence" and "full speech,"[24] reminiscent of Auden's identification of poetry as "a way of happening."[25] However, the aspiration for such presencing experience, or what T. Clark determines as "an experience of total immediacy," is bound to clash with its realization as "powerlessness" or "ecstasies." The inexorable interrelation between the experience of "powerlessness" or "ecstasies" is clarified by Clark by being associated with "an experience of impossibility,"[26] traceable to Derrida's deconstructive notion of the "poetic," according to which the subject ceases to be itself,[27] if ever it had been itself, and is prone to the overpowering desire, "apprendre par coeur"; such desire, Clark argues, gives precedence to "alterity" over "auto-affection" as its condition of possibility; without the "other"/"otherness," subjectivity would not be conceivable.[28] The "poematic" experience is the experience of the impossibility of "identity-to self"[29]; it supplants subjectivity by otherness; the poem is entrusted to the "other" as an utterance which bespeaks his/her most intimate concerns: "[...] the poem is a [...] voyage toward the other as if toward the being lost in anonymity, [...] an imparted secret, at once public and private, *absolutely* one and the other, absolved from within and from without...."[30]

Accordingly, it seems that poetry is not conceivable outside such a duality, or what Derrida defines as both a "double restraint" and "aporetic constraint."[31] Poetry, according to him, is constrained by that insoluble contradiction, a twofold double bind: first, it commits itself to language, that which imperils its very survival. In this sense, Derrida defines poetry as "a thing beyond languages, even if it sometimes recalls itself in language."[32] In this sense, Clark argues while quoting Derrida: "The poetic takes place only at the risk of disappearing into the very economy of language which it needs and unsettles, those 'sentences that circulate risk-free through the interchanges and let themselves be translated into any and all languages.'"[33] From another angle, poetry's "autotelic"[34] vocation suggested by the hedgehog figure rolled up onto itself can only be conceived of as directed towards the other to whom the hedgehog points its spines.[35] Hence, the double law which is ascribed to poetry's "autotelic" nature is manifested in the poem's vocative essence by intrinsically seeking to reach out for the other to penetrate his flesh by irresistibly attending to his bodily participation. As a "hedgehog" figure pricking up its spines, poetry, similarly, imposes its "incision"[36]; that is, it punctures absolute subjectivity. In this sense, poetry is defined by Derrida as "…a silent incantation, an aphonic wound that, of you, from you, I want to learn by heart."[37] Such "wounding" power of poetry can be considered as, among other things, "the inscriptive force" of its rhythm[38] which punctures subjectivity and leads, as Lacoue-Labarthe would contend, to its "desistance,"[39] or in Derrida's terms, its realization as a "syncope."[40] Both notions designate a fracture in subjectivity, as Derrida explains in his introduction to Labarthe's book "Typography":

> We are constituted by ... rhythm, in other words *(de-)constituted* by the marks of this "ceasured" stamp, by this "rhythmo-typy" which is nothing other than the divided idiom in us of desistance [...] The "character" it imprints or prescribes is not the attribute of the being we are, not an attribute of our existence. No, before the stance of our being-present, before its consistency, its existence, and its essence, there is rhythmic desistance.[41]

Auden's poem "September 1, 1939" evinces both criteria of Derrida's notion of the heart: intimacy and mnemotechniques. It broaches the heart of the "Collective Man" and opens a deep wound, the ever-whirling spiral of persecution and xenophobia.[42] The compelling three-beat rhythm of its eleven-lined stanzas makes it resound in the reader's mind and heart as an "aphonic wound," a "silent incantation" meant to make an incision in language.[43] This wound releases both "the deaf" and "the dumb," "commuters" and "governors"[44] from their debilitating, stultifying habits and the self-righteous doctrines of the moral and historical determinism they are inexorably caught up in.

Auden's poem is replete with allusions, notably to thinkers of the Renaissance and the Enlightenment, like Luther for instance, along with, though not mentioned in this poem, but referred to by Auden elsewhere, other thinkers like Machiavelli and Descartes who have ensconced the notion of the "Economic Man."[45] What has ensued, according to Auden, from such individualistic doctrines is an oppressive, deeply entrenched self-love and egotism nourished by glaring greed and impudent ambitions, as is suggested in the sixth stanza of "September 1, 1939."

Auden's poem, as Anthony Hecht argues, "is about the curse and the cure."[46] The curse lies in the chain of violence, as is echoed in the twenty-first and twenty-second lines which allude to the notion that one returns evil for evil. The cure which Auden proffers in his poem for the whole toil of humanity is simply "universal love."[47] The poem's much debated line, by both Auden and critics, "We must love each other or die." enacts Derrida's notion of the "syncope," that is a fracture of subjectivity,[48] through its appeal to unconditional mutual love with its vocative apostrophe "we" and imperative modal "must." Without the other's hearkening to Auden's "voice,"[49] the whole poem cannot follow the twofold rule of the heart which brings into joint play "pure interiority" and the "exteriority of the automaton."[50] Thus the poem can ensure its survival only by being taken up and cherished by the other, to whom it "is confided like prayer"[51]; the poem as a hedgehog-figure rolled up with its outward-pointing spines resists "death," the "catastrophe"/the "accident"[52] of oblivion only when it cuts through to the heart of the other/reader and its latent anxieties; only then does it remain in both the heart and memory of the other/reader as both an indelible trace and a haunting "incantation," which is certainly the case of many poems of Auden's, notably "September 1, 1939."

Derrida's hedgehog figure compellingly suggests poetry's twofold resistance: first, its propensity to defend itself against being entirely subsumed into language,[53] as it is altogether something beyond language. Poetry's second form of resistance consists in its operating against the notion of subjectivity as "identity-to-self or presence-to-self of consciousness."[54] The poetic as Derrida identifies it, "absolute non-absolute," which constitutes the very essence of Auden's appeal to "universal love" in his poem "September 1, 1939," thus substitutes the "normal heart"[55] for Derrida's "poematic heart,"[56] which opens to the other, and can be offered like a precious present.

"Spain, 1937" is arguably written in the same 'vein' as "September 1, 1939." It is incontestably a powerful call to resistance, a cry from the "heart," associating "Madrid" with the "heart" in stanza nineteen. It admirably illustrates Derrida's laws of the heart, through the heightened sense of empathy and the recitation made possible through its tight-knit metrical and blend of sonorities. With its peculiar, complex metrical patterning, haunting refrain-like lines and compelling call to action, Auden's poem resounds as an overpowering "incantation,"[57] an exaltation of the reader's predisposition to resistance which he/she can barely resist. In "Spain, 1937," Auden is no longer content with bringing about a change of attitude in the reader as is the case with his poem "September 1, 1939." Rather, he is intent on enacting such change by a resoundingly persuasive call to action (and arms) to allow such a "heart" to enact its most cherished precepts, ensconcing the "Just City."[58] The poet and critic Hecht highlights the exhorting tone, and "embattled" quality of Auden's poem, making of it a genuine, outspoken "call to action."[59] His insightful comment on the connection between the thematic dimension and rhythmic aspect of Auden's poem "Spain, 1937," and more precisely on how the concept of history is articulated, is worth quoting in its entirety for it shall provide a pertinent illustration of Derrida's envisioning of the poem as "a prayer," "a dictated dictation"[60] through the twofold power of the "heart"[61]: "It ["Spain, 1937"] is built rhetorically around the historical trinity of past, present and future, which recur as rhythmic refrains throughout the poem under the names of "Yesterday," "Today," and "Tomorrow," and in rhythmical, repetitive patterns that are little short of ecclesiastical."[62] Not only is history articulated in thrice recurring rhythmic patterns, the whole poem is forcefully orchestrated into a relentlessly repetitive stanza pattern in the form of quatrains in stressed verse that follows the same stress pattern — 4/3/4/4 — reminiscent of the ballad's enticing tempo.

The stanzas sketch out some past facts and their unfathomable logic by listing a plethora of miscellaneous events that have marked human history. Before putting forward this varied chronicle, Auden invokes three representatives of humanity: the poet, the scientist and the destitute who stand helplessly hesitant before the startling legacy of the past and the foreboding future awaiting them, as is suggested in the seventh, eighth and ninth stanzas of "Spain, 1937."

While the poet focuses on his intuitively prescient, visionary speculations, being fundamentally a visionary, the scientist counts on meticulous examination, whereas the poor seem closest to finding a way out of humanity's predicament. However, changing the course of history is far from being an easy task for it works according to a mystery, "a hidden law," as Auden claims in "The Hidden Law."[63] His claim that "Poetry makes nothing happen," may be understood as meaning that the incommensurable scope of history's power and tyranny makes it infinitely hard to resist its unfathomable logic.[64] However, by no means does Auden extol complacency and submission; he advocates both the verbal and physical involvement of artists so that they enact his most intimate convictions; his trip to Spain in 1937 to take part in the "struggle" and resolve both physically and verbally to support the Republican cause evince his eagerness for a long-awaited "change of heart,"[65] evoked in his earlier poem "September 1, 1939." Hecht points out:

> But Auden himself was perfectly aware that this ["Poetry makes nothing happen"] was not the case, for in May 1937 the poem "Spain, 1937" was issued as a pamphlet, with all royalties going to Medical Aid for Spain; and quite apart from whether or not the poem changed anyone's mind about the Spanish conflict, or even played the smallest part in anyone's decision to enlist against Francisco [Franco], the very fact of the contribution of the royalties to even so politically neutral a cause as Medical Aid signifies that, for all its irrelevance to the practical world of political action, *poetry can make and has made something happen.*[66]

According to the speaker of the poem, the only way to resist history's ruthless impassiveness and undo its puzzling schemes is to respond to the call of the heart. In the second line of stanza nineteen, the speaker associates "Madrid" with the "heart," which implies that what affects Spain/Madrid should affect all humanity, for only the "heart" can foster such solidarity.

Humans are also invited by Auden to discard all leisurely trifles, and postpone them to the "future," because the present priority lies in "struggle," as is suggested by the relentlessly recurring, refrain-like "But to-day the struggle."[67] In his "utopian"[68] vision of the future, Auden expects poets to detonate like "bombs"; their words shall resound like "bombs" in the conscience of the young as their unbridled verve shall be most prolific ever. However, in time of war, deeds are needed, more than words, though the latter may trigger them. "Struggle" becomes a vital necessity and can only affect history's intransigent course by rallying all forces, as is suggested from stanza eleven to stanza nineteen.[69]

For Auden, history should be perpetually (re)-molded by personal choice and action. He regards the Spanish Civil War more as a catalyst which is meant to sensitize humans to the ugly sides of their history and to the inevitable price to pay to preserve their survival and dignity through "struggle" which constitutes the very essence of their existence. Otherwise, and in the absence of action and resistance in a time of urgency, only bitterness and utter disarray are all that is left to humanity, as is hinted at in the last two stanzas.

Poetry's rallying power and its resistance to reduction have also been broached differently by Aviram who, drawing on Lyotard's thought,[70] ascribes to poetry the power to resist "an economy of disposability and planned obsolescence," thanks to poetry's endemic use of rhythm.[71] Aviram argues that poetry's resistance to reduction is heightened in the case of "traditional metric poetry" because metrical rhythms are more apt to call upon the reader's sensibility, to "...appeal to the body in its fundamental existence, prior to or outside the ideologies that construct the body within any social code."[72] Poetic meaning is to be understood only as an allegory[73] or an attempt "to rationalize the physical energy of poetic rhythm"[74]: this energy is the bodily experience of poetic rhythm, and it intrinsically exceeds discursive/linguistic reduction. Such an allegorical relation between the "meaningful" (images and metaphors) and the "meaningless"[75] (poetic rhythm) imparts to poems their unfathomable quality; they are to be read as "self-reflexive allegories of their own failure to speak their own message, which is the energy of their rhythmic being ... a speaking of the inability to speak the unspeakable."[76] Each poem recounts, in its own way, through its own semantic message, a sort of scenario, which may bear on a variety of themes. However, all poems do convey the notion of language's inadequacy before "the sublime infinitude of rhythm — that is, of life's [own] infinite possibilities."[77] Poems testify to their "inability to speak the unspeakable." This is not negative, for it points to "a vitality outside language."[78] By calling into question the validity of its own linguistic medium, poetry proffers a momentary liberation from the oppressive political, social and cultural constructs and prejudices which this very medium ensconces.[79]

"This Lunar Beauty" is rooted in the subversive possibilities of rhythm. In this poem, composed presumably upon Auden's seeing a photograph of the loved one as a child,[80] Auden portrays a particular type of unalterable beauty, a beauty that could be described in Nietzschean terms as "originary" or "primal"[81]; it is wraithlike, otherworldly, exceeding the bounds of reality and the mutability of human sensations and psyche; in a word, it is incommensurable, in the very image of the poem's own rhythm. We, as readers, stand mesmerized by the incommensurability of the type of beauty evoked and the poem's own ethereal, almost hypnotic two-beat rhythm, whose overpowering resonance seems to ward off the "ghost" of mortality that hovers over the poem.[82]

Auden composed this poem at an early period of his poetic career, during which he was still reserved about his homosexuality[83] which he wished to consider as outside the established oppressive social and political constructs. His use of a compellingly simple but almost esoteric language (like his cryptic use of "lover" and the ambiguous demonstrative pronoun "this" or possessive adjective "His"),[84] and a forcefully cadenced rhythm may be thought of as testifying to the speaker's aspiration for some transcendental experience. The latter may be mediated by the sublime[85] power of the poem's own rhythm which exceeds the confines of linguistically and culturally mediated reality and prejudices, so that poems are to be perceived as "allegories of the sublime power of their [own] rhythm," disclosing, as such, their own inability to represent what is by essence beyond semantic/linguistic reduction. The poem comes to "challenge socially prevalent concepts, dislodging them momentarily so that they can change as part of historical processes."[86] It is all these features which mean that "This Lunar Beauty" stands outside the realm of the reducible, testifying, as such, to the incommensurability of the speaker's experience of his homosexuality and the reader's experience of the poem's own rhythm.

Accordingly, whether overt or understated, thematic or allegorical, resistance is almost ubiquitous in Auden's poetry. His allegation that "Poetry makes nothing happen"[87] is not meant to dwarf poetry's status, but rather implies that its essence is not factual, but rather experiential. The enduring quality of many of Auden's poems is traceable to the power of their rhythms, as well as to the poet's unique treatment of miscellaneous issues, and ability to confer upon them a curious universality.

Notes

1. S. Y. A. Gotlieb, *Regions of Sorrow: Anxiety and Messianism in Hannah Arendt and W. H. Auden* (Stanford: Stanford University Press, 2003), 82.
2. W. H. Auden, *The Dyer's Hand and Other Essays* (New York: Vintage Books, 1989), 71.
3. A. F. Aviram, *Telling Rhythm–Body and Meaning in Poetry* (Michigan: The University of Michigan Press, 1994), 325.
4. See *The English Auden-Poems, Essays and Dramatic Writings 1927–1939*, Ed. E. Mendelson (Great Britain: Redwood Burn, 1982; first edition, 1977): "September 1, 1939" (245–247), "Spain, 1937" (210–212), "This Lunar Beauty" (52); other poems mentioned in this essay include "In Memory of W. B. Yeats" (241–243) and "The Hidden Law" (156).
5. Jacques Derrida, *Points.... Interviews, 1974–1994*, Ed. ElizabethWeber, transl. Peggy Camuff and others (Stanford: Stanford University Press, 1995), 289–299.
6. Aviram, 5.
7. Derrida, *Points...*, 289.
8. Aviram, 35.
9. Derrida, *Points...*, 97.
10. Derrida's claim reminds us of Auden's statement in his "Elegy to W. B. Yeats" that "Poetry makes nothing happen."
11. Derrida, *Points...*, 97.
12. Martin Heidegger, *Poetry, Language, Thought*, Transl. Albert Hofstadter (New York: Harper Colophon Books, 1975), 48.
13. Derrida, *Points...*, 304.
14. Derrida, *Points...*, 291.
15. Timothy Clark, *The Theory of Inspiration* (Manchester: Manchester University Press, 1997), 270.

16. Derrida, *Points...*, 286.
17. Derrida, *Points...*, 291.
18. Clark, 264.
19. C. Malabou clarifies: "The motif of the heart links those of intimacy and the mechanical"; cf. Claire Malabou and Jacques Derrida, *Counterpath—Traveling with Jacques Derrida,* Transl. David Willis (California: Stanford University Press, 2004), 268.
20. Jacques Derrida, *Points...*, 295.
21. Derrida, *Points* ..., 293.
22. Derrida, *Points...*, 293; 295.
23. Jacques Derrida, *The Derrida Reader,* Ed. Julian Wolfreys (Edinburgh: Edinburgh University Press, 1998), 285.
24. Derrida, *The Derrida Reader,* 285.
25. "Elegy to W. B. Yeats."
26. Clark, 265.
27. Philippe Lacoue-Labarthe, *Typography–Mimesis, Philosophy and Politics* (California: Stanford University Press, 1989), 196.
28. Clark, 265.
29. Clark, 267.
30. Derrida, *Points...*, 295.
31. Derrida, *Points...*, 293; 295.
32. Derrida, *The Derrida Reader,* 284.
33. Clark, 263.
34. Derrida, *Points...*, 293.
35. Clark, 265.
36. Clark, 277.
37. Derrida, *Points...*, 297.
38. Lacoue-Labarthe, 34.
39. Lacoue-Labarthe, 35.
40. Clark, 265.
41. Lacoue-Labarthe, 31.
42. "September 1, 1939."
43. Clark, 277. Clark evokes "the incision of the poetic mark in language."
44. "September 1, 1939."
45. John Fuller, *A Reader's Guide to W. H. Auden* (London: Thames and Hudson, 1970), 260.
46. Anthony Hecht, *The Hidden Law–The Poetry of W. H. Auden* (London: Harvard University Press, 1993), 161.
47. "September 1, 1939."
48. Clark, 265.
49. "September 1, 1939."
50. Malabou and Derrida, 264.
51. Derrida, *Points...*, 292.
52. Derrida, *Points...*, 293.
53. Derrida, *Points...*, 297.
54. Clark, 265.
55. "September 1, 1939."
56. Derrida, *Points...*, 304.
57. Derrida, *Points...*, 297,
58. "Spain, 1937."

59. Hecht, 122.
60. Derrida, *Points...*, 289.
61. Derrida, *Points...*, 291.
62. Hecht, 122.
63. "The Hidden Law."
64. "Elegy to W. B. Yeats."
65. "September 1, 1939."
66. Hecht, 121–122 (italics mine).
67. "Spain, 1937."
68. Hecht, 129.
69. "Spain, 1937."
70. Aviram, 32.
71. Aviram, 34.
72. Aviram, 35. Aviram adds: "Given the importance of rhythm as already resistant to reduction, clearly the more powerful the rhythm and the more strongly it resists being coopted into meaning, the more effective it will be in achieving the postmodernist goal."
73. Aviram, 225.
74. Aviram, 35.
75. Amittai. F. Aviram, *Telling Rhythm–Body and Meaning in Poetry*. (Michigan: The University of Michigan Press, 1994), 21.
76. Aviram, 24.
77. Aviram, 285.
78. Aviram, 25.
79. Aviram, 244.
80. Fuller, 45.
81. Frederick Nietzsche, *The Birth of Tragedy*, Transl. Douglas Smith (Oxford: Oxford University Press, 2000), 35.
82. Fuller, 45.
83. Hecht, 446.
84. N. F. Blake, *An Introduction to the Language of Literature* (Singapore: Macmillan Education Ltd., 1990), 137.
85. Aviram, 239.
86. Aviram, 223.
87. "Elegy to W. B. Yeats."

Works Cited

Auden, W. H. (1989), *The Dyer's Hand and Other Essays*. New York: Vintage Books.
_____ (1974), *Forewords and Afterwords*. Ed. E. Mendelson. New York: Vintage Books.
_____(1977), *The English Auden — Poems, Essays and Dramatic Writings 1927–1939*. Ed. E. Mendelson. London: Faber and Faber.
Aviram, A. F. (1994), *Telling Rhythm–Body and Meaning in Poetry*. Michigan: The University of Michigan Press.
Blake, N. F. (1990), *An Introduction to the Language of Literature*. Singapore: Macmillan Education Ltd.
Clark, Timothy (1997), *The Theory of Inspiration*. Manchester: Manchester University Press.

Derrida, Jacques (1998), *The Derrida Reader*. Ed. Julian Wolfreys. Edinburgh: Edinburgh University Press.

_____(1995), *Points.... Interviews, 1974–1994*. Ed. Elizabeth Weber, translated by Peggy Camuff and others. Stanford: Stanford University Press.

Gotlieb, S. Y. A. (2003), *Regions of Sorrow: Anxiety and Messianism in Hannah Arendt and W. H. Auden*. Stanford: Stanford University Press.

Fuller, John (1970), *A Reader's Guide to W. H. Auden*. London: Thames and Hudson.

Hecht, Anthony (1993), *The Hidden Law—The Poetry of W. H. Auden*. London: Harvard University Press.

Heidegger, Martin (1975), *Poetry, Language, Thought*. Transl. Albert Hofstadter. New York: Harper Colophon Books.

Lacoue-Labarthe, Philippe (1989), *Typography–Mimesis, Philosophy and Politics*. California: Stanford University Press.

Malabou, Claire, and Derrida, Jacques (2004), *Counterpath: Travelling with Jacques Derrida*. Transl. David Willis. California: Stanford University Press.

Nietzsche, Friedrich (2000), *The Birth of Tragedy*. Transl. Douglas Smith. Oxford: Oxford University Press.

14. Hugo Williams
Standing the Test of Time?
Adrian Grafe

In the conclusion to an appreciation of the poetry of John Betjeman, Hugo Williams quotes the first stanza of Betjeman's from the poem "Ireland with Emily," beginning: "Has it held, the warm June weather?" Williams goes on to praise Betjeman's mastery of memory and language, and ends: "Has it held? Has it held? I think we can say it has."[1] Betjeman's is the only poetry, as far as I know, for which Williams has written an introduction and from which he has made a selection. Though his own poetry differs from Betjeman's in many ways, what it shares with it can be seen as a kind of resistance. The aim of this chapter is to discover and explore what kind or kinds of resistance this could be, and what the object(s) of such resistance are. Despite his gripe against manifestoes in this piece, in some ways his introduction to Betjeman stands as a manifesto of his own: the deeper he explores the spirit of Betjeman's poetry, the closer he comes to the spirit of his own. This is partly because he feels that Betjeman always remained true to his own identity and wrote out of it, rather than taking his cue from what Williams sees as the bookishness of the Modernists. This is not to say, however, that for all the crucially autobiographical dimension of Williams's work, he views poetry as self-expression. Far from it: he denies the latter definition, insisting rather that poetry is "making something."[2] This makes Williams's own analogy between making a dam and making a poem, discussed below, all the more understandable. The poetry is as it were in the making: the shaping into lines of poetry of, in Williams's case, what is presented as autobiographical material, whether it is factually so or not. There is a certain pleasing smoothness to Williams's poetry: he calls his poems "rather streamlined," like a fast car, perhaps.[3] Yet this very smoothness can also be seen as an artistic effect, hard to achieve. His poetry shuns both the facile traps of self-expression and the complexities of Modernism. He isn't averse to intertextuality, but only uses it sparingly: it is not a literary principle in itself, as it is for Modernism, but must be required by the context.

The Movement, that loose grouping of fifties poets including Kingsley Amis, Philip Larkin, Thom Gunn, John Wain, Elizabeth Jennings, and others, with the spirit of which Williams aligns himself, aimed at a low-key rhetoric: it "turned the volume down" (a phrase from Williams's poem "Some R & B and Black Pop"[4]), wanting to stay close to the everyday, choosing (relatively) straightforward language, and in that respect was a reaction to the Modernism of Eliot and Auden. If it had an icon, rather than poets of the past it was Thom Gunn's "Elvis Presley," a poem celebrating an artist who was a contemporary, popular cultural figure — just as Larkin celebrated Sidney Bechet and seemed to love Louis Armstrong as much for his connection with his audience as for his artistry, which Larkin deeply admired. Williams actually defines poetry as "a subtle form of entertainment."[5] In one brief phrase he thus strips the poet of the vatic function he or she has enjoyed since time immemorial down to Eliot and on to Ted Hughes and Geoffrey Hill. By seeing poetry as entertainment, Williams is able to pick up on the entertainment value in Modernism; at least, that is how one might interpret his completely original linking of Eliot and Betjeman. He compares Betjeman's "Clash Went the Billiard Balls" to Part II of the *Waste Land*: both poems feature pub voices saying goodnight in demotic tones.[6] Hugo Williams has said that he considers Larkin to be the greatest twentieth-century poet, followed by MacNeice.[7] What is notable about this statement is not the choice of these particular poets so much as the fact that it conspicuously omits both Eliot and Auden, who would probably be many if not most people's first choices. (Ted Hughes, whose poetry and thought do not seem to bear much witness to the influence of the poetry of Eliot, described the latter as the greatest and most inspired poet in the English language since Shakespeare).[8] Williams is a poet of wit and verve — the wit more often than not at his own expense, which makes it all the more endearing — but beneath it all, beneath the relish for the "sweeter things of life"[9] and the jokey English Hugh-Grant-type pretend incompetence and diffidence, there is not only the mastery of language he finds in Betjeman but also a current of regret and melancholy — symptoms of loss indeed. There is a kind of friction between these two dimensions of Williams's writing, friction due to the fact that each dimension as it were resists the other. Resistance to Modernism, and indeed other literary trends, does not wholly define the special quality of Hugo Williams's poetry, but it certainly contributes to doing so.

There are no poems featuring Betjeman's bohreens or fuschias in Hugo Williams's own poetry. But what he does have is three dam poems: the first is "A Dam" from the 1994 volume *Dock Leaves*; the third, "Washing My Hands," revisits "A Dam," and closes the *West End Final* collection of 2009. Its position at the end of the volume, as a kind of coda casting its clarity back over the whole volume, makes the metaphor even clearer all the same: "The dam seems to be holding."[10] This is an image of the poem as resistance. The dam makes the stream back up, reminiscent of Harry Fainlight's line "That miraculous stream that flows uphill," defying nature in a magical way, or taking part in nature in the only way that makes any sense: by playing with it and in it.[11] And for the dam to be effective, human hands have to be able to let it go, so that it literally holds its own. The image of the overflowing banks is a sign that the dam is successful. Making the dam is not pointless; it's not competitive; it requires concentration; it's riveting, the most riveting moment being the one where the poet takes his hands away. It's child's play. The involuntary surge of memory at the beginning of the poem, brought on by the vision of the hands in the water leads on to an act of resistance to what Bowie in "Changes" calls "the stream of warm impermanence": that act being making the dam, making the poem. The dam dams up the stream. The poem dams up the flow of time. But will it last? Will it hold?

Similar water imagery crops up, incidentally, in passing, in Williams's introduction to his Betjeman selection: "Nowadays everything passes away so quickly on the tide that there is no time for Betjeman's brand of lyricism even to recognize it, let alone pin it down so fervently."[12] An earlier poem, "A New Page," begins with the poet writing his lover's name "on a new sheet" which he goes on to describe as zigzagging like ice on a lake which will not break if only he "keep[s] moving."[13] The decisive iambic meter, stress on key words like "stand," "weight," and "crack," and hard, aggressive consonantal rhymes give the lines a decisive feel: the ice is harder than it looks. This ice, like the dam, is an image of resistance; it functions elsewhere in the poem as an image of the coldness standing between the poet and the addressee; the ice stands between them but the ice, the resistance, is more on the side of the addressee. Does he keep moving? Will the ice hold? After all, like the child's dams in Williams's poems, the ice here is portrayed as fragile. Perhaps it is the fragility of these things that paradoxically gives them their resistance, their capacity to survive as poetic creations.

In order to attempt to answer such concerns, one needs to be aware of the kind of poet Williams is. In connection with this, some words of Philip Larkin's, writing about Hardy, come to mind: "He's not a transcendental writer, he's not a Yeats, he's not an Eliot." Larkin goes on: "When I came to Hardy it was with a sense of relief that I didn't have to try and jack myself up to a concept of poetry that lay outside my own life."[14] The style of the early Movement was partly a reaction to the abstractions and complexities of Eliot. If one read Williams's poetry against Eliot's programmatic critical statement, "Poets in our civilization, as it exists at present, must be difficult," one could see the kind of poetry Williams writes as resistance to Eliot's statement. The reason why poetry must be difficult is because "our civilization comprehends great variety and complexity, and this variety and complexity, playing upon a refined sensibility, must produce various and complex results."[15] What is especially relevant here is the phrase "playing upon a refined sensibility." To what extent does Hugo Williams allow "our civilization" to "play upon" his sensibility? Many of his poems insist on his physical seclusion: in *Writing Home*, he "tuck[s] himself" into a "deep basement calm," with "windows [...] sealed," so as to be able of "absorb[ing] the shock" of looking back at his father's life and his life with his father.[16] One might see him as blocking out everything here but this one poetic obsession. On a slightly different plane, he's also known not to own a computer or mobile phone, things which have arguably increased the "variety and complexity" of civilization. It would be an exaggeration to claim that Williams cuts himself off entirely from this. Nevertheless, he does not try to reflect it nor does he depend on it. His world is his "dear room"[17] and the happiness that comes from writing in it: the language and feeling of poetic creation, and not the trappings of outward "civilization."

But a further question arises. Apart from cutting himself off from the outside world, the poet describes himself as "dawdling."[18] Such "dawdling" can in itself be called a sort of resistance — resistance to worldly ambition, resistance to a world in which speed is all, and which allows no time for, or views as weak or fatal, the slightest modicum of hesitation. But has he really been "dawdling?" Hugo Williams published his first poetry collection *Symptoms of Loss* in 1965 at the age of 23, and his first prose book, the traveler's tale *All the Time in the World*, the next year. In the years and decades that followed, he published seven further volumes of verse. All eight came out in *Collected Poems* in 2002. He was one of the youngest poets to be included in Larkin's *Oxford Book of Twentieth Century English Verse* (1973). In 1981, he published a second piece of travel writing, an account of a reading-tour in America, *No Particular Place to Go*. His *Selected Poems* appeared in 1989. A collection of pieces from his TLS "Freelance" column came out in 1995 as *Freelancing: Adventures of a Poet*. The poet hoped his *Collected* would not be a *Complete*, and it isn't. He's brought out two volumes since then, *Dear Room* in 2006, and *West End Final* in 2009 — for this poet an unusually brief gap between two collections, and which heralds a fruitful "late Williams" period. He also edited *Curtain Call: 101 Portraits in Verse* (Faber, 2002) and the afore-mentioned Betjeman edition. These volumes all taken together form a body of work and a literary achievement both remarkable and unique. He's gone from strength to strength, and his poetic powers show no sign of waning. His technical mastery and openness to experience may mean that his best work is still to come.

One reader, however, who has proved resistant to Williams's poetry is the critic Robert Potts who, assessing Williams's T.S. Eliot Prize-nominated *Billy's Rain* in the Guardian in 2002, called him a "one-club golfer," meaning his style and subject matter were limited. Williams went on to win the prize for the volume. Potts, interviewed when Williams's *Collected Poems* came out, stuck to his guns: "one-club golfer is the right phrase."[19] This in itself reveals a limited, blinkered approach to Williams's poetry which, given its formal and thematic variety — easily resists criticism on this basis.

If there is thematic resistance within the poetry of Hugo Williams, one form in which it manifests itself is his speaker's self-avowed reluctance to work. His poetry from *Writing Home* onwards began to suggest that he didn't want to work, though one finds traces of this in earlier poems: we find him "Sheltering from work" in the first "Bar Italia"[20]; "I didn't want to work" he says in "Man and Superman."[21] Poems such as "Tipping My Chair" and "A Start in Life" make the same point.[22] Though his alter ego, Sonny Jim, seems to have a job in construction in "The World of Work," six poems later the reader is relieved to learn that Jim's now "out of work."[23] Shirking, in the form of sleeping in, is the order of the day in the Larkin-inspired "Religion."[24] Such poems, some published in the Thatcherite era, chime with Raymond Carver, who amid the Reaganomics of the mid-eighties published the two poems "Loafing," where we find the poet "doing nothing at all," and "Shiftless," in which he claims he "never liked work."[25] In a study of Charles Bukowski, the American critic Gay Brewer insists on the fact that Bukowski enjoys "the subversive leisure that is a reclamation of one's own life."[26] Brewer also says: "Bukowski's work places a high premium on free/freed time. Although mandatory for the writer's craft, leisure constitutes [...] a passive aggression toward a society that it implicitly rejects."[27] Although Williams is not exactly a socially rebellious writer in the way that Bukowski presents himself as being, Williams's attitude to work as he expresses it in his poetry often seems to carry with it a sense of the passive aggression Brewer hints at here.

Despite claiming not only to dislike work but to be "[D]awdling in peacetime/Not having to fight...," Hugo Williams is in fact a war poet (he was born in the middle year of World War II, 1942). He began a piece for the Poetry Book Society Quarterly in 1970, presenting his collection *Sugar Daddy*:

"One of my themes is the war between objects and people." The war between objects and people, and the danger of turning people into objects, would be the subject of another debate. Nevertheless war is there. In the fine autobiographical piece, "Sex and Poetry," Williams says:

> What was so hot about an education which had never once touched on poetry except as parrot-fashion "saying lessons?" And even then in antique diction? Politics, philosophy, criticism, sex, money, conversation, dancing were other essential omissions in a gentleman's education. Don't imagine I didn't enjoy myself, but how did they hope to win us? It was Them and Us forever, six-guns blazing, a weird legacy.[28]

This list is worth lingering over. It contains many of the things that go to make up his poems, things that his elders thought it better he knew nothing about. If we are to take the poet at his word, it seems that a "Them and Us" attitude "forever" informs his poems. This dimension of his poems — as opposed to what he says about them — is hard to pin down, but it's there nonetheless: *us* writing against *them*, perhaps even us *reading* against them. A touch of cheek in the tone, sheer wit, his paradoxically devil-may-care, reckless if ironic attitude to revealing what he sees as his own failures or his cautiousness. The wry, knowing humor — humor the very essence of resistance, as when he resists the end of an affair, incredulous that his lover would accuse him of "loitering without intent."[29] Ever since his early teens, poetry has been his very own act of resistance. Poetry was not on his school curriculum which, as has been made clear by now, he responded to feelingly as being of absolutely no use to him. This is not because he is averse to learning in itself: his TLS "Freelance" columns show what a stickler for facts and history he is. He often works in much erudition to these columns, such as the history of new places he visits, so modestly and smoothly one hardly notices he's doing it. Yet he learns about the world first hand — from experience. His poetry is thus valuable for his ability to put words to his experience and to the feelings that his experience gives rise to. Poetry for the teenage Williams was opposition to school, his own mode of revolt: hence his opposition to Modernist poetry, which in Williams's eyes was the kind of poetry that was more taught on exam syllabuses than read for pleasure.

Williams has built a number of his poems around — if not war directly — the subject of truces at least; nor is it strange that it is precisely through his father's wartime letters that he should choose to let his father, as it were, speak through him. His poems and poem titles reveal a fondness for military or quasi-military metaphors: "Truce," "A Parting Shot," "Another Shot," "Deserter."[30] His fondness for memory is mingled with repression of memory — what he calls in "In the Blindfold Hours" "the memory wars."[31] In

Williams's own words, "themes of resistance/and surrender" ("A Pillow Book," 8), war and truce, echo throughout Hugo Williams's work.[32]

The father in Williams's poems is a demolition expert. The poem is there to show the poet as one of those old-style cartoon characters who get flattened by a steamroller and immediately bounce back up into two dimensions. His father/son poetry is a reckless record of stinging humiliation and shame — reckless because the poet does not spare himself, as when, in "Walking Out of the Room Backwards," he depicts his shame as the father punishes or humiliates his son by making him do the eponymous action.[33] Such moments are among the most poignant and memorable — the most resistant — in his poetry. When he gets caned in front of the School Debating Society the boy does not tense up as the master takes aim, nor does he resist during the caning itself. Rather he "absorbs," "storing away" his "tears" and "cries."[34] Rather than non-violent resistance, he practices violent non-resistance.

In some ways his speakers present themselves as taking the path of least resistance: doing nothing, saying nothing, flying, floating, drifting.... And that, paradoxically, is a sort of resistance in itself: resistance to whatever is heavy, monumental, impressive, self-important. Yet some things just won't go away. Poem titles and lines recur at different stages in his career. These might be called nodes of resistance. The Sonny Jim poems spanning several decades of Williams's poetic output, are among his most resistant poems, his toughest. Sonny Jim makes his first entry into Williams's poetry in the 1970 *Sugar Daddy* collection. He keeps cropping up off and on over the next few decades, latterly in 2006's *Dear Room*. If his poems are "self-satires" as he calls them,[35] they work precisely because the self—most selves, at least — resist being satirized, while calling out to be satirized. The American poet Reed Whittemore's poem "Clamming" says that the self refuses to "let go of its even most fictional grandeur...."[36] Hence the interest of having an alter ego: Chinalski for Bukowski, Henry for Berryman, Sonny Jim for Williams. There are three poems entitled "Everyone Knows This," and two poems entitled "Bar Italia."[37] The three truce poems from collections from different times —1975's *Some Sweet Day*, 1994's *Dock Leaves*, and 1999's *Billy's Rain*— enact that difficult space, and would tend to confirm that Hugo Williams is a kind of war poet.[38] The songs in his 1994 *Dock Leaves* poem "Untitled" return five years later in *Billy's Rain*'s "Blank Pages": "two-note songs without refrains."[39] "Blank Pages" finally gives way to "the sensation of falling," a phrase that had already appeared in "Lightly Clenched Fists."[40] These things help to structure the whole of Williams's work; they act as a kind of scaffolding, giving it solidity and resistance.

"Clenched fists" are a sign of resistance, but they are clenched "lightly" and anyway the poem "goes floating past on a lilo." As "Self-Portrait with a Slide" makes clear, the adult speaker does occasionally try to resist.[41] He can't get hold of his pencil stub or nudge it into upright position. "Everything," in fact, "slips through [his] fingers," as he tries not to slide down to the kitchen. He does dig in his heels but has soon lost his footing as the medium of time proves too slippery for him. He clings to the table-cloth but down he goes at the end of the poem. His poems are not the products of the will. They are the "involuntary cries" his speaker utters in the last line of that poem. Those cries could be those of hilarity or joy or horror, or all those things mingled together, as in a photo at the Explora exhibition at the *Cité des sciences* in Paris showing some little girls sliding down a huge, steep slide with a mixture of all these emotions on their faces, their mouths wide open so the spectator could hear their cries.

The self, "what a brute it is," tells itself fictions, lies. It places these lies between itself and reality, or what really happened. They're all there: curtains, trap doors, walls, reflections in lieu of the real thing. These things are obsessions, and in that respect they resist. Exactly twenty years after the first "Bar Italia" (1979), he's back in the "Bar Italia," reflections taking the place of the absentee, and therefore making her present. She could be one and the same person addressed in the first "Bar Italia," or different, or perhaps both, like the poet himself. It is the place and the situation, the waiting, that resist. Perhaps the speaker likes the "long mirror" in the "Bar Italia" because it reminds him of that other "long mirror," that of his boyhood; the "long mirror" in which he spends his time on his own at home playing his father. Many of Hugo Williams's poems enacting his boyhood are not only about his father but rather about his wanting to be his father. He doesn't want to be himself, he wants to be his father. His father resists. The poems stage confrontations — battles in the war between the boy and his father. His father's resistance to his claim to wanting to be an actor like him, is in fact what frees the speaker of these poems to be himself: to be a poet even if, to paraphrase Bowie, he seems "immune" to his father's "consultations." There is as much drama in clenched fists as in a punch, if not more so. Williams's poems are every bit as dramatic as those poems of Robert Lowell's in which he reverts obsessively to his attack on his father. Lowell writes in "Anne Dick, 1. 1936": "I knocked my father down." "I struck my father": the blow, and the speaker's apology, are "never to be effaced." ("Mother and Father 1").[42] In the 1994 collection *Dock Leaves*, the father challenges the boy on his knowledge of London theater. Again the boy hides his frustration, clenching his fists "under the table," muttering "something about television."[43] In the recent poem, the second of the dam poems mentioned above, "The Mouthful," the military images come thick and fast: the poem begins with "steel-tipped arrows," while the father's widow's peak is "pulled down," resembling "a Norman helmet"; he has eyes of "shrapnel." The boy is making "dams out of mashed potato" on his plate: these dams are his unspoken emotion, compounded, when his father scolds him for his damming, when, as in "Man and Superman," he "clench[es] [his] fists under the table."[44] Dams and hidden clenched fists are the boy's resistance, his anger, expressed in verse half a century later. Hugo Williams's poetry is the man answering his father back: something he couldn't do as a boy, in the face of his father's cruelty: "My father never opened his mouth unless it was for some perfectly cruel witticism."[45] Resistant to, and angry at, the father, all "air of sealed regret,"[46] Hugo Williams breaks the seal on the regret; the poem is his fists unclenching; the dam overflows its banks, and turns into "Death of an Actor" and the other father poems of *Writing Home* and other poems. The lyricism of the nine brief lines of the third section of "Death of an Actor," beginning "Gold on the doorstep" — with the last line, in which the father's throat is "torn to sand," literally pulverizing that lyricism — has rarely if ever been surpassed in contemporary English poetry. Gold as resistance, sand as fragility. Tony Harrison's well-known poem "Timer," about his mother's wedding-ring, offers another reminder of gold's resistance, the ring surviving the crematory fire in which the mother's body is placed. Behind Williams and Harrison stands Donne's gold in "A Valediction Forbidding Mourning":

> Our two soules therefore, which are one,
>   Though I must goe, endure not yet
> A breach, but an expansion,
>   Like gold to ayery thinnesse beate.

You can beat gold to an "airy thinness" and it will still resist. Its resistance lies in its malleability — in Donne's poem, in its very ability to be fragile. It is not strange that Williams should pick up on a similar strand in Betjeman's poetic: he writes of his elder's "emotional nakedness," his "rawness," the "confessional details" that fill his work, his "moments of weakness" and "odd failures."[47] Gold is also at the origin of the expression "the acid test," because unlike all other metals it won't dissolve in nitric acid. Gold: beautiful, tough and malleable. Of a favorite poem of his in 1985, Williams said: "Dowson writes so beautifully [...] that he eliminates all trace of effort from his work."[48] This doesn't mean that there is no effort. Of Betjeman, Hugo Williams writes: "if he ever permitted us to pause we might glimpse a more recalcitrant material from which such casual brilliance had been persuaded to unfold. I wonder from what inauspicious lump of rock he carved the unforgettable image of the couple 'In a Bath Teashop.'"[49] Williams assumes, with his allusion to effort, and with this sculpting metaphor, that resistance lies as it were behind the poem, forming its hinterland. This isn't the way we usually think of

Betjeman. Dams, ice, gold: not the usual things that are associated with Hugo Williams's poetry. With the one exception of gold — what better or more precious? — he doesn't much pause to give us a glimpse of "more recalcitrant material": he doesn't pause much, he keeps on moving in case the ice gives way beneath him. Will his gold pass the acid test? He is, in Bowie's words, "much too fast to take that test." "The dam seems to be holding." And it *is* holding. But will it last? Will it go on holding? I think we can say it will.

Notes

1. John Betjeman, *Poems selected by Hugo William* (London: Faber and Faber, 2006), xvii.
2. In a talk given at Artois University in France on June 3, 2010.
3. Hugo Williams, "Freelance," in TLS, June 25th, 2010, 16.
4. Hugo Williams, *Some R&B and Black Pop* (Warwick: The Greville Press, 1998), 7.
5. Hugo Williams, Artois University.
6. John Betjeman, x.
7. Hugo Williams, Artois University.
8. Cf.. Ted Hughes, *Winter Pollen: Occasional Prose* (London and Boston: Faber & Faber, 1995), 291: Eliot is "a poet who stands in English with maybe only one other name."
9. A phrase the poet used in private correspondence with the author to describe the kind of music he liked and was able to get hold of at Ray's Jazz record shop in Soho.
10. Hugo Williams, *West End Final* (London : Faber and Faber, 2009), 57.
11. Harry Fainlight, *Selected Poems*. Edited and introduced by Ruth Fainlight (London : Turret Books, 1986), 51.
12. John Betjeman, ix.
13. Hugo Williams, *Collected Poems* (London: Faber & Faber, 2005), 79 (2002).
14. Philip Larkin, *Required Writing: Miscellaneous Pieces 1955–1982* (London: Faber and Faber, 1983), 175.
15. T.S. Eliot, *Selected Essays,* 3rd edn. (London: Faber, 1951), 289.
16. Hugo Williams, *Writing Home* (Oxford, New York : Oxford University Press, 1985), 56–57.
17. Cf. the title of Hugo Williams's 2006 poetry collection, *Dear Room* (London : Faber and Faber). One is reminded of Pascal: *Tout le malheur des hommes vient d'une seule chose, qui est de ne pas savoir demeurer en repos dans une chambre.* (All human unhappiness comes from one thing only: the inability to stay peacefully in a room).
18. Hugo Williams, *Writing Home*, 60.
19. Potts first called him a "one-club golfer" in a brief review of *Billy's Rain* when it was on the Eliot short-list: *http://www.guardian.co.uk/books/2000/jan/15/poetry.award sandprizes*. Potts stuck to the description when asked to contribute to a Guardian Profile of Williams by James Campbell http://www.guardian.co.uk/books/2002/sep/07/featuresreviews.guardianreview10.
20. Hugo Williams, *Collected Poems,* 75.
21. Hugo Williams, *Collected Poems,* 214.

22. Cf. Hugo Williams, *Writing Home* (Oxford, New York: Oxford University Press, 1985), 15.
23. Cf. "Sonny Jim's House," *Collected Poems*, 166.
24. Hugo Williams, *West End Final* (London: Faber and Faber), 29.
25. Cf. Raymond Carver, *Ultramarine* (New York: Random House, 1986), 59 and 105 respectively.
26. Gay Brewer, *Charles Bukowski*. Twayne : New York, 1997, 145.
27. Brewer, 143.
28. Hugo Williams, "Sex and Poetry" (Autobiographical Essay) in *Poetry Review*, Vol. 73, N° 2, (June 1983, 30–38), 36.
29. Cf. Hugo Williams, *Dear Room*, "Playing Safe," 24.
30. Cf. *Collected Poems*, 57, 218 ("Truce"), 128 ("A Parting Shot"), 138 ("Another Shot"), 191 ("Deserter").
31. Hugo Williams, *Collected Poems*, 228.
32. Hugo Williams, *West End Final*, 43.
33. Hugo Williams, *Writing Home*, 27.
34. Cf. Hugo Williams, "A Suitable Cane," *West End Final*, 17–18.
35. Hugo Williams on *Writing Home*, in Clare Brown and Don Paterson (eds.), *Don't Ask Me What I Mean: Poets in their own words* (London: Picador, 2004; first edition 2003), 310: "My own poems are best described as self-satires."
36. Cf. Reed Whittemore, "Clamming," in *The Penguin Book of American Verse*, Ed. Geoffrey Moore (Harmondsworth: Penguin, 1979; first edition, 1977), 475.
37. Cf. Hugo Williams, *Collected Poems*, "Everyone knows this," 183, 238, 273; "Truce," 57, 218
38. Cf. Hugo Williams, *Collected Poems*, "Truce," 57, 218; "Early Morning," 273.
39. Cf. Hugo Williams, *Collected Poems*, ""Untitled," 240, "Blank Pages," 272.
40. Cf. Hugo Williams, *Collected Poems*, 167.
41. Cf. Hugo Williams, "Self-Portrait with a Slide," *Self-Portrait with a Slide* (Oxford, New York: Oxford University Press, 1990), 55–58.
42. "Anne Dick, 1. 1936," "Mother and Father I," Robert Lowell, *Selected Poems* (New York: The Noonday Press, 1992; first edition 1976), 194, 195 respectively.
43. Hugo Williams, *Collected Poems*, 214.
44. Cf. Hugo Williams, "The Mouthful," *West End Final* (London: Faber & Faber, 2009), 10.
45. Hugo Williams in a *Guardian* interview with him by Emma Brockes, "On leaving my mistress": http://www.guardian.co.uk/culture/1999/oct/27/artsfeatures
46. Cf. Hugo Williams, "Death of an Actor," *Writing Home*, 55.
47. John Betjeman, xii–xv.
48. Hugo Williams, "Ten Desert Island Poems," *Poetry Review*, Vol. 75, N° 3, 1985, 21–28 (26).
49. John Betjeman, xiv.

Works Cited

Betjeman, John (2006), *Poems selected by Hugo Williams*. London: Faber and Faber.
Brockes, Emma (1999), "On leaving my mistress" (interview with Hugo Williams), http://www.guardian.co.uk/culture/1999/oct/27/artsfeatures

Brewer, Gay (1997), *Charles Bukowski*. Twayne : New York.
Brown, Clare, and Paterson, Don (eds.) (2004; first edition, 2003), *Don't Ask Me What I Mean: Poets in Their Own Words*. London: Picador.
Carver, Raymond (1986), *Ultramarine*. New York: Random House.
Eliot, T. S. (1951), *Selected Essays*. Third edition. London: Faber and Faber.
Hughes, Ted (1995), *Winter Pollen: Occasional Prose*. London and Boston: Faber & Faber.
  Larkin, Philip (1983), *Required Writing: Miscellaneous Pieces 1955–1982*. London: Faber and Faber.
Lowell, Robert (1992; first edition 1976), *Selected Poems*. New York: The Noonday Press.
Moore, Geoffrey (ed.) (1979; first edition 1977), *The Penguin Book of American Verse*. Harmondsworth: Penguin.
Potts, Robert (2000), "Best in the Language" (review of the T.S. Eliot Prize short-listed volumes), http://www.guardian.co.uk/books/2000/jan/15/poetry.awardsandprizes
Williams, Hugo (2005), *Collected Poems*. London: Faber and Faber.
_____ (2010), "Freelance," *TLS* (June 25th), 16.
_____ (1990), *Self-Portrait with a Slide*. Oxford, New York: Oxford University Press.
_____ (1983), "Sex and Poetry" (Autobiographical Essay), in *Poetry Review*, Vol. 73, N° 2, June 1983, 30–38.
_____ (1998), *Some R&B and Black Pop*. Warwick: The Greville Press.
_____ (1985), "Ten Desert Island Poems," in *Poetry Review*, Vol. 75, N° 3, 21–28.
_____ (2009), *West End Final*. London: Faber and Faber.
_____ (1985), *Writing Home*. Oxford, New York: Oxford University Press.

15. "Wi Naw Tek Noh More a Dem Oppreshan"[1]
Linton Kwesi Johnson's Resistant Vision
Emily Taylor Merriman

Given his long and public opposition to various ideologies and powers, including racism, economic inequality, and social injustice, Linton Kwesi Johnson (born in 1952, often called LKJ) unquestionably falls into the category of "British poets of resistance." From his earliest work, his radical stance establishes him as a writer whose rhythms and narratives deliberately oppose economic exploitation and social inequality, especially on the basis of race and class. While the interests of Johnson's work have shifted over time with changing historical and social circumstances — becoming more global, for example, as well as more inwardly meditative[2] — he remains an artist whose creative work and other professional pursuits (as an activist, journalist, and record label manager[3]) are directed to resisting oppressive cultural and political forces.

Johnson is often critically and publicly associated with the term "resistance" in its political sense. Rebecca Dyer, for example, contrasts him with Caribbean-British novelist Sam Selvon as an exemplary creator of "overt forms of literary resistance."[4] Today, Johnson's YouTube presence (among a wide range of performances, both accompanied and unaccompanied by music) includes an interview for "People, Signs & Resistance ... a [2009] participatory arts & oral history project" about Brixton[5] and a poetry reading at the 2008 Marxism and Resistance Conference.[6] With reference to a quotation from the poet himself, Hugh Hodges claims, "Poetry may never be a substitute for concrete political action, but in the case of Linton Kwesi Johnson's poetry it is never far *from* the action."[7] Acknowledging the much wrestled-with paradox at the heart of consciously political poetry, however, Johnson himself says, "I've never been under the illusion that art changes anything."[8] Art's modes of political resistance are not directly, or at least not measurably, successful.

Yet Johnson's voice of activist resistance, represented on the cover of the

Penguin *Selected Poems* by his distinctive trilby-hatted silhouette speaking into a megaphone, is not political in a narrow sense. (The Johnson trademark profile, with or without megaphone, owes something to visual representations of another boundary-stretching artist, Thelonius Monk.[9]) Johnson's concerns are not confined to inequitable relations of power, or even to issues of culture and identity; he is profoundly concerned with entire worldviews and human behaviors. His modes of resistance operate to protect and promote his understanding of the meaning of human life — an understanding that runs counter to capitalism and consumerism not out of blind loyalty to socialism (although he is a socialist) but because of the joylessness that exploitative materialism engenders. His poetry is founded — even if this is only perceptible at certain moments — on a hopeful vision of pleasure, fun, and peace, and on an assertion of the human right to enjoyment.

Johnson moved from Jamaica to England as an eleven-year-old boy in 1963. His life as a socially-engaged young working-class man of Jamaican origin in late twentieth-century Great Britain shaped his poetic voice. It developed partly out of resistance to the political, educational, legal, and media forces that saw him and his black community as inferior to broader British society and sometimes as legitimate targets for exploitation and brutality. Johnson was involved with the British arm of the Black Panthers and then the Race Today Collective, but he was inspired to write poetry by reading W.E.B. Dubois, *The Souls of Black Folk*.[10] As Alex Pryce puts it, quoting Johnson's own verse, "The 'musik of blood / black reared' ("Bass Culture") is part of community, but it is one *forced into resistance*, at war with itself because of its subordinate class status and the many social problems that causes" (emphasis mine).[11] I would underscore that this "musik" is not only at war with itself, but also with subordinating social forces of long and broad standing. In a 2006 interview with Michael North, Johnson himself states clearly his early means and purposes: "My very choice of language was political. I saw poetry as a weapon in our struggle for black liberation."[12]

In the context of this history and biography, literary critical discussions of Linton Kwesi Johnson's work have understandably focused on three main areas: language, history, and form. First, critics have discussed how and why Johnson chooses to write almost exclusively in a Black British derivative of Jamaican creole — or to use Kamau Brathwaite's term, "nation language"[13] — rather than in Standard English, the culturally dominant dialect of Great Britain. Johnson deploys variant spelling in order to represent the Jamaican accent. In distinctively voiced poems/songs such as "Inglan is a Bitch," the poet's decision to use the language of his home community enables him to both maintain a stronger cultural connection to the indigenous artistic forms of his country of origin and to write lyrics that represent the immigrant experience in Britain. Second, critics have analyzed his work in its historical contexts, for example the Notting Hill Carnival[14] and the Brixton riots of April 1981 ("The Great Insohreckshan" as Johnson called them). Third, there has been considerable debate about his artistic forms, particularly the relationship between his verse and his music.[15]

Johnson is renowned as the founder of a new hybrid genre form called "dub poetry" (a term he coined in 1976),[16] which can be simply defined as the composition or performance of verse to a reggae beat. The meaning of "dub" as a musical term is more complex than this, however. In fact, the website *Classical Reggae Interviews* has compiled a page of quotations from Johnson on the meaning and significance of dub, including the assertion that it is a "deconstructive art" because it involves a studio engineer breaking down the different musical elements and stripping levels of instrumentation away.[17] It is also a constructive art, however, as it involves the laying down of other instruments on the track, or, in the case of dub poetry, the incorporation of the speaking voice. Johnson has tried to clarify his use of the term "dub poetry" by saying that he was talking about what DJs in the early to mid–1970s were doing, and that he in fact prefers to call what he does "reggae poetry."[18]

Reggae today, globally speaking, is a much more popular art form than poetry, which leads Esther Pereen to note that Johnson's work is hard to categorize in relation to high or low culture.[19] As reggae, it has at least the potential for appeal to a wide and varied audience; as poetry, even as performance poetry, it is less evidently attractive. Johnson's work inherently resists cultural categorization, and this commitment has influenced its presentation in practical terms. At times, Johnson has sought to reverse his poetry's social marginalization by performing it with a dub band; at others, he has rejected public performance and musical accompaniment in order to focus attention on his lyrics, which — as separate forces of meaning-making — are sometimes overshadowed by the power of the music. The music operates on emotional and sensual levels that can drown out the semantic declarations.

As a consequence of this range of concerns, there are intrinsic tensions within Johnson's modes and purposes. The music (usually some form of reggae) that often accompanies Johnson's verse in performance tends to reinforce this hopeful, even joyous vision, but such reinforcement can be problematic, as the relaxed enjoyment of the music easily turns into an end in itself. If and when that happens, the effect is to reduce the quality of mindful resistance that generated the pleasure-giving form in the first place, even while it engenders the very enjoyment which ranks high in Johnson's scale of values. The creatively instigated resistance can be swallowed up in the relatively passive reception of the artistic product.

One critic who has wrestled with this dilemma in specific reference to Linton Kwesi Johnson is Walter Bernhart. Prompted by Johnson's own words and choices about performance, Bernhart argues that music can actually "destroy" the political message that the lyrics are seeking to convey. This is particularly so under four conditions: when the words really do wish to communicate something specific rather than to arouse an emotional state, when the music is not itself in interpretive dialogue with the text, when there is a large (and so more anonymous, less intimate) audience, and (not surprisingly) when individual listeners are more interested in music than words.[20] Bernhart cites one particular but representative incident when an audience in Zurich (usually an enthusiastic venue) was not interested in Johnson's unaccompanied spoken word poetry, and he felt that "his words had lost all their impact, as expressions of his strong moral concerns, through the addition of music."[21] It is possible to go too far, however, in the assertion that the reggae "kills" the message. Bernhart accuses a commentator of naiveté in the assertion that "'Johnson uses the rhythms of reggae to get his message across,'" but the truth is that the reggae both enhances the appeal of his message and, at least under certain circumstances, interferes with its communication.[22]

The relationship between words and music in reggae poetry can be put into a wider sociological context by drawing on the work of Simon Frith, who proposes that in the context of culture's political role, "the concept of 'resistance' is [...] slippery." He asks,

> How should we distinguish between the ways in which people use culture to "escape," to engage in pleasures that allow them a temporary respite from the oppressive relations of daily life (a function of working class leisure that the bourgeoisie have always encouraged), and those uses of culture which are "empowering," which bring people together to change things?[23]

Frith acknowledges that it is "not a simple matter of either/or: 'resistance' shifts its meaning with circumstance."[24] Similarly, Johnson's work tries to provide pleasure while arguing vociferously for political change. It also makes an implicit but powerfully unifying argument: this political change must happen so that opportunities for rest and pleasure and joy (such as that an audience might experience in listening to Johnson) can be both maximized and fairly distributed.

As previous commentators have noted, popular culture is not necessarily an arena of resistance to hegemonic culture, although it may have that capacity.[25] Both as an activist and as a poet, Johnson has an interest in finding ways to make his spoken word available and attractive to audiences despite as well as because of his use of reggae music. In this he has been reasonably successful: if his work is considered to be popular music, it does not have a huge listenership, but Johnson has at times garnered audiences as large as 10,000[26]—an enormous audience for the work of a poet. Johnson has written eloquently of how, without music, the poem is both "unadorned" (less attractive, perhaps) and "unfettered"—freer to express what only words alone can say.[27] It is one of the limitations of critical prose (limitations, in this instance, reinforced by my own lack of training in music) that the analysis in this chapter must be restricted for the most part to a consideration of the plain "unfettered" verse.[28]

In one of Johnson's earlier poems, "Want fi Goh Rave," a speaker sets up a frame narrative in which, while moving on foot through an urban environment, he overhears a series of three young men discussing their situation. Amor Kohli astutely notes and discusses the similarity of the poem to William Blake's "London."[29] The opening of "Want fi Goh Rave"[30] is calm and ordinary, a past tense recollection that belies the present intensity of the actual circumstances at the heart of the poem:

> I woz
> waakin doun di road
> di adah day
> when I hear a likkle yout-man say
> him seh:

The quoted first speaker protests his unhappy circumstances, which are the consequence of economic deprivation and social inequities, and which lead to his feeling of existential emptiness:

> yu noh si mi situation
> mi don't have noh acamadeshan
> mi haffi sign awn at di stayshan
> at six in di evenin
> mi seh mi life gat noh meanin
> I jus livin widout feelin

The quoted youth has a sense of what would help him: enough money to be able to party, dance, and meet other young people in a way appropriate to his years:

> still
> mi haffi mek a raze
> kaw mi come af age
> an mi want fi goh rave

In the two subsequent vignettes of the triptych, Johnson presents an escalation of the characters' desperation for the things that young men in Western society believe they need to feel alive and be of value. The second young man refuses to labor for an inadequate wage ("mi naw wok fi noh pittance") or to rely on self-esteem-destroying government dole-outs ("mi naw draw dem assistance"). Instead, he enterprisingly sets up a "lickle rackit," but it is stopped by the police, and he too runs up against a dead end in his quest to "goh rave." The quotation from the third young man, who narrates his increasingly large crimes of theft, illustrates how deprivation can lead both to the deepening moral corruption of the individual and to negative consequences for others, who are subjected to pick-pocketing, stealing, and burglary:

> mi haffi pick a packit
> tek a wallit fram a jackit
> mi haffi dhu it real crabit
> an if a lackit mi haffi pap it
> an if a safe mi haffi crack it
> ar chap it wid mi hatchit

The frame narrator, who introduces this third speaker with a subtly weary "I woz / waakin doun di road / yet anadah day," does not return to close the frame at the end of the poem, so it ends with the chorus again: "mi haffi mek a raze / kaw mi come af age / an mi want fi goh rave." The verse implies that this speaker will have some opportunities to "goh rave" at least for a while, but at costs that include the stimulation of his own material greed ("crabit" is a Jamaican word for "greedy," extant in England till the eighteenth century[31]) and his likely eventual incarceration. Additionally, other people will lose their wallets or have their homes broken into, and banks will be robbed. The succession of increasingly violent verbs underscores this progression of non-bodily violence: "pick," "pap," "crack," and "chap."

Teaching this poem in the early 1990s at a sixth form college in Walthamstow, northeast London, proved an edifying experience for me. Students enjoyed working with the non-standard language, with which (in some instances) they were more familiar than the teacher. In the intellectual and intimate classroom environment, where close attention to and consciousness about language use were required, the music (on a tape recording) reinforced the interest and appeal of the poem's message rather than distracted from it. Most notably, sixteen- to eighteen-year-olds were gratified to read, experience, and discuss quality verse concerning circumstances that some of them knew only too well.

In "It Noh Funny," a poem from the same era as "Want fi Goh Rave," Johnson talks (or, to be more precise, talks about how people talk) about how young men will take chances without counting the costs. Johnson suggests that their desires (at least some of them) are the legitimate desires of young people, and natural desires unfulfilled will turn dangerous:

> dem wi' tek chance
> fi get a likkle kile
> dem wi' tek chance
> fi live-it-up in style
> dem wi' tek chance
> fi goh jump and prance
> dem wi' tek chance
> far dem love blues dance
> dem wi' tek chance
> an dem don't count di cauce

The dancing rhymes, mostly "-ance" but a little "-ile," underscore the inevitability of the young people's choices, and the unrhymed ominous final line of the stanza points toward worrisome consequences that the poem's audience must then consider. If the "yout af today" are "carryin on a way" (and they get up to more serious shenanigans involving drugs and sex later in the poem), then what is the responsibility of the wider society for the understandable if risky choices of these young people? Part of Johnson's vision of resistance involves waking up or educating his readers so they can perceive the operative forces in society, both those forces that are inevitable and those that may be stopped or changed. (Readers will be unsurprised to learn that Johnson holds a degree in sociology.) It is not possible to resist anything if you aren't aware that there is anything to resist.

These questions about listener or reader response and responsibility raise further questions about the nature of Johnson's audience. Who reads him? Who listens to him? To put the questions in terms of the theme of this volume — to what extent is Johnson a representative speaker on behalf of community resistance in which his audience is already engaged? Or, to what extent does he resist his own (wider?) audience, and to what extent does his audience resist him? To some degree these are unanswerable questions. Johnson's use of Black British English identifies him closely with his community of origin. Yet to be published by Penguin — for a while, Johnson was one of only two living authors published in their Modern Classics series (*Mi Revalueshanary Fren*, 2002) — is to suggest full entry into the literary establishment and access to its range of readers. Yet I suspect that some readers still think of his work as belonging to minority interests, either people of color or white people who want to be "politically correct" (one of the negative labels that can enable shortcuts in thinking).

According to Miranda Moore, Johnson's current audience (like the audience for most poetry) is white and middle-class.[32] (One might add, also, probably female — but reliable statistics on any of these variables are hard to come by.) However, Johnson is also often spoken of as a leader of the black community, someone whom "the West Indian community rallied behind" in the context of the racially conflictual events of the 1970s and 1980s.[33] In the

1970s, his audience was primarily black communities in London.[34] Since then, his dub poetry tours have taken him all over the European continent and to America, although he is not very well-known in the United States. When students as far afield as San Francisco are introduced to his work, however, they are extremely receptive. In general, the homeland of Beat poetry is delighted to encounter dub poetry.

It is reasonable to make a comparison here with the world's most famous reggae artist, Bob Marley; one can see Johnson's primary audience as being to a large extent ethnically and nationally constituted, but acknowledge that his work appeals to many people in Great Britain, parts of Europe, parts of the Caribbean, and potentially all over the globe — mostly people who would define themselves as politically left and perhaps resistant to hegemonic or standard Western consumerist culture as they see it.

Much Western culture at the end of the twentieth and beginning of the twenty-first century is marked by the increasingly rapid pace of production, information-gathering, work, consumption, entertaining diversions, and even activities as basic as eating. Resisting this acceleration is difficult for many reasons, including the anxious sense that one is being left behind — in business, in technology, in social relationships, in knowledge. Yet such acceleration is marked by self-evident dangers: superficiality, loss of self-awareness, and loss of human connection and community. The media regularly publishes articles about the negative consequences of new technologies that speed things up, and there has been a rise of movements advocating a return to "slow food" or a slower life in general.[35]

In "More Time," the title work of Johnson's 1998 album, the poet combines his traditionally socialist approach to working hours and conditions with a sense of how the changing era might open up new possibilities for a better way of life. After an opening stanza that discusses how technology might reduce working hours, he includes a first section that lists the potential rewards of such a development:

> more time fi leasure
> more time fi pleasure
> more time fi edificaeshun
> more time fi reckreashan
> more time fi contemplate
> more time fi ruminate
> more time fi relate
> more time

This Biblically-influenced anaphora of "more time" (demonstrating Johnson's familiarity with the King James Version) reinforces the poem's requests, and the rhymes underscore their righteousness. When the lyrics are performed with the Dennis Bovell Dub Band, Johnson's musical backing group of long-standing, the reggae beat sets up a time-taking tempo so that for the duration of the song, at least, there is an impression of "more time" — enough time to do all the things we need to do, and many of those we want to do (and indeed, the song itself lasts longer than the regulation three-minute pop song). A second list reveals that what we really need is a life of love, family, service, creativity, and (even though Johnson is an atheist[36]) spirituality:

> more time fi di huzban
> more time fi di wife
> more time fi di children
> more time fi wi fren dem
> more time fi meditate
> more time fi create
> more time fi livin
> more time fi life

None of this message is original or unusual, or even very interestingly stated, but that doesn't mean it isn't valuable and necessary. Sometimes resistance consists of the repetition of ideas that the distractions of daily labor and easy pleasures might otherwise erase from consciousness.

Such messages have often been uttered from pulpits over the decades. Johnson spent many childhood and adolescent hours in Baptist church services and in forming a relationship with the Bible in English. There is a strong Christian undercurrent in his vision of social justice as the advent of peace and joy for all. When he talks, in one of his rare Standard English poems about life being the "greatest teacher" and the lesson being love ("Seasons of the Heart"), he is building a sermon out of common clichés in a way designed to "correspond to, or represent, a generous common humanity."[37]

Other English poets have uttered similar (often unheeded) messages. To give but one example, there is the end of Edmund Spenser's "Easter": "— Love is the lesson which the Lord us taught." Johnson's adaptations of the English literary tradition both adopt and resist its divided legacies. Russell Banks, in his introduction to *Mi Revalueshanary Fren*, rejects earlier critical comparison of Johnson to John Clare and instead cites a wide range of other voices who work with underlying musical traditions, including "the great Renaissance song-poets like Skelton, Wyatt and Herrick," Robert Burns, Emily Dickinson, Langston Hughes, Amiri Baraka, Michael Harper, and Paul Muldoon.[38] In noting how Johnson reworks the ballad form, Kohli remarks, "Literary resistance here is found in a reconfiguration — into an idiomatic transformation — rather than in a complete rupture."[39] Kohli intriguingly compares Johnson to William Blake; the two poets' radical visions of the human right to joy are strikingly similar.

More surprisingly, one of only five inspirations that Johnson recently cited (he has cited many others in the past) was Gerard M. Hopkins. The others were the Bible, Derek Walcott, Kamau Brathwaite, and Count Ossie & the Mystic Revelation of Rastafari; Hopkins's is the only influence to have originated in England, rather than beyond it.[40] As a Jesuit priest and a patriot, Hopkins might well have taken exception to claims like "Inglan is a Bitch." In what ways has Hopkins inspired Johnson, then? Johnson says that Hopkins's "strange diction really struck a nerve with me as soon as I heard it" but striking word choice is only part of Hopkins's style. Informed by Geoffrey Hill's reading of Hopkins in his essay "Redeeming the Time," I believe the answer lies in certain kinds of rhythmic and linguistic resistance to culturally dominant patterns of language, resistance that might partially define what makes noteworthy poetry. While Hopkins turned to sprung rhythms to enact what Hill calls his "dogged resistance,"[41] Johnson turned to reggae rhythms. Johnson is also practiced in what Hill calls "the antiphonal voice of the heckler."[42] Although the heckling is mostly externally directed rather than being an internal self-questioning, a general distrust of rhetoric, because of its power to mislead, becomes implicit even within the texture of the poem's own rhetorical strategies. In the language of "Fite Dem Back," for example, Johnson takes on the language of British racists, especially those who beat and intimidate people of color on the streets, and turns it against them by ironically quoting their threats and boasts.[43] Johnson said that it, "tried to turn on its head the kind of fascist boot-boys chant that one would hear."[44] He uses the verbal violence of artistic protest against their actual violence, and yet this art (as it knows) also could be accused of encouraging violence.

It is worth asking not only what any poet is resisting (and how), but what he or she is trying to create or protect through resistance. Often it is quite clear what writers are opposed to, but how do they establish and promote whatever it is they are open to? Resistance for resistance's sake risks being swallowed up in its own self-interested territory. In Linton Kwesi Johnson's case, despite his profound seriousness, resistance has definite purposes, and he would be happy for it to become redundant through the accomplishment of its aims. There are some obvious things that Johnson seeks to establish: racial equality, economic justice, and freedom from police brutality. There are times when his pursuit of such goals means that his work acts as propaganda, as he has himself said in an interview:

[In] "Independent Intervenshan."... I was just being a propagandist, basically, was enunciating the position of the alliance of the Race Today Collective, the Black Parents Movement and the Bradford Collective, which was more or less saying that we're not victims and we don't need to be led by the Socialist Workers Party and the Communist Party, and all these parties who were preying and trying to exploit the oppression of black people, and we had a history of resistance and rebellion, and that we could organize our own selves ... quite a few of my verses and recordings in those days were simply serving a propaganda function.[45]

Although sometimes wryly funny ("If I Woz A Tap-Natch Poet" is hilarious[46]) and not difficult in terms of literary allusiveness or complexity of syntax, Johnson's poetry is nevertheless challenging to read. Surprisingly, his difficulty does not arise from his use of Black British dialect, which is mostly comprehensible to a Standard English speaker when heard or read aloud and is instantly accessible to speakers of that dialect. Yet Johnson makes demands of his audience as listeners, thinkers, and moral agents: pay attention, learn about history and society, and accept some responsibility for our own life circumstances and those of our fellow human beings. His role as modest but determined spokesperson for those unjustly served by society renders him resistant to easy accommodation or appropriation.

Yet his work, alongside its life-and-death ethical seriousness, is enjoyable to experience aurally even when unaccompanied by reggae. An underlying motivation for Johnson's righteous anger about racism, economic inequalities, and stunted, warped lives is his vision of the human capacity for joy. In Johnson's work, young people's irrepressible desire to "Goh Rave" should be met, not negated, while adults also have the right to "More Time" for leisure, pleasure, education, and relation. As Russell Banks says at the end of his introduction to the first Penguin edition of Johnson's work, the poems are "redemptive and life-affirming."[47] In an interview, Johnson says (again in one of life's necessary clichés): "you have to have hope and be optimistic."[48] Interviewed by Sue Lawley on Desert Island Discs, Johnson chose John Lennon's "Imagine" as a favorite piece of music. Another (also a choice of Derek Walcott on the same show) was Bob Marley's "Redemption Song."[49]

Johnson's resistance, then, seeks to eliminate unnecessary and unjust suffering *and* to further righteous and uncomplicated human enjoyment. As an older man, he acknowledges that he has become "a little more patient, a little wiser, a little more tolerant,"[50] but he remains uncompromising about the need to value and improve the quality of all human life. Combining wise tolerance with life-long determination requires walking a tight rope, a rope that offers sufficient resistance; slackness rather than tension in the line will make the walker wobble or fall. Johnson's rope is strung along the narrow contiguity of pleasure and protest — step to one side and pleasure becomes self-indulgent passivity rather than righteous joy; step to the other side and protest becomes its own end, blinkered if not blinded to the big view of human life as an opportunity for love.

In a short questionnaire in the *New Statesman* in 2008, Linton Kwesi Johnson wrote, "The creative imagination is a defining characteristic of what it means to be human. Art offers us a vision of how we could be" and "Art has often been the only means for ordinary people to voice their suffering, hopes and aspirations and their vision of change."[51] Alongside the poetry's considered, performative rejection of injustice, the pleasurable elements of Johnson's art resist the joylessness that plagues people of all races and classes in unjust societies. This is not to subsume Johnson's work under a homogenizing universalism that would assimilate and weaken his claims, however. Johnson's voice remains distinctively that of a black British man of Jamaican descent, one whose poetic patterns of resistance have helped to counteract the racist and exploitative aspects of British culture. His example shows how pleasure and protest sometimes work at odds in art's vision of "how we could be," and how they sometimes work together. The voice that resists suffering in the long-term may also alleviate it in the moment; the danger is only that the momentary alleviation obscures the greater vision.

Notes

1. "Di Great Insohreckshan," *Selected Poems* (London: Penguin, 2006), 60. (See "Darcus Howe remembers the 'insohreckshan'" in *The New Statesman*, <http://newstatesman.com/200604030015>, accessed 2 September 2010.)

2. Laurie Taylor, "Leggo Relijan: Laurie Taylor interviews Linton Kwesi Johnson" in *New Humanist* 118:1 (Spring 2003), <http://newhumanist.org.uk/583/leggo-relijan-laurie-taylor-interviews-linton-kwesi-johnson>, accessed 2 September 2010.

3. LKJ Records, <http://lintonkwesijohnson.com>, accessed 2 September 2010.

4. Rebecca Dyer, "Immigration, Postwar London, and the Politics of Everyday Life in Sam Selvon's Fiction" in *Cultural Critique* 52 (2002, 108–144), 139.

5. See the interview at "Linton Kwesi Johnson — People, Signs & Resistance," 23 March 2009, <http://youtube.com/watch?v=mz0etGNTAE0>, accessed 2 September 2010. For more information about the project, see "Sam the Wheels: Local Brixton Films 1960–2008," <http://samthewheels.co.uk/3>, accessed 2 September 2010.

6. "Linton Kwesi Johnson: Marxism 2008: Cultures of Resistance," <http://youtube.com/watch?v=J09FRtkyZ6k>, accessed 2 September 2010.

7. Hugh Hodges, "Text Version: Linton Kwesi Johnson's Dub Poetry in Print" in *Xavier Review* 22:2 (Fall 2002, 60–79), 60. See Burt Caesar, "Linton Kwesi Johnson talks to Burt Caesar" in *Critical Quarterly* 38.4 (1996, 64–77), 77.

8. Taylor interview with Johnson, "Leggo Relijan."

9. See, for example, the front cover of Robin D. G. Kelley, *Thelonious Monk: The Life and Times of an American Original* (New York: Free Press, 2009).
10. Jason Gross, "Interview with Linton Kwesi Johnson" in *Perfect Sound Forever* (January 1997), <http://www.furious.com/perfect/lkj.html>, accessed 2 September 2010.
11. Alex Pryce, "Linton Kwesi Johnson," British Council: Contemporary Writers, 2009, <http://www.contemporarywriters.com/authors/?p=auth58>, accessed 2 September 2010.
12. Michael North, "Linton Kwesi Johnson," *Times Higher Education Supplement* 1749 (2006, 23).
13. Kamau Brathwaite, *History of the Voice: The Development of Nation Language in Anglophone Caribbean Poetry* (London: New Beacon Books, 1984).
14. See, for example, Ashley Dawson, "Linton Kwesi Johnson's Dub Poetry and the Political Aesthetics of Carnival in Britain" in *Small Axe* 21 (2006, 54–70).
15. See Sarah Lawson Welsh's review of *Tings an Times*, for example ("Linton Kwesi Johnson, *Tings an Times; Selected Poems*" in *Bête Noire* 12.13 [1991, 406–424]), or Walter Bernhart's analysis, discussed in more detail below.
16. Ian Dieffenthaller, "Locating Linton Kwesi Johnson in a West Indian British Context" in *Bridges Across Chasms: Towards a Transcultural Future in Caribbean Literature*, Ed. Bénédicte Ledent (Liège, Belgium: Liège Language and Literature, English Department, Université de Liège, 2004), 127–138.
17. "Linton Kwesi Johnson Interview — DUB" in *Classical Reggae Interviews* (September 1998), <http://www.classical-reggae-interviews.org/lkj-dub.htm>, accessed 2 September 2010.
18. James Ferguson, "'Revalueshanary Voice': Interview with Linton Kwesi Johnson" in *Caribbean Beat* (July/August 2003), <http://www.meppublishers.com/online/caribbean-beat/archive/index.php?id=cb62-1-68>, 2 September 2010.
19. Esther Pereen, *Intersubjectivities and Popular Culture: Bakhtin and Beyond* (Stanford, CA: Stanford UP, 2008), 23.
20. Walter Bernhart, "The 'Destructiveness of Music': Functional Intermedia and Disharmony in Popular Songs" in *Cultural Functions of Intermedial Exploration*, Ed. Erik Hedling (Amsterdam, Netherlands: Rodopi, 2002), 247.
21. Bernhart, 249.
22. Bernhart, 250, quoting Nancy Rawlinson, "Linton Kwesi Johnson: Dread Beat An' Blood: Inglan Is A Bitch," in *Spike Magazine*, <http://www.spikemagazine.com/1298kwes.php> accessed 3 September 2010.
23. Simon Frith, *Performing Rites: On the Value of Popular Music* (Cambridge, MA: Harvard University Press, 1996), 40.
24. Frith, 40.
25. Esther Pereen, *Intersubjectivities and Popular Culture: Bakhtin and Beyond* (Stanford, CA: Stanford UP, 2008), 23.
26. Burt Caesar, "Linton Kwesi Johnson talks to Burt Caesar" in *Critical Quarterly* 38.4 (1996, 64–77), 71.
27. Linton Kwesi Johnson, *LKJ A A Capella Live*, liner notes, quoted in Amor Kohli, *The Demands of a New Idiom: Music, Language, and Participation in the Work of Amiri Baraka, Kamau Brathwaite, and Linton Kwesi Johnson* (Doctoral Thesis, Tufts University, 2006), 168.
28. A full discography can be found at "Lincoln Kwesi Johnson Discography," LKJ Records, <http://www.lintonkwesijohnson.com/linton-kwesi-johnson/discography/>, accessed 2 September 2010.

29. Kohli, 187–89.
30. Linton Kwesi Johnson, "Want fi Goh Rave," *Selected Poems* (London, Penguin 2006), 33–34.
31. "Crabbit, adj.": "cruel, rough, grasping, greedy." Frederic G. Cassidy and R. B. Le Page, *A Dictionary of Jamaican English* (S.l.: University of the West Indies, 2002).
32. Miranda Moore, "New World Hawdah?" in *Linguist* 41:4 (2002), 114.
33. Dieffenthaller, 34.
34. Burt Caesar, 67.
35. To cite but one example: Carl Honoré's *In Praise of Slowness: How a Worldwide Movement is Challenging the Cult of Speed* (2004).
36. Nicholas Wroe, "'I Did My Own Thing.' Interview with Linton Kwesi Johnson," *The Guardian* 8 March 2008, <http://www.guardian.co.uk/books/2008/mar/08/features reviews.guardianreview11>, accessed 2 September 2010.
37. Geoffrey Hill, "Dividing Legacies," *Collected Critical Writings* (Oxford: Oxford University Press, 2008), 378. Hill quotes Christopher Ricks, *T.S. Eliot and Prejudice* (Berkeley: University of California Press, 1988), 255 [Ricks was quoting Leavis]).
38. Russell Banks, "Introduction," *Mi Revalueshanary Fren: Selected Poems* by Linton Kwesi Johnson (London: Penguin, 2002), iii.
39. Kohli, 139.
40. Wroe, "I Did My Own Thing."
41. Geoffrey Hill, "Redeeming the Time," *Collected Critical Writings* (Oxford: Oxford University Press, 2008), 108.
42. Hill, 94.
43. Linton Kwesi Johnson, *Forces of Victory* (1979), Vinyl LP Album.
44. Caesar, 69.
45. Burt Caesar, 69–70.
46. A video recording is available online at "Linton Kwesi Johnson performs If I Woz A Tap Natch Poet," *The Guardian* 11 December 2008, <http://guardian.co.uk/books/video/2008/dec/05/linton-kwesi-johnson-poetry>, accessed 2 September 2010.
47. Banks, v.
48. Graham Brown-Martin, "Interview with Linton Kwesi Johnson," *Music and Media* 2 June 2004, <http://ammocity.com/artman/publish/printer_175.shtml>, accessed 2 September 2010.
49. "Factual—Desert Island Discs—2 December 2002," BBC Radio 4, <http://www.bbc.co.uk/radi04/factual/desertislanddiscs_20021208.shtml>, accessed 2 September 2010.
50. Ferguson.
51. Linton Kwesi Johnson, "The Way I See It" in *New Statesman* 137.4888 (2008), 41.

Works Cited

Banks, Russell (2002), "Introduction," *Mi Revalueshanary Fren: Selected Poems* by Linton Kwesi Johnson. London: Penguin, i-v.
Bernhart, Walter (2002), "The 'Destructiveness of Music': Functional Intermedia and Disharmony in Popular Songs," in *Cultural Functions of Intermedial Exploration*. Ed. Erik Hedling. Amsterdam, Netherlands: Rodopi, 247–253.

Brathwaite, Kamau (1984), *History of the Voice: The Development of Nation Language in Anglophone Caribbean Poetry*. London: New Beacon Books.

Brown-Martin, Graham (2004), "Interview with Linton Kwesi Johnson," in *Music and Media* (2 June). <http://ammocity.com/artman/publish/printer_175.shtml>. Accessed 2 September 2010.

Caesar, Burt (1996), "Linton Kwesi Johnson talks to Burt Caesar," in *Critical Quarterly* 38.4, 64–77.

Cassidy, Frederic G, and Le Page, R. B. (2002), *A Dictionary of Jamaican English*. S.l.: University of the West Indies.

Dawson, Ashley (2006), "Linton Kwesi Johnson's Dub Poetry and the Political Aesthetics of Carnival in Britain," in *Small Axe* 21, 54–70.

Dieffenthaller, Ian (2004), "Locating Linton Kwesi Johnson in a West Indian British Context," in *Bridges Across Chasms: Towards a Transcultural Future in Caribbean Literature*. Ed. Bénédicte Ledent. Liège, Belgium: Liège Language and Literature, English Department, Université de Liège, 127–138.

Doumerc, Eric (2002), "La *dub poetry*: évolution d'un genre," in *Anglophonia* 11, 179–84.

Du Bois, W.E.B. (2008), *The Souls of Black Folk*. Oxford: Oxford University Press.

Dyer, Rebecca (2002). "Immigration, Postwar London, and the Politics of Everyday Life in Sam Selvon's Fiction," in *Cultural Critique* 52, 108–144.

"Factual — Desert Island Discs — 2 December 2002" (2002), BBC Radio 4. <http://www.bbc.co.uk/radio4/factual/desertislanddiscs_20021208.shtml>. Accessed 2 September 2010.

Ferguson, James (2003), "'Revalueshanary Voice': Interview with Linton Kwesi Johnson," in *Caribbean Beat* (July/August). <*http://www.meppublishers.com/online/caribbean-beat/archive/index.php?id=cb62-1-68*>. Accessed 2 September 2010.

Frith, Simon (1996), *Performing Rites: On the Value of Popular Music*. Cambridge, MA: Harvard University Press.

Gross, Jason (1997), "Interview with Linton Kwesi Johnson," in *Perfect Sound Forever* (January). <*http://www.furious.com/perfect/lkj.html*>. Accessed 2 September 2010.

Hill, Geoffrey (2008), "Dividing Legacies," *Collected Critical Writings*. Oxford: Oxford University Press, 366–379.

_____ (2008), "Redeeming the Time," *Collected Critical Writings*. Oxford: Oxford University Press, 88–108.

Hodges, Hugh (2002), "Text Version: Linton Kwesi Johnson's Dub Poetry in Print," in *Xavier Review* 22:2 (Fall): 60–79.

Johnson, Linton Kwesi (1998), "Linton Kwesi Johnson Interview — DUB," in *Classical Reggae Interviews* (September). <http://www.classical-reggae-interviews.org/lkj-dub.htm>. Accessed 2 September 2010.

_____ (2008), "Linton Kwesi Johnson: Marxism 2008: Cultures of Resistance." <http://youtube.com/watch?v=J09FRtkyZ6k>. Accessed 2 September 2010.

_____ (2009), "Linton Kwesi Johnson — People, Signs & Resistance." <http://youtube.com/watch?v=mz0etGNTAE0>. Accessed 2 September 2010

_____ (2008), "Linton Kwesi Johnson Performs "If I Woz A Tap Natch Poet," *The Guardian Online* (11 December). By *Shehani Fernando*. <http://www.guardian.co.uk/books/video/2008/dec/05/linton-kwesi-johnson-poetry>. Accessed 2 September 2010.

_____ (2002), *Mi Revalueshanary Fren: Selected Poems*. London: Penguin.

_____ (2006), *Selected Poems*. London: Penguin.

_____ (2008), "The Way I See It," in *New Statesman* 137.4888, 41. *Academic Search Premier*. Web. Accessed 21 April 2010.

Kelley, Robin D. G. (2009), *Thelonious Monk: The Life and Times of an American Original*. New York: Free Press.
Kohli, Amor (2006), *The Demands of a New Idiom: Music, Language, and Participation in the Work of Amiri Baraka, Kamau Brathwaite, and Linton Kwesi Johnson*. Doctoral Thesis. Tufts University.
LKJ Records (undated). <http://lintonkwesijohnson.com>. Accessed 2 September 2010.
Moore, Miranda (2002), "New World Hawdah?," in *Linguist* 41:4, 114–15.
North, Michael (2006), "Linton Kwesi Johnson," *Times Higher Education Supplement* 1749, 23.
Peeren, Esther (2008), *Intersubjectivities and Popular Culture: Bakhtin and Beyond*. Stanford, CA: Stanford University Press.
Pryce, Alex (2009), "Linton Kwesi Johnson," British Council: Contemporary Writers. <http://www.contemporarywriters.com/authors/?p=auth58>. Accessed 2 September 2010.
Rawlinson, Nancy. "Linton Kwesi Johnson: Dread Beat An' Blood: Inglan Is A Bitch," in *Spike Magazine*. <http://www.spikemagazine.com/1298kwes.php> accessed 3 September 2010.
Ricks, Christopher (1988), *T.S. Eliot and Prejudice*. Berkeley: University of California Press.
"Sam the Wheels: Local Brixton Films 1960–2008" (2008). <http://samthewheels.co.uk/3>. Accessed 2 September 2010.
Taylor, Laurie (2003), "Leggo Relijan: Laurie Taylor interviews Linton Kwesi Johnson," in *New Humanist* 118:1 (Spring). <http://newhumanist.org.uk/583/leggo-relijan-laurie-taylor-interviews-linton-kwesi-johnson>. Accessed 2 September 2010.
Welsh, Sarah Lawson (1991), "Linton Kwesi Johnson, *Tings an Times*; Selected Poems," in *Bête Noire* 12.13, 406–424.
Wroe, Nicholas (2008), "'I Did My Own Thing' Interview with Linton Kwesi Johnson," in *The Guardian* (8 March). <http://www.guardian.co.uk/books/2008/mar/08/featuresreviews.guardianreview11>. Accessed 2 September 2010.

About the Contributors

Shona M. **Allan** holds a Ph.D. in German and English literature from the University of Glasgow. She has published extensively on Anglo-German cultural relations in the eighteenth and nineteenth centuries, particularly on Byron and Goethe. Formerly at the University of Glasgow and the University of Mainz, Germany, and she teaches at the University of Cologne.

Galia **Benziman** is a lecturer in the Department of Literature, Language and the Arts at the Open University of Israel, and specializes in nineteenth-century British literature. Her essays have been published in *Dickens Quarterly, SEL, JNT: Journal of Narrative Theory, Partial Answers* and other journals, and her book *Narratives of Child Neglect in Romantic and Victorian Culture* is forthcoming.

Sarah **Bouttier** is a specialist of the non-human in the poetry of D. H. Lawrence. She has authored articles on Lawrence's poetry and engagement with the non-human in the French journal *Etudes Lawrenciennes* and she has taught at the Sorbonne Nouvelle, Cambridge University, and Stockholm University.

Elise **Brault-Dreux** teaches English literature at Valenciennes University. A specialist in D.H. Lawrence and T.S. Eliot, her research focuses especially on the concepts of voice, personae and masks.

Suzanne **Bray** is a professor of English at Lille Catholic University in the north of France. She specializes in literature and theology in 20th century Britain and has published extensively, in English and in French, on C.S. Lewis, Dorothy L. Sayers and Charles Williams. A recent publication is an annotated collection of Dorothy L. Sayers's religious writings, translated into French, with a critical introduction.

Charlotte **Estrade** is a former student at the Ecole Normale Supérieure. She is teaching at the University of Maine in Le Mans (France), where she specializes in the study of myth in Modernist poetry.

Adrian **Grafe** is a poetry specialist living in Paris. He holds a B.A. (Hons.) degree from Oxford, postgraduate degrees from the University of Paris VII, and a post-doctoral diploma from the University of Caen. He wrote *Hopkins: la profusion ténébreuse* (2003) and *Emily Dickinson: Poems* (2009) and he edited *Ecstasy and Understanding* (2008), essays on modern poetry. With Emily Taylor Merriman he co-edited *Intimate Exposure: Essays on the Public-Private Divide in British Poetry 1950–2008* (McFarland, 2010).

Claire **Hélie** teaches at Panthéon-Sorbonne University, and specializes in poetry from or about the North of England since the 1960s. She has published articles on Basil Bunting, Ted Hughes, Tony Harrison and Simon Armitage.

Boutheina Boughnim **Laarif** is an Auden specialist, and lectures at the Higher Institute of Applied Humanities at Gafsa, Tunisia. She is interested in the relationship between literature and philosophy, and has worked on Nietzsche and Heidegger.

Emilie **Loriaux** teaches English at Lille Catholic University and is a doctoral candidate at Artois University, working on the language of poetry in Thomas Hardy and William Barnes.

Emily Taylor **Merriman** is an assistant professor of English at San Francisco State University, where she teaches 20th century poetry. She has degrees from Oxford, London and Boston universities. Her published work includes essays on Gerard M. Hopkins, William Blake, Geoffrey Hill, and Adrienne Rich and she is writing a book, *Poetry's God*, on the theology in Geoffrey Hill, Derek Walcott, and Charles Wright.

Anne **Mounic** is an associate professor at Paris 3 Sorbonne Nouvelle and the author of several volumes of criticism, among them *Jacob ou l'être du possible* (2009), and *Counting the Beats: Robert Graves' Poetry of Unrest* (2011) and *Monde terrible où naître: La voix singulière face à l'Histoire* (forthcoming).

Elizabeth **Muller** is an associate professor in English at the University of Nantes. A Yeats specialist, she is the author of numerous articles and a monograph on the poet. She is writing a book titled *Yeats and the Greeks*.

Catherine **Phillips** is a fellow in English at Downing College, Cambridge. Her publications include a biography of Robert Bridges (1992), an edition of the manuscripts of W. B. Yeats's play *The Hour-Glass* (Cornell, 1994), editions of Gerard Manley Hopkins's poetry and prose and a monograph, *Gerard Manley Hopkins and the Victorian Visual World* (2007). She is co-editing Hopkins's letters and preparing an edition of his poems for the *Collected Works of Gerard Manley Hopkins*.

Jessica **Stephens** is an assistant professor of English at Paris 3 Sorbonne Nouvelle University, where she teaches translation. She holds a Ph.D. from the Sorbonne in contemporary Irish poetry and her published work includes essays on Seamus Heaney and John Montague. Formerly co-director of the English Department at Angers University, she is writing a book on translating Rimbaud, Coleridge, and Derek Walcott.

Index

activism 218, 221
Adorno, Theodor 5
Agamben, Giorgio 106, 111
agon 109, 137
allegory 168–169, 194, 201–202
"Almond Blossom" 59–64 *passim*
ambiguity 17, 24, 25, 30, 26n5, 36, 37, 73, 74, 80, 113, 115, 127, 131, 143, 155, 174, 201
Amis, Kingsley 207
"Among School Children" 10, 171
amorphos 155
The Amulet 79
"Ancestral Houses" 171, 172
"The Ancient Briton Lay Under His Rock" 143
"The Angel" 140
"Another Shot" 211
antagonism 61, 196
Anxiety of Influence 26n5
Aristotle 131
Armitage, Simon 145, 182, 186
"The Assault Heroic" 76, 81
"At Central Station" 184
"Attis: Or Something Missing" 123
Auden, W.H. 8, 11, 194–205, 207; "Elegy to W. B. Yeats" 196, 199, 202; "The Hidden Law" 199, 202n4; "September 1, 1939" 194, 197, 198–200; "Spain, 1937" 194, 198, 199, 200, 202n4; "This Lunar Beauty" 194, 201–202
"An August Midnight" 30–33 *passim*, 36, 38
Aüslander, Rose 4
Autobiography 166, 167, 170, 171, 173, 174, 177n13
Aviram, Amittai F. 194, 200

ballad 37, 136, 150, 168, 199, 226
"Bar Italia" 210, 212, 213
Bataille, Georges, *Le coupable* 104
Bate, Jonathan 140
Beat poetry 225
"Beautiful Lofty Things" 174
Bell, Bishop George 91
Benjamin, Walter 115
Bergson, Henri 7, 53, 57–59, 118n88, 144
Berryman, John 221
Betjeman, John 206, 207, 208, 210, 214–215
Bible 8, 71–73, 80, 106, 113–114, 225–227;
Adam 79, 98; Babel 83, 111, 116; "Deuteronomy" 72; "Ecclesiastes" 85n21, 108–109, 114; Ephesians (St. Paul's Epistle to) 2; "Genesis" 2, 58, 82; "Isaiah" 79; Jacob 2, 11, 71, 77, 82, 84; "Leviticus" 74; Lilith 79; Moses, in Rosenberg's poetry 70, 78, 79; New Testament 2; Old Testament 142; "Revelation" 50; St. Matthew's Gospel 2
Birthday Letters 140
Black Panthers 219
"The Black Tower" 10, 149–151, 158, 159
Blake, William 5, 20, 54n22, 81, 222, 227
"Blank Pages" 212
Bloom, Harold, *Anxiety of Influence* 26n5
Bowie, David, "Changes" 208, 213, 215
Bradbury, Ray, *Fahrenheit 451* 6
Brathwaite, Kamau 219, 227
"Break of Day in the Trenches" 81
"Briggflatts" 121, 123, 124, 126–128
Brittain, Vera 91
Brixton riots 220
"A Bronze Head" 161
Bruegel 108
La Bruyère 42
Buber, Martin 74
Bukowski, Charles 210, 212
Bunting, Basil 9; "Attis: Or Something Missing" 123; "Briggflatts" 121, 123, 124, 126–128; conscientious objector 9, 120; "The Spoils" 124–125; "The Well of Lycopolis" 121–124
"Butterfly" 65
"Byzantium" 151

"The Caged Goldfinch" 36
Camus, Albert, *La peste* 112
capitalism 42–49 *passim*, 219
Cartesianism 142, 145
Carver, Raymond 210
Casement, Roger 10, 173
Cat O'Mary 93
"Childhood Among the Ferns" 17, 18, 20, 22, 23, 25
Chopin, Frédéric 93–94
Christianity 8, 10, 16, 26n5, 45, 58, 62, 88–99, 109, 113, 142, 226; Anglicanism 99, 127; Baptist church 226; Catholicism 10, 78, 149,

153, 169, 177n13; Judeo-Christian 2; Methodism 137, 141, 142; Puritanism 142
Churchill, Winston 90–92, 125
"The Circus Animals' Desertion" 174
City of Dreadful Night 184
Civil Rights Movement 1
Clare, John 6, 226
"Clamming" 212
"Climbing into Heptonstall" 143
Coleridge, S.T. 107
Collected Poems 168
Compagnon, Antoine 145
condensation 9, 59–63, 66, 121, 127, 131–132
conscience 71, 200
consciousness 19, 45, 95, 107–108, 141, 198
consumerism 219, 225
"Corot" 57, 58
Count Ossie & the Mystic Revelation of Rastafari 227
The Countess Cathleen 167, 177n13
"Counting the Beats" 84
Le coupable 104
Crazy Jane poems 175
Crossways 168, 169, 176
"Cuchulain Comforted" 149, 150, 159, 160
"Curlews in April" 139
Cyrulnik, Boris, *Un merveilleux malheur* 106

"A Dam" 208
Dante 111, 150, 159
"The Darkling Thrush" 15, 30–34, 36
Darwin, Darwinian 50
"Daughters of War" 80, 81, 83
"Dead Man's Dump" 82
"Death Duke Street" 184
"Death of an Actor" 214
Derrida, Jacques 11, 194–199
"Deserter" 211
dialect 30, 36, 37, 125, 136, 145, 184, 219, 228; Black British English 219, 224; non-standard language 37, 223
Didi-Huberman, Georges 106–111 *passim*
Dionysos, Dionysian 53, 77
disobedience 1, 4, 46–47, 49, 50
Dissenting tradition 5, 9
dissolution 7, 55–69 *passim*, 75–76, 79, 83
"Divine Sacrifice" 75, 83
Donne, John, "A Valediction Forbidding Mourning" 214
"Drummer Hodge" 30, 34–38
Dub poetry 12, 220, 225
Dubois, W.E.B. 219
Duffy, Carol Ann 179
Dunkirk 89, 91

"Easter 1916" 164n49, 173
Eco, Umberto 111
Edwards, Michael 31, 32, 34
"Ego Dominus Tuus" 149, 159
"Elegy to W.B. Yeats" 196, 199, 202
Eliot, T.S. 8–10, 88, 99, 104–119, 127, 130, 150, 180, 194, 207, 208, 209, 215n8; *Four Quartets* 104–119, 169; "objective correlative" 138, 140, 151; "The Social Function of Poetry" 105; "Thoughts After Lambeth" 99; "Tradition and the Individual Talent" 169; *The Waste Land* 151, 162n10, 173, 207
Elmet 13, 136, 137, 139, 140, 141, 143, 144, 145
Elyot, Thomas 109
"Emily Brontë" 139
Empedocles 153
Empson, William 131
"The English War" 89, 90, 91
the Enlightenment 87, 139, 141, 142, 145, 198
"Escape" 76
"Everyone Knows This" 212
evil 2, 42, 73, 96, 155, 198; good and evil 30, 74
evolution 58

Fahrenheit 451 6
fascism 127
"Fight! O my Young Men" 43, 44, 47, 52
"The First Men on Mercury" 180, 184
"Fish" 56, 64
"The Fisherman" 149, 156
"Fite Dem Back" 227
flow, flux 3, 7, 12, 43, 47, 56–67 *passim*; flow of time 208
"Football at Slack" 144
"The Founding of the Company" 97
Four Quartets 104–119, 169
Frazer, James, *The Golden Bough* 53, 77
free verse 42, 46, 47, 150, 194
Freud, Sigmund 2, 22
Futurism 44, 53n16

Gallipoli 140
Gandi, Mohandas 1
Gardner, Helen 137n41
"Genius" 82
"Glasgow Green" 184
"Glasgow Sonnets" 180, 185
God 2, 26n5, 43, 58, 73, 74, 78, 83, 91, 93, 96, 97, 99, 110, 116, 142, 154
"God Made Blind" 73
Goethe, Johann Wolfgang von 80
The Golden Bough 53, 77
"Goliath and David" 75
Goodbye to All That 77
Graves, Robert 8, 70–87; "The Assault Heroic" 76, 81; "Counting the Beats 84; "Divine Sacrifice" 75, 83; "Escape" 76; "Genius" 82; "Goliath and David" 75; *Goodbye to All That* 77; *The Hebrew Myths* 71, 79; "In Broken Images" 81; "In the Wilderness" 74; "Nine Hundred Iron Chariots" 81; "On Portents" 84; *Over the Brazier* 74; "The Philosopher" 80; "Two Fusiliers" 71; *The White Goddess* 71, 77, 79, 80, 84, 164n53; "Youth and Folly"74
Gray, Alasdair 179
The Green Helmet and Other Poems 171

Guernica 4
"The Gulf" 45, 47
Gunn, Thom 6, 207

Haeckel, Ernst 7, 61, 62
Hardy, Thomas 6, 7, 15–40; "An August Midnight" 30–33 *passim*, 36, 38; "The Caged Goldfinch" 36; "Childhood Among the Ferns" 17, 18, 20, 22, 23, 25; "The Darkling Thrush" 15, 30–34, 36; "Drummer Hodge" 30, 34–38; *Jude the Obscure* 20, 21, 29; *Life* 20, 22, 26–27n20; "The Oxen" 16; "The Self-Unseeing" 17, 22, 23, 25, 27n24; "Shelley's Skylark" 15; "To Outer Nature" 16, 17
Harrison, Tony 136, 214
The Hawk in the Rain 144
Heaney, Seamus 5, 105, 141, 144–145, 162, 179, 186
The Hebrew Myths 71, 79
Heidegger, Martin 136, 195
"Heptonstall" 137
"Heptonstall Cemetery" 139
Heraclites (or Heraclitus) 43, 47, 109, 153
"The Heroic Theme" (editorial) 89
"The Hidden Law" 199, 202n4
Hill, Geoffrey 1, 5, 207, 227
Hitler, Adolf 90, 91, 93, 96, 98
Hölderlin, Friedrich 136
Homer 159, 160
Hopkins, Gerard M. 6, 227
"The Horses" 144
"Hound Voice" 149, 150, 158, 159
The Hour Glass 175
Hughes, Ted 5, 6, 9, 10, 135–148, 207; "The Ancient Briton Lay Under His Rock" 143; "The Angel" 140; *Birthday Letters* 140; "Climbing into Heptonstall" 143; "Curlews in April" 139; *Elmet* 13, 136, 137, 139, 140, 141, 143, 144, 145; "Emily Brontë" 139; "Football at Slack" 144; *The Hawk in the Rain* 144; "Heptonstall" 137; "Heptonstall Cemetery" 139; "The Horses" 144; "A Masque for Three Voices" 140; *Remains of Elmet* 9, 193, 194, 197, 203, 204, 205; "The Rock" 9, 136–138, 140, 143, 145; "Sacrifice" 144; "Two Photographs at Top Withens" 140; "Where the Mothers" 139; "You Claw the Door" 139
"Humming-Bird" 60–61
humor 4, 31, 32, 33, 34, 112, 144, 211
Huxley, Aldous 42

"If I Woz a Tap-Natch Poet" 228
The Iliad or the Poem of Force 75–76
"Imagine" 228
"In Broken Images" 81
"In the Blindfold Hours" 211
"In the Snack Bar" 184
"In the Wilderness" 74
industrial revolution 48, 137, 141, 142
inertia 44, 45, 57, 58, 59, 61, 62, 66

interstitial 20, 31, 106
Ionesco, Eugène, *Journal en miettes* 105
irony 6, 15, 16, 21, 22, 34, 50, 74, 80, 125, 211, 227
irresistibility 181, 187
"It noh funny" 223–224

Jennings, Elizabeth 207
"The Jew" 79
John of the Cross, Saint 109, 110
Johnson, Linton Kwesi 12, 218–233; "Fite Dem Back" 227; "If I Woz A Tap-Natch Poet" 228; "It noh funny" 223–224; "More Time" 225–226; "Seasons of the Heart" 226; "Want Fi Goh Rave" 222–223
Journal en miettes 105
Jude the Obscure 20, 21, 29
Julian of Norwich 111
The Just Vengeance 95

Kangaroo 64
Kant, Emmanuel 110
Keats, John 15, 142
Kierkegaard, Soren 71–72
King, Martin Luther 1, 2

Lacoue-Labarthe, Philippe 104, 197
Lady Chatterley's Lover 64, 78
"Lapis Lazuli" 173
Larkin, Philip 207, 208, 209, 210
Last Poems 47, 63, 66, 149, 153, 175
Lawrence, D.H. 5, 7, 8, 41–69; "Almond Blossom" 59–64 *passim*; "Butterfly" 65; "Corot" 57, 58; "Fight! O My Young Men" 43, 44, 47, 52; "Fish" 56, 64; "The Gulf" 45, 47; "Humming-Bird" 60–61; *Kangaroo* 64; *Lady Chatterley's Lover* 64, 78; *Last Poems* 47, 63, 66; "Let the Dead Bury Their Dead" 42, 44, 47; "Lucifer" 66; "Michael Angelo" 58, 59; "Nemesis" 46, 47; "Only the Best Matters" 65, 66; *The Plumed Serpent* 64; "Poetry of the Present" 46, 48, 59; *The Rainbow* 78; *Study of Thomas Hardy* 51, 59; "To Let Go or to Hold On —?" 49, 50, 51; "Trees in the Garden" 63; "The Triumph of the Machine" 50, 52; "Turkey-Cock" 63; *Women in Love* 56; "Wonderful Machine" 44
Lawrence, Frieda 42, 68n27
Lennon, John, "Imagine" 228
"Let the Dead Bury Their Dead" 42, 44, 47
Levinas, Emmanuel 71, 83
Lewis, C.S. 98
Leyris, Pierre 9, 104, 112–116
Life 20, 22, 26–27n20
"Lightly Clenched Fists" 212
"The Loch Ness Monster's Song" 188
Lochhead, Liz 179, 188, 189n2
Longenbach, James, *The Resistance to Poetry* 5
"The Lover Mourns for the Loss of Love" 166
"The Lover Tells of the Rose in His Heart" 155
Lowell, Robert 213

Lubitsch, Ernst 112
"Lucifer" 66
Luddites 44
Luther, Martin 198
Lyotard, J.-F. 200

Machiavelli 198
MacNeice, Louis 207
Mallarmé, Stéphane 110, 111
"Man and Superman" 210, 214
Maquis 1
Marin, Claire 2–3
Marinetti, F.T. 44
Marley, Bob 225; "Redemption Song" 228
Marvell, Andrew 6
Marxism 218
"A Masque for Three Voices" 140
materialism 58, 219
matter, materiality 55, 57–66 *passim*, 138, 155
Mayakovsky, Vladimir 10, 180, 181, 187
mechanization 7, 32, 41–51 *passim*, 196, 203n19
"Meditations in Time of Civil War" 156, 169, 171, 172, 173, 174
Memoirs 166, 170
Un merveilleux malheur 106
meter 7, 34, 36, 37, 150, 208
"Michael Angelo" 58, 59
Milton, John 5, 37
Minkowsky, Eugène 70
Modernism 5, 8, 12, 15, 34, 41, 126, 130, 138, 150, 157, 206, 207, 211
Monism 61, 63
"More Time" 225–226
Morgan, Edwin 10–11, 179–193; "At Central Station" 184; "Death Duke Street" 184; "The First Men on Mercury" 180, 184; "Glasgow Green" 184; "Glasgow Sonnets" 180, 185; and Hungarian poetry 180–187 *passim*; "In the Snack Bar" 184; "The Loch Ness Monster's Song" 188; "Spacepoem 1: from Laica to Gagarin" 180; "Spacepoem 3: Off Course" 180; "Stobhill" 184
Morin, Edgar 1, 4
Moses 78–79
Motion, Andrew 30, 37
"The Mouthful" 213
The Movement 207
music 23, 33, 34, 104, 126, 129, 220–223, 226, 228
"The Municipal Gallery Revisited" 174
"My Days Are But the Tombs of Buried Hours" 71
mysticism 2, 3, 109, 154
mythology 8, 9, 120, 122, 123, 125, 129, 130, 131, 136, 140, 141, 151, 152, 158, 159, 167, 168, 169, 186

"Nemesis" 46, 47
"A New Page" 208
Nietzsche, Friedrich 52, 62, 68n27, 68n28, 201
"Nine Hundred Iron Chariots" 81

non-resistance 50, 212
nostalgia 6, 16, 17, 19, 22, 23, 25, 30, 35, 81, 123, 145, 151, 174

"Ocean-1212-W" 138
Olson, Charles 126
"On Hearing That the Students of Our New University Have Joined the Agitation Against Immoral Literature" 171
"On Portents" 84
On the Boiler 152, 161, 162
"Only the Best Matters" 65, 66
opposition 2, 3, 5, 7, 8, 31, 32, 37, 38, 46, 55, 110, 123, 137, 140, 142, 161, 170, 173, 211, 218
oppression 3, 77, 90, 228
Order of the Coinherence 97
Orwell, George 71
Over the Brazier 74
"The Oxen" 16

pacifist, Sassoon as 80, 81
parody 26n5
"A Parting Shot" 211
Pascal 42, 215n17
Pasolini, Paolo 107, 181
pastoral 6, 18
Penn Warren, Robert 34
"Percivale at Carboneck" 89, 96–97
performance poetry 220
performativity 43, 229
La peste 112
Phaedrus 155
"The Philosopher" 80
physical resistance 7, 55, 56, 144
"A Pillow Book" 212
Plath, Sylvia 9, 137–140; "Ocean-1212-W" 138
Plato 149, 155, 162n13; *Phaedrus* 155
"Playing Safe" 211
pleasure 12, 31, 33, 219, 220, 221, 225, 226, 228, 229
Plotinus 163n13, 164n66
Plutarch 164n66
The Plumed Serpent 64
poematics 11, 194–196, 198
poethics 136, 145
"Poetry of the Present" 46, 48, 59
politics 1, 3, 4, 5, 10, 12, 38, 42, 44, 45, 46, 52, 72, 88–91, 99, 120, 121, 125, 127, 131, 132, 141, 156, 158, 161, 163n37, 164n64, 167, 170–171, 173, 176, 180, 181, 183, 184, 186, 187, 188, 194, 200, 201, 211, 218, 219, 221, 225; politically correct 224
"Politics" 175–176
postmodernism 204n72
Pound, Ezra 10, 72, 121, 126, 127, 129, 130, 133n42, 164n66, 180, 194; "The Return" 158, 159
"The Prayers of the Pope" 8, 89, 98, 99
prophecy 5, 42, 43, 45, 46, 47, 48, 49, 50, 51, 52, 80, 96, 163n23, 185
prosody, rhythm 11, 34, 37, 42, 46, 47, 48,

49, 50, 51, 58, 60, 77, 81–84 *passim*, 106, 109, 114, 115, 130, 145, 168, 194, 195, 197, 199, 200, 201, 202, 204*n*72, 221, 227; cadence 51, 110, 114, 210
protest 6, 8, 10, 12, 34–36, 227, 229
Protestantism 5, 10, 74, 170
Proust, Françoise 3
Prynne, J.H. 5, 128
Purgatory 155, 156

racism 12, 218, 227, 228, 229
Raftery 157
The Rainbow 78
Raine, Kathleen 151, 161
realism 31, 32, 34, 66, 75, 185
rebellion 8, 10, 38, 44, 50, 51, 79, 150, 173, 228
"Redemption Song" 228
regeneration 9, 78, 108–110, 140, 141, 143, 144
Reggae 220, 221, 222, 225, 226, 227, 228
regionalism 37, 120–148 *passim*
religion 8, 58, 75, 88, 89, 122, 125, 127, 131
"Religion" 210
Remains of Elmet 9, 193, 194, 197, 203, 204, 205
Renaissance 136, 198, 226
resilience 1, 9, 52, 104, 106, 151
Resistance Movement, French 1
The Resistance to Poetry 5
"The Return" 158, 159
"Reveries Over Childhood and Youth" 170
revolt 6, 25, 211
revolution 37, 42, 158, 180
rhyme 7, 33, 34, 37, 38, 58, 130, 150, 159, 168, 208, 224, 226
Rimbaud, Arthur 111
"The Rock" 9, 136–138, 140, 143, 145
Romanticism 6, 15–25 *passim*, 26*n*15, 31, 33, 138
The Rose 167
Rosenberg, Isaac 3, 8; *The Amulet* 79; "Break of Day in the Trenches" 81; "Daughters of War" 80, 81, 83; "Dead Man's Dump" 82; "God Made Blind" 73; "The Jew" 79; *Moses* 78–79; "My Days Are But the Tombs of Buried Hours" 71; "Soldier: Twentieth Century" 83; "Trench Poems" 71; *The Unicorn* 79–80
Rosenzweig, Franz, *Der Stern der Erlösung* 71, 74
Rosicrucianism 151
Rousseau, Jean-Jacques 20
Russell, Bertrand 45

"Sacrifice" 144
Sassoon, Siegfried 71, 75, 80, 81
satire 122, 123, 124, 144; Hugo Williams's poems as "self-satires" 212
Sayers, Dorothy L. 8, 88–103 *passim*; *Cat O'Mary* 93; "The English War" 89, 90, 91; "The Heroic Theme" (editorial) 89; *The Just Vengeance* 95; "Target Area" 8, 92, 93, 94, 95, 99

Schopenhauer, Arthur 72
"Seasons of the Heart" 226
Secker, Martin 42
"Self-Portrait with a Slide" 212–213
"The Self-Unseeing" 17, 22, 23, 25, 27*n*24
Selvon, Sam 218
Semprun, Jorge 112
"September 1, 1939" 194, 197, 198–200
"September 1913" 173
The Shadowy Waters 167
Shakespeare, William 84, 207
Shelley, P.B. 3, 15
"Shelley's Skylark" 15
skepticism 22
"The Social Function of Poetry" 105
Socrates 3
Soelle, Dorothee 2, 3
"Soldier: Twentieth Century" 83
"The Song of the Happy Shepherd" 168
sonnet 180, 185
Sophocles 162
"Spacepoem 1: from Laica to Gagarin" 180
"Spacepoem 3: Off Course" 180
"Spain, 1937" 194, 198, 199, 200, 202*n*4
Spencer, Herbert 7, 61
Spenser, Edmund 226
Spinoza, Baruch 73
"The Spoils" 124–125
Standard English 36, 38, 187, 189, 226, 228
standardization 1, 10, 157, 171
"A Start in Life" 210
"The Statues" 153, 154, 161
Steiner, George 4, 112, 130–131
Der Stern der Erlösung 71, 74
Stevens, Wallace 131
"Stobhill" 184
"The Stolen Child" 169
Study of Thomas Hardy 51, 59
subversion 2, 4, 6, 7, 17, 44, 126, 130, 187, 201
"A Suitable Cane" 212
Swinburne, Algernon 169

Taoism 142, 144
"Target Area" 8, 92, 93, 94, 95, 99
Taylor, Dennis 26*n*4, 26*n*5, 26*n*13, 34–38 *passim*
Tennyson, Alfred Lord 89
Thatcherite 12, 210
"This Lunar Beauty" 194, 201–202
Thomson, James, *City of Dreadful Night* 184
"Thoughts After Lambeth" 99
"Tipping My Chair" 210
"To Let Go or to Hold On—?" 49, 50, 51
"To Outer Nature" 16, 17
Tolstoy, Leo 72
The Tower 151
"Tradition and the Individual Talent" 169
Traherne, Thomas 6
translation: as cultural/linguistic resistance 104–119 *passim*; Edwin Morgan as translator 179–193 *passim*

"Trees in the Garden" 63
"Trench Poems" 71
"The Triumph of the Machine" 50, 52
"Truce" 211
"Turkey-Cock" 63
"Two Fusiliers" 71
"Two Photographs at Top Withens" 140
Tyndall, John 55

the unconscious 2, 3, 137
"Under Ben Bulben" 149, 150, 152–159 *passim*, 175
the *Unheimlich* 31
The Unicorn 79–80
"Untitled" 212
utopia 200

"A Valediction Forbidding Mourning" 214
via negativa 109, 111, 113
Vigée, Claude 9, 104, 112, 113–116, 117n54
Villon, François 129
violence 71, 72, 76, 83, 159, 160, 172, 174, 198, 223, 227; brutality 219, 227
A Vision 163n27, 160, 164n66, 173
vitality 42, 43, 45, 46, 51, 53, 56, 57, 58, 61–66 *passim*, 122, 123, 175, 201; *élan vital* 44, 53, 53n16, 57–59

Wain, John 207
Walcott, Derek 227, 228
"Walking Out of the Room Backwards" 212
The Wanderings of Oisin 168, 169, 177n13
"Want Fi Goh Rave" 222–223
war 4, 8, 11, 16, 123, 124, 125, 131, 137, 140, 141, 142, 143, 151, 152, 153, 154, 159, 161, 173, 176, 200, 211–213 *passim*; Boer War 30, 33, 35, 38; First or Great War 70, 72, 74, 75, 76, 77, 78, 79, 80, 83, 91, 95, 120, 129, 140, 141 Second World War 8, 71, 77, 88–119 *passim*, 120, 124, 140, 141, 175, 177n11, 210; Spanish Civil War 200; Wars of the Roses 136
"Washing My Hands" 208
The Waste Land 151, 162n10, 173, 207
Weil, Simone, *The Iliad or the Poem of Force* 75–76
"The Well of Lycopolis" 121–124
"Where the Mothers" 139
The White Goddess 71, 77, 79, 80, 84, 164n53
Whitman, Walt 42, 46
Whittemore, Reed, "Clamming" 212
Williams, Charles 8; "The Founding of the Company" 97; "Percivale at Carboneck" 89, 96–97; "The Prayers of the Pope" 8, 89, 98, 99
Williams, Hugo 11–12, 206–217; "Another Shot" 211; "Bar Italia" 210, 212, 213; "Blank Pages" 212; "A Dam" 208; "Death of an Actor" 214; "Deserter" 211; "Everyone Knows This" 212; "In the Blindfold Hours" 211; "Lightly Clenched Fists" 212; "Man and Superman" 210, 214; "The Mouthful" 213; "A New Page" 208; "A Parting Shot" 211; "A Pillow Book" 212; "Playing Safe" 211; "Religion" 210; "Self-Portrait with a Slide" 212–213; "A Start in Life" 210; "A Suitable Cane" 212; "Tipping My Chair" 210; "Truce" 211; "Untitled" 212; "Walking Out of the Room Backwards" 212; as war poet 210–212; "Washing My Hands" 208; "The World of Work" 210
Wilson, Woodrow 91
The Wind Among the Reeds 172, 173
Women in Love 56
"Wonderful Machine" 44
Wordsworth, William 15–28 *passim*, 138, 140
"The World of Work" 210
Wuthering Heights 139

Yeats, John Butler 171
Yeats, W.B. 10, 107, 110, 141, 149–178; "Among School Children" 10, 171; "Ancestral Houses" 171, 172; *Autobiography* 166, 167, 170, 171, 173, 174, 177n13; "Beautiful Lofty Things" 174; "The Black Tower" 10, 149–151, 158, 159; "A Bronze Head" 161; "Byzantium" 151; Roger Casement poems 173; "The Circus Animals' Desertion" 174; *Collected Poems* 168; *The Countess Cathleen* 167, 177n13; Crazy Jane poems 175; *Crossways* 168, 169, 176; "Cuchulain Comforted" 149, 150, 159, 160; "Easter 1916" 164n49, 173; "Ego Dominus Tuus" 149, 159; "The Fisherman" 149, 156; *The Green Helmet and Other Poems* 171; "Hound Voice" 149, 150, 158, 159; *The Hour Glass* 175; "Lapis Lazuli" 173; *Last Poems* 149, 153, 175; "The Lover Mourns for the Loss of Love" 166; "The Lover Tells of the Rose in His Heart" 155; "Meditations in Time of Civil War" 156, 169, 171, 172, 173, 174; *Memoirs* 166, 170; "The Municipal Gallery Revisited" 174; "On Hearing That the Students of Our New University Have Joined the Agitation Against Immoral Literature" 171; *On the Boiler* 152, 161, 162; "Politics" 175–176; *Purgatory* 155, 156; "Reveries Over Childhood and Youth" 170; *The Rose* 167; "September 1913" 173; *The Shadowy Waters* 167; "The Song of the Happy Shepherd" 168; "The Statues" 153, 154, 161; "The Stolen Child" 169; *The Tower* 151; "Under Ben Bulben" 149, 150, 152–159 *passim*, 175; *A Vision* 163n27, 160, 164n66, 173; *The Wanderings of Oisin* 168, 169, 177n13; *The Wind Among the Reeds* 172, 173
"You Claw the Door" 139
"Youth and Folly" 74

Zukofsky, Louis 126, 132n12

www.ingramcontent.com/pod-product-compliance
Lightning Source LLC
Chambersburg PA
CBHW051219300426
44116CB00006B/630